M000247587

IN THE TRENCHES
WITH JESUS AND MARX

Lynd Ward's 1963 wood engraving "Portrait of My Father"

RELIGION AND AMERICAN CULTURE

Series Editors
David Edwin Harrell Jr.
Wayne Flynt
Edith L. Blumhofer

IN THE TRENCHES
WITH JESUS AND MARX

Harry F. Ward and the Struggle for Social Justice

DAVID NELSON DUKE

The University of Alabama Press • Tuscaloosa and London

Copyright © 2003
The University of Alabama Press
Tuscaloosa, Alabama 35487-0380
All rights reserved
Manufactured in the United States of America

Typeface: ACaslon

Frontispiece: Lynd Ward's 1963 wood engraving "Portrait of My Father" was
created for the program cover for Harry F. Ward's ninetieth-birthday celebration at Carnegie Hall. May McNeer and Lynd Ward's children's book *Armed
with Courage* (New York: Abingdon Press, 1957) includes chapters on Jane
Addams and Mahatma Ghandi, two persons who strongly influenced Harry
Ward. (Courtesy of Nanda Ward and Robin Ward Savage)

∞

The paper on which this book is printed meets the minimum requirements
of American National Standard for Information Science-Permanence of
Paper for Printed Library Materials, ANSI Z39.48-1984.

Library of Congress Cataloging-in-Publication Data

Duke, David Nelson, 1950–
In the trenches with Jesus and Marx : Harry F. Ward and the struggle for
social justice / David Nelson Duke.
    p.   cm. — (Religion and American culture)
Includes bibliographical references and index.
ISBN 0-8173-1246-3 (alk. paper)

1. Ward, Harry Frederick, 1873–1966. 2. Methodist Church—Clergy—
United States—Biography. 3. Communists—United States—Biography.
I. Title. II. Religion and American culture (Tuscaloosa, Ala.)

BX8495.W2464 D84 2003
261.8′092—dc21

                                                                    2002010879

British Library Cataloguing-in-Publication Data available

For Marcia, who never seemed to tire of stories about Harry and Daisy

CONTENTS

ILLUSTRATIONS

PREFACE

RECONSTRUCTING HARRY WARD's life is not an easy task. He was a very private man who left no diaries or autobiography. Thanks to the foresight of his son and daughter-in-law, Lynd Ward and May McNeer Ward, many boxes of Harry Ward's correspondence, sermons, class notes, and writings have survived. Still, important gaps persist, especially for Harry Ward's English boyhood. Other than a birth certificate, a school graduation certificate, and photographs, no documents survive from his first seventeen years. Therefore this book is heavily indebted to Ward's descendants, who have been willing to share the oral tradition maintained by the family and answer my numerous questions.

Nanda Ward and Robin Ward Savage, Harry Ward's only grandchildren, demonstrated long-suffering patience with my visits, letters, e-mails, and phone calls. Due to their grandfather's long life, they knew him well, and they listened attentively to their parents, thereby developing a rich, reliable oral tradition, which they graciously passed on to me. Robin maintains the family photographic archives, and she and Nanda have generously shared other items in their possession. Their mother, May McNeer Ward, though advanced in years when I interviewed her, was a veritable font of information on Harry Ward, for she and her husband Lynd remained over the years very close to "Dad," as the family called him. I conversed with Lynd Ward only once in the late 1970s, before Alzheimer's claimed his mind and life. I regret that I did not know enough about his father at the time to ask the questions that puzzle me now. Lynd Ward and May McNeer Ward were important persons in their own right—he an artist and she an author—and their papers at Georgetown University contain valuable documents for reconstructing the family history. In the early 1980s Harry's elder son, Gordon, responded in detailed letters to a number of my questions. Though Gordon Ward is no longer living, his correspondence has continued to provide valuable information and clues for this project. Nanda Ward discovered some letters of Muriel Ward, the youngest child of Harry and Daisy Ward, and thus one more piece of the puzzle fell into place.

As I learned from reading and listening to David McCullough, especially during a memorable dinner in our home when he was researching his biography of Harry Truman, photographs can reveal a great deal about a person. Thanks to the care of Harry Ward's family, a number of photographs from his long life survive, even a few from his boyhood. Coupled with the family oral tradition and other documents, they do far more than illustrate the story. They help the researcher (and, I hope, the reader) understand the biographical subject and his times far better.

Historical research is always indebted to libraries and librarians. I am particularly grateful for the attentive assistance of Seth Kasten and his staff on the several occasions I worked with the Ward Papers at Union Theological Seminary, New York City. It is impossible to forget how much Dr. Kenneth Rowe and his assistants provided during my stay at Drew University's Methodist Archives, Madison, New Jersey. The Ward research has taken me many places, and I am indebted to numerous other librarians who gave advice and secured documents: the Library of Congress, Washington, D.C.; Georgetown University, Washington, D.C.; Yale University Archives, New Haven, Connecticut (especially Joan Duffy); John Rylands Library, Manchester, England; Chiswick [Public] Library, Chiswick, England (especially Carolyn Hammond); Hammersmith and Fulham Library, London, England; Hampshire County Library, Winchester, England; Ealing Library, London, England; State Historical Society of Wisconsin, Madison, Wisconsin; American Baptist-Samuel Colgate Historical Library, Colgate Rochester Divinity School, Rochester, New York (especially Dana Martin); Central Methodist

College Archives, Fayette, Missouri; and Kansas City Public Library, Kansas City, Missouri. The librarians, especially Elise Fisher, at my home institution, William Jewell College, have provided invaluable assistance locating and securing numerous and often quite rare books and articles through interlibrary loan services. Though underpaid and overworked, these many librarians obviously relish historical preservation and research. How impoverished our culture would be without them, though we persist in underfunding their best efforts.

Again taking a cue from David McCullough, I have roamed the physical space that Harry Ward inhabited during his long life. Though over a century has passed since he was born in London and roamed the forests of southern England as a boy, and though, of course, those places have changed physically and culturally, there was much to be learned from the sights, sounds, and smells of those places even today.

Thank goodness for institutions that support such projects. I am indebted to William Jewell College for sabbatical leave and to the Center for the Study of Religion and American Culture, Louisville, Kentucky, for a grant that enabled the final research and initial writing to take place. Finally I am grateful for the encouragement of friends—who often spoke the right word at the right time—and family, especially my wife, Marcia, to whom this book is dedicated.

> David Nelson Duke
> Professor of Religion
> William Jewell College

David signed the contract for publication of this book in January 2000. He completed all substantive changes to the manuscript before cancer claimed his life in December of that year. Since he did not live to see his book go into production, David had no opportunity to thank those who facilitated the process.

I am very grateful to Wayne Flynt for his enthusiasm for publishing David's manuscript in this distinguished series and for his very positive place in David's life. My thanks to the kind and helpful people at the University of Alabama Press, and special thanks to Sandra Williamson for her very careful copyediting and wonderful sense of humor.

Elise Fisher's persistence in tracking down answers to bibliographical questions that emerged once the manuscript moved into production was invaluable. I underscore David's gratitude to Elise.

Warmest thanks to Nanda Ward and Robin Ward Savage for their kindness to David and me, for their interest in this project, and for sharing family photographs and Lynd Ward's wood engravings for inclusion in David's book.

David's own "never failing friend" Samuel E. Balentine encouraged and guided me and generously invested his time as we worked together to conform David's finished manuscript to the technical requirements for publication. David would want to thank Sam for "every step of the way" and beyond.

Marcia S. Duke

IN THE TRENCHES
WITH JESUS AND MARX

Prologue

The World of an Outsider

ENTERING THE BUILDING in the middle of the day, when New York City's lunchtime traffic was at its height, a slightly built, eighty-year-old man found the receptionist at the Macmillan Publishing House. She had a package for him. It was not a package he wanted, for it signaled rejection of his labor of love, a manuscript he regarded as his legacy to the world. It was a sad moment, and though he was a very private person, he was not able to keep that disappointment and sadness to himself.

He heard a familiar voice: "What are you doing here, Dad?"

It was his granddaughter Nanda, who had begun working at Macmillan not so long ago. How he cherished this young woman and her sister Robin, his only grandchildren. Over the course of their brief lifetimes, he had been an important, and sometimes controversial, public figure. As a little girl, Nanda had watched him address a packed Madison Square Garden. Back then people listened intently and applauded vigorously his carefully reasoned oration. Why, not much more than twenty years earlier Macmillan had been more than happy to publish his manuscripts. His books sold well then, and one was a book-of-the-month selection for the Religious Book Club. Back then people were eager to read what he wrote and hear what he had to say. He had been, after all, Professor of Christian Ethics at America's most prestigious Protestant seminary of the day, chairman of the American Civil Liberties Union board for two decades, an influential leader in Methodist circles, and much in demand as a speaker for labor groups and activist organizations.

Now times were different. This was a different America, and he stood outside the mainstream. Too many friends and colleagues of earlier years had become distant from him, some even bitterly alienated. This was Senator Joe McCarthy's cold war America, and Macmillan was not interested in a manuscript entitled "Jesus and Marx," especially by an author widely known for his Soviet sympathies. The rejection letter insisted that the decision had not been colored by his controversial political alliances, but he remained suspicious.

His eyes looked moist as he answered, "Oh, Nanda. I've just come to retrieve my manuscript." The diction was clipped, and the accent decidedly British, though there were traces of American influence as well. He looked so very sad to his granddaughter, but not defeated. This was not a man who allowed himself to accept defeat. He was a warrior on a holy mission, and the fire would not die in his belly until he passed from this earth some thirteen years later.

That fire had been kindled in another century in another country, and though his commitments were very different from those he learned from his Methodist shopkeeper parents in suburban London, the temperament and values remained firm. Perhaps on that sad day in 1953 Harry F. Ward remembered an earlier time in his life when he looked at another culture from the outside, when from the window of his family's butcher shop he looked out on the busy traffic of Chiswick's High Road and wondered if he would ever realize his dreams. Perhaps on that sobering day in 1953 Harry Ward remembered how far he had come in those eighty years, even as he wondered what lay ahead for a person regarded by many as out of step with his culture.

1

An English Methodist Shopkeeper's World
1873–1891

> I am not ungrateful to my peasant forefathers, nor to the tradition of duty and self-discipline, for the little blue imp who is most of the time on my shoulder, whispering: "Get on with the job."
> —Harry F. Ward, "Why I Have Found Life Worth Living"

HARRY FREDERICK WARD entered this world 15 October 1873, the firstborn of Harry and Fanny Jeffrey Ward of Chiswick, England. In 1873 Chiswick was a suburb of greater London, a quiet village on the Thames known for its orchards and stately homes, but the town was changing. Ambitious merchants like the Wards were quickly transforming it into a middle-class suburb of shopkeepers. Their Queen's Row shop opened onto the High Road, an ancient thoroughfare to London dating back to the Roman era and, in Harry's day, an increasingly busy road, part of greater London's burgeoning transit system.

The Ward family was part of the influx of merchants who were building commerce along the High Road in a Chiswick hamlet called Turnham Green. The 1870s saw the population of Chiswick almost double in size.[1] In 1891, the year when young Harry Ward immigrated to the United States, an observer of Chiswick noted that though there was "a flavour of aristocracy about Chiswick; Turnham Green, on the contrary, sounds distinctly plebeian."[2] Without question Fanny and Harry Ward were part of this "plebeian" tide lamented by the Chiswick aristocracy and middle class.

Harry's father, probably as a teenager, had immigrated to London from southern England's New Forest area, where for decades, perhaps centuries, his ancestors worked the land as "agricultural laborers," as the census labeled them. Once in the London area it is likely that this young man apprenticed himself to a trade. By the time of his son Harry's birth he was listed as a cheesemonger in Turnham Green.[3]

Only a handful of pictures survive of the elder Harry Ward, all but one taken when he was quite aged. Typically he sits uncomfortably in his coat and tie, the way working men often look. In two of the photographs one notices in particular his very large, swollen, and gnarled hands. As a young adult, Harry described his father as "an upright and godly man and the kindest of parents," the latter a rather striking comment in light of the impersonal authoritarianism often associated with Victorian fathers.[4]

As with most women of ordinary standing, Fanny Jeffrey Ward's life is difficult to reconstruct. Ward family tradition remembers her as the daughter of a French lady's maid. She was born in nearby Hammersmith,[5] a suburb immediately adjacent to Chiswick on the east. She and Harry Ward must have met after he moved to the London area, probably in the early 1870s. Ward family tradition retains the memory of her alienation from her own family because she abandoned her religious tradition (Anglican or Catholic) to join her husband's Methodist chapel.

Her life was not easy in several respects. She was blind in one eye due to an accident with scissors. Subsequent to Harry's birth, she lost an infant daughter, Nall. In the late 1870s she bore three other children, apparently no more than a year apart: Hugh, Elizabeth, and Beatrice. She would live only long enough to see one of her children leave home— Harry, just months before her death. Her son Harry would remember fondly going to midweek prayer services with her at the Methodist chapel. One of her few surviving portraits shows a slightly built woman and gives the impression of gentleness. Her face is very plain, with her hair pulled straight back, revealing rather large ears. Her partial blind-

Harry F. Ward at age six.
(Courtesy of Nanda Ward
and Robin Ward Savage)

ness is not immediately evident, though her left eye strikes the viewer as off-center and unfocused. With her receding chin and thin lips, she is not a beauty, but her countenance expresses a pleasant softness. The earrings and lace handkerchief high on her neck do not seem natural to her appearance; one can more easily picture her in an apron, holding her children or tending customers in the shop.

Like her life's story, only a fraction of her tombstone remains: "In loving memory, Fanny, wife of Harry Ward, [pa]ssed away Dec. 29th 1891, aged 42 years."[6] A father-to-son letter on the day of her death painfully reports that during her final hours only one member of her biological family was in attendance to offer her "a word of spiritual comfort."[7] Fanny Jeffrey Ward's bulldog persistence in the face of adversity would be a prominent characteristic of her son Harry. And he, too, would struggle with poor health.

Harry F. Ward at age
thirteen. (Courtesy of
Nanda Ward and Robin
Ward Savage)

We know little of the Ward family dynamics. As an adult Harry described himself as growing up in a family that rarely expressed deep feelings: "I come of a breed that is stark in speech and used to stand[ing] mute when greatly moved."[8] Certainly there is something very English here, though reticence may also stem from the limited family interaction allowed by long hours maintaining a shop. Harry remembered his mother as "one of the best mothers God ever gave a man; the influence of her life still lingers with a benediction."[9] While Harry would always find heartfelt expressiveness difficult, it is obvious that he was raised by parents who nurtured sensitivity.

Appropriate to his hometown's original name, Cheesewick, Harry's parents had their commercial beginnings as cheesemongers. Hard workers, they shared Chiswick's growing prosperity, eventually becoming the proprietors of a butcher shop. Young Harry's education reflected this prosperity, for at seven years of age he was sent to a boarding school catering to "the landed gentry, lower aristocracy, and successful business men," according to Ward family oral tradition.[10] It might have been one of a number of schools newly created for the rising middle class.

We do not know how long Harry remained at this school, but we do know that it was a difficult experience for him. According to family tradition, young Harry, slightly built like his mother, was victimized by the class bully. As the story goes, Harry took boxing lessons—readily available in Chiswick, a town famous for the sport—and he ultimately defeated his antagonist. But Harry was not strong enough to overcome the effects of the poor diet offered by the school, and he fell victim to rheumatic fever. Two photographs from his childhood starkly reveal the serious impact of this illness. As a six-year-old, before starting school, Harry stands straight and confident, with the full face of a healthy youngster. As a thirteen-year-old he looks thin and sad, with dark circles under his eyes. As a result of his illness, Harry was withdrawn from the school and sent to live with relatives for two years in Lyndhurst, at the center of southern England's beautiful New Forest.

In this land of his Ward ancestors he found not only health but a love for the outdoors which he would maintain throughout his long life.[11] The area is charming, with villages like Lyndhurst nestled among the heath and forest. Ponies, once wild, graze on the heath. The forests abound with a large variety of vegetation. One sees broadleaf as well as evergreen, saplings and scrub brush along with venerable, thick-trunked oaks. In some places the green canopy is so thick that even at midday the forest is like twilight, with the occasional white-striped birch standing out like a signpost. Here young Harry Ward could hike miles and miles of forest paths over heath, through dense forests, and past thick patches of fern, shiny holly bushes, and bright green moss on ancient logs. Within minutes of Lyndhurst there were places where each bird's voice could be heard distinctly, as if one were hundreds of miles from the nearest human outpost. Harry had not lived in London's squalor but in a suburb, where he could gaze out on orchards and large gardens, some directly across the High Road from his father's shop; yet by comparison with Chiswick, Lyndhurst's beauty was extraordinary. More importantly, the New Forest became a healing paradise for the boy's sick body and a solace for the worries that attended his illness.

Here also Harry heard stories about his ancestors, how for centuries commoners such as they were forbidden to hunt in the New Forest—a domain specially reserved for nobility since the time of William the Conqueror, who in 1079 made this area his own private deer preserve. The penalty for encroachment was severe, including mutilation, blinding, and, for frequent offenders, death. The law also prohibited commoners' ownership of hunting dogs, and in the Lyndhurst Verderers' Hall Harry could see the Rufus Stirrup, a device used to discourage illegal hunting. A dog whose feet were too large to fit through the stirrup would have its paws maimed so as to destroy its hunting prowess.

Perhaps even more compelling were the stories of smuggling. Apparently smuggling was so common among the inhabitants of the south coast villages and countryside that one nineteenth-century historian claimed "every labourer was either a poacher or a smuggler."[12] It seems that the economic benefits were not the only aspect of smuggling that appealed to New Forest inhabitants; there was also the thrill of adventure as the commoners tried to outwit the authorities. As an adult, Harry remembered with admiration the exploits of these New Forest folk, who, in a kind of class war, "smuggled the king's brandy and measured their wits and their strength with those of the king's officers." He recalled the story of the "buxom dame" who sat in a pony-drawn cart, covering a keg with her skirts, while coyly chatting with a representative of the Crown.[13]

Another story about smuggling featured a Ward ancestor who emigrated from Ireland to the New Forest "one jump ahead of the sheriff," as Ward later recalled with a smile. Riding a steed named Satan, this outlaw habitually smuggled rum and poached the king's deer in the New Forest, but all that changed after he heard the preaching of John Wesley,[14] who sometimes evangelized in the area.[15]

This story of an ancestor's Methodist conversion is crucial for understanding Harry Ward and his family. For the children—Harry, Hugh, Elizabeth, and Beatrice—this tale, together with reminders of their mother's alienation from her own relatives, reinforced a certain kind of evangelical Methodist subculture in suburban London that provided their family identity. The Wards' social and economic status corresponded to that of many Methodists of the time. Indeed, one historian of Victorian England referred to Methodists as a "sect of shopkeepers and small businessmen."[16]

Following the death of John Wesley in 1791, Methodism experienced what new religious groups often undergo after the death of the founder: a certain amount of fragmentation as religious tradition faces new challenges and struggles to interpret the founder's legacy for subsequent generations in different cultural contexts. Whereas splinter groups such as Primitive Methodism each claimed to be the true representative of Wesley's heritage and found niches in England's religious and social spectra, the mainstream expression came to be known as Wesleyan Methodism. Even within Wesleyan Methodism, however, there was often a good deal of dissension, though usually this stopped short of a formal breach in the ranks. The Ward family represents one such case.

Though there is no evidence that the family shifted their allegiance from Wesleyan Methodism to the more revivalistic Primitive Methodism, apparently there were times when the Wards' Wesleyan identity was sorely tested. In particular, Harry's father was put off by his congregation's increasingly formal liturgy.

The Wards were not alone in their dissatisfaction. In the late 1870s, for example, when Harry was just a young child, Methodism's Second London District wrestled with proposed revisions in the Methodist liturgy. It is probably no accident that in 1879 the district minutes describe "serious losses occasioned by the large number of members who have removed or ceased to meet."[17] A real crisis seems to have developed ten years later, for Methodist periodicals of the time feature letters and articles from concerned lay folk and lay preachers about the coldness of formal liturgy.[18]

Lay preachers, commonly known as "local preachers," were scandalized by and frequently suspicious of educated clergy, partly because of their unhappiness with read prayers and learned, passionless sermons, and partly because of the derision—real and perceived—they suffered at the hands of their "betters." Though criticism by the professional Methodist clergy was painful, it did not alter the conviction of these stouthearted lay preachers. As one of them said: "If zeal and fire—deep piety and bold aggression—are but the marks of vital life in Methodism—then it will need that every man a flame of fire shall be, fitted by heaven for mighty deeds, and noble conquests win o'er Satan's kingdom."[19]

The elder Harry Ward, himself a lay preacher, was cut from this same bolt of Methodist cloth. Together with his family, he found ways to withdraw without leaving the Wesleyan fold. The Wards joined a mission band, a group devoted to revivalistic, open-air meetings attended by members of London's working classes. Mission band participants like the Wards could remain Wesleyan Methodists even as they engaged in a style of religious practice more in keeping with their beliefs. Through their membership in the mission band and the elder Ward's itinerant preaching, the Wards could avoid the formal mode of worship that prevailed in their Chiswick congregation and still retain their adherence to Wesleyan Methodism. The legacy of this dissident membership style would last throughout son Harry's long life.

Many lay people such as the senior Ward preached regularly, filling pulpits as they were assigned in their circuit. If the 1891 quarterly circuit plan is typical, Harry's father, a local preacher in the Ealing and Acton Circuit, had ample opportunities. He is listed there as preaching among four different chapels at least three times each month, including Sunday mornings, Sunday evenings, and mid-week services.[20]

These religious gatherings played a key role in defining young Harry's sense of place and commitment in Victorian society. Church life among Wesleyan Methodists was the principal feature of his social life and, most likely, the primary context within which he made friends and learned customs of social interaction. Indeed, a significant portion of each week was lived in the company of his fellow Wesleyans. There were Sunday services and midweek prayer meetings to be attended with his mother, in addition to preaching forays with the mission band into working-class districts of London.

Reports and advertisements for the mission bands reveal their revivalist ethos. For example, in Harry's sixteenth year, mission bands associated with the London Wesleyan Mission Band Union made a day of it on a Bank Holiday. The observance began with a prayer meeting at 10 A.M., followed by a "Consecration Meeting," a time of inspiration and challenge—or, as a Methodist reporter saw it, "a time of heart-searching and holy resolve with very many [people]. . . . [P]rayers were offered by workers full of fire and faith, and the meeting closed, every heart aglow." Early afternoon provided an opportunity for "Prayer and Praise." As to music, "The singing went with a swing, the old-time hymns and tunes firing the hearts of all." Testimonies followed. "Hearts throbbed, pulses beat quicker and quicker still, tears of gladness mingled with shouts of praise." This was followed at 3:15 by an open-air procession of mission band workers led by two of their brass bands (instruments and singing comprised a principal strategy for drawing a crowd to hear the forthcoming sermon). One picks up the flavor of this religious subculture: "Thank God the devil is not having his own way on Bank Holidays. The singing and speaking were of the right stamp, and the good results of our meetings will presently appear." The size of the crowd is evident by the report that 500 persons stayed for tea (supper). The day ended with an "Evangelistic Meeting" at 6:30 P.M. A "sea of bright faces" nearly filled chapel, and people listened attentively to the preaching and sang vigorously as "the chorus was taken up again and again." Both ordained and lay preachers addressed the audience, "pleading with the sinners [and] inspiring the saints. . . . It was far from a silent gathering. The shouts of 'Glory' and 'Hallelujah' will not be readily forgotten." The meeting ended with another prayer and a call to the altar. Some eleven hours after the day's first session had begun, the crowd left for home, "but the workers were jubilant still."[21]

This was the sort of religious atmosphere in which Harry Ward was raised. It was emotional and utterly committed to the dissemination of truth as its adherents understood that truth, no matter how differently the larger culture might see it. These Methodist folk believed they were engaged in a holy war with a corrupt world. As the Methodist reporter described that mission band union meeting: "We are no longer alone, fighting against desperate odds; we are a mighty army, full of an unconquerable enthusiasm."[22]

It is not surprising that these Methodists created their own religious setting as well as their own social milieu. For these pious folk, many of the popular Victorian diversions were unsavory, what they termed "worldly." In 1891 a Methodist representative spoke proudly of "our ancient opposition to card-playing, theatre-going and dancing."[23] This "Nonconformist conscience," as it was labeled by a Wesleyan minister in 1890, was heavy on prohibitions, especially "against drinking, against gambling, against the music halls."[24] Is it any wonder that in a rare moment of recorded self-analysis Harry would later describe his childhood as one in which those around him were "inclined to take things too seriously"?[25]

It is one thing for an adult to embrace this alternative way of life. It is quite another for young people, whose developing identities depend a great deal on peer approval. It would be rare for a young person of any culture and time to choose to be an outcast. Therefore it is important for religious subcultures like Wesleyan Methodism to create alternative social experiences for their young people.

Methodist temperance societies, for example, had a juvenile version, Bands of Hope. Advertisements in Methodist publications encouraged readers to join the Young People's Bible and Prayer Union. The Wesleyan Methodist Book-Room lists not only works on Christian doctrine, biblical studies, Methodist history, and personal holiness, but also a number of titles appealing to young people's desire for stories of adventure and romance. For an English society which, as Anthony Trollope observed in 1870, had "become a novel-reading people, from the Prime Minister down to the last-appointed scullery maid,"[26] this was necessary if Methodists hoped to maintain their religious subculture against the pressures of the dominant society. In the year Harry became a teenager, one Methodist commentator declared: "The fact is our young people must have amusement. If the Church will not provide it, the Devil will."[27] Opportunities for "rational recreation," developed as alternatives to worldly options for young people, were a critical part of young Harry's life in Chiswick. In suburbs like Chiswick, lawn tennis was promoted during Harry's boyhood as yet another "counter-attraction" to worldly pursuits.[28]

Of course, these alternative forms of recreation were not always enthusiastically embraced by young people, even the pious ones. Little wonder then that in the year Harry turned sixteen, "Our Young Men's Column" in the *Methodist Times* featured a response to teenage correspondents' inquiries about the Methodist prohibition against social dancing, even ballroom dancing. The columnist listed several arguments against it: dancing undermines one's reputation; it allows the "animal" side of the human creature a loose rein; and it leads to other evils, especially drinking.[29]

Together with its many prohibitions, this religious subculture also emphasized a divinely ordained work ethic. A Methodist hymn of the era reflects the mind-set:

Full well the labour of our hands
With fervency of spirit stands;

For God, who all our days hath given,
From toil excepts but one in seven:
And labouring while we time redeem,
We please the Lord, and work for him.[30]

Small wonder that over half a century later Harry would still be repeating a motto of his childhood family: "A situation is either inevitable or it is not. If it is inevitable endure it gracefully. If it is not inevitable change it."[31]

Methodists of that period also embraced a virtue in which Victorian public schools put great stock: "manliness." Popular magazines and comics glorified manly values through exciting stories of heroic individuals. Recognizing the effectiveness of these media, churches adopted these popular forms to promote Christian manliness among its young men. "Muscular Christianity" had become part of the redefinition of gentlemanliness in Victorian England,[32] and surely a pious, ambitious young man like Harry aspired to be a true Christian gentlemen. One such muscular Christian was General Charles "Chinese" Gordon, who demonstrated great courage and personal compassion while leading his army against overwhelming odds at the battle of Khartoum. Gordon's heroic leadership and death during Harry's twelfth year was forever etched in the mind and heart of this impressionable adolescent.

It is evident that throughout his life Harry was quite taken by all sorts of dramatic stories of courage and integrity, not just those of the General Gordons. There was more to this than the influence of Victorian culture: it was a personal matter as well. Yet by the standards of Victorian manliness, Harry failed the test as a young man. He was physically weak, hardly the sturdy specimen represented in most depictions of Victorian heroes. It is no wonder that the story of his boxing triumph survived in family oral tradition, for that experience may have been one of the few occasions during Harry's boyhood when he felt he measured up to the standards of manliness.

Harry always relished a challenge, especially a physical one. In a rare moment of public autobiographical candor about his struggles with poor health, he once defined his physical limitations as an opportunity for courage—the premier virtue of those Victorian manly figures.[33] And despite physical and educational limitations, Harry was determined not to be denied his dreams. In December of 1887, at age fourteen, he received a certificate from the Ealing Centre indicating completion of his formal education.[34]

Harry wished to pursue his education further, and perhaps he did so through personal reading and maybe even the odd evening class while he worked days in his parents' butcher shops (by this time the Wards owned two such establishments), but his inferior formal education made him an unlikely candidate for a university education. Though two generations earlier Nonconformist families such as his could not have even contemplated entering a British university, a limited number of university slots were now open to Nonconformists. Just two years before Harry's birth all religious tests for university matriculation and graduation were abolished. Nevertheless, this did not matter to Harry; he was not qualified. His frustrated ambition must have gnawed at him as he performed the menial tasks of butcher's work year after year.

In order to appreciate Harry Ward's dramatic transformation into a radical social activist, it is important to be very clear about the socioeconomic standing of this young man and his family. Descriptions of Ward growing up among London's East End working class and poor are erroneous,[35] for he was the beneficiary of a middle-class shopkeeper's growing prosperity. By 1887 the family had added another butcher shop on the High Road, just a few doors west of the original one. The 1881 census reports that there were two teenage women domestic servants and three young men—ages twenty-two, seventeen, and fourteen— serving as the Wards' shop assistants.

Of course, young Harry had to work hard; that was part of the Methodist shopkeeper ethos of Victorian England. But he experienced no Dickensian-like working-class boyhood. Harry Ward received an education superior to many working-class folk of his day, though to be sure he did not achieve the level he desired. On the whole, his life in Chiswick was very middle-class. Photographs of the High Road during that era show wide, paved sidewalks lined with trees in front of neat shops. Though it was a busy thoroughfare, with horse-drawn trams running one right after another up the tracks to London, curbs and street lights provided safety for the stream of shoppers. Kew Gardens lay just across the river, and just south of Turnham Green Common the Royal Horticultural Society maintained thirty-five acres of gardens to which thousands flocked every year.

In a setting that combined suburban commercial development and natural beauty, Harry grew up not wanting for any material necessity. The solid brick structures of Queen's Row rise three stories above the shops, and the Wesleyan chapels with which the family was associated were not insignificant structures. It must be emphasized that despite the limitations imposed by English society's class consciousness, Harry Ward grew up in comfortable, middle-class surroundings. He knew economic deprivation and exploitation only by observation.

Perhaps one of the most difficult things Harry had to deal with in his teen years was the shop assistants' increasing dissatisfaction with the work schedule set by his father. Mr. Ward considered himself to be a fair man, and he allowed the assistants two days off each week, but apparently they did not perceive this arrangement as equitable. Their discontent seems a reflection of events in the world around them.

The late 1880s saw a great deal of labor unrest in England, including "the first successful mass strike by unskilled labour,"[36] the dockworkers' strike in 1889. When the Ward shops experienced a shortage of meat, the teenage Harry became curious and went to the docks to see for himself what the situation was. Though later in life he became a strong advocate of organized labor, there is no evidence that this strike had an immediate impact on his notions of social justice. Instead, as the local shop assistants' union became more and more vocal about working hours, Harry shared some anxiety, and perhaps some anger, with his father.

In March of 1890 nearby Hammersmith saw a demonstration of trade union members and shop assistants in support of "the demands of the Shop Assistants against the selfish minority of employers opposed to the limitation of the hours of labour." One of the speakers at the meeting compared the situation to slavery and called for a boycott of certain shops.[37] It is likely that Harry Ward's butcher shops were among those listed, for there is a family story of young Harry sending pickets into retreat as he pummeled them with sacks of flour and soot, probably from the windows of the family quarters above the shop. When in July the Shop Assistants Union met in Turnham Green, the vicar of the

Anglican Church just a few blocks west of the Wards' shops expressed his sympathy and support for an eight-hour workday. The *West London Observer* reported that Chiswick's Radical Club had "passed a resolution pledging itself to support the Shop Assistants Union of Chiswick in their efforts to shorten their hours of labour."[38] Perhaps this is the occasion when pickets distributed handbills which read:

> WE, THE SHOP ASSISTANTS OF THIS DISTRICT, appeal to you, whose servants we are, to refuse your custom to the shopkeeper whose name is given below. . . . [B]y his refusal to co-operate with their Fellow Tradesmen in shortening the Hours of Labour, he is making our lives one weary long round of toilsome, monotonous labour, working as we are 14 to 16, and sometimes 16 to 18 hours a day. . . . After reading this, you, as self-respecting men and women, with a sense of duty towards others, will BOYCOTT this SWEATER of your Oppressed Brothers and Sisters.
>
> SWEATER, HARRY WARD, Butcher and Provision Merchant, High Road, Chiswick.[39]

Such accusations must have caused great pain for son Harry. He had grown up in a context of piety that obligated the believer to pursue holiness and a life of honesty, hard work, and fairness. His father was not a "sweater," for had he not already bent over backward by providing his workers two days off each week? Why shouldn't his father refuse to negotiate with these ungrateful workers?

In 1891, the year of Harry's immigration to America, shop workers in England formally unionized. Though they achieved some gains in subsequent years, it was not until 1912, with the passage of the Shops Act, that they could claim victory in their efforts to limit legally the number of hours they were required to work.[40] By that time the Chiswick butcher's son had become a vigorous supporter of the labor movement. His journey from sweater's son to friend of labor required that he travel far from *home* in every sense of the word.

2

Discovering New Worlds in America
1891–1898

I belong to a generation of uplifters and converters; without apology.
. . . It was the need of people that called my generation. We were not
after self-expression or self-realization. I remember how I wrote it
down one day in college—our obligation to help those who had not
our opportunities.
  —Harry F. Ward, "Why I Have Found Life Worth Living"

AN ARTICULATE, BRIGHT young man who loves learning, is an
excellent public speaker, and has ambition may very likely avoid following in his father's shopkeeper footsteps. The only reason ever given for
Harry's immigration to America in May of 1891 was a desire for the
education he could not acquire in his English homeland.

Harry had been promised a job on his uncle's ranch near Provo, Utah,
to fund his educational aspirations, but before heading west he spent
some time with another uncle who owned a butcher shop in the Chicago
suburb of Wilmette. (Later he would work for a third uncle, who ran an
irrigated farm in Idaho, producing potatoes and alfalfa for cattle feeder
lots; there Harry learned how to catch trout from mountain streams.)
It is obvious that young Harry had no more intention of becoming a

rancher than a butcher. Perhaps that is why he sought employment in Salt Lake City, applying for a secretarial job at the Latter Day Saints Board of Education. According to a family story, when his prospective employer asked if he could take dictation, Harry responded that he could type as fast as the employer could talk. Harry got the job.[1]

Whether or not this story has been embellished is irrelevant for understanding Harry Ward, for its theme is a refrain in his own self-definition: no task is too difficult for those with enough commitment, drive, and effort (and talent!). His Wesleyan perfectionist heritage contributed to this mind-set, not to mention the inherited Victorian middle-class moral prudence: those who work hard can achieve much. Now as a participant in the pageant known as "the making of the American West," Harry was committed to achieving great things even against overwhelming odds. Looking around Salt Lake City and seeing how people had carved beauty and prosperity from a barren wilderness must have inspired him. He believed that he was up to any challenge, though he was only eighteen years old, on his own, and thousands of miles from parents, siblings, friends, and home. A true Victorian *man* must overcome all obstacles.

In one respect, at least, Harry followed in his father's footsteps: he became a lay preacher. He was listed as a "preacher on trial" at the time he emigrated,[2] so it is likely that the following event occurred not long before then. The story goes that on one occasion[3] when the Wards' mission band was evangelizing on the streets of London, the mission band leader leaned over to Harry and informed him that he would be preaching on the next street corner. The group sang their hymns; the usual crowd gathered, and the teenager launched into his first sermon. It was well received—so much so that Harry became one of the group's regular preachers and sought formal approval of his lay preacher status. The three Wesleyan judges who heard his trial sermon "declared him a natural Preacher."[4] Once again, a challenge had been met and overcome.

Harry continued his lay preaching in America. In Mormon Utah, mainstream Protestant ministers may have been in short supply, for when persons at a local army base learned of Harry's preaching credentials, they asked him to serve as chaplain. Thereafter he preached to the soldiers every Sunday afternoon.[5]

Seven months after his arrival in America, Harry received word from his father that his mother had died. His father's letter was written on the very day of her death, and it became the only piece of correspondence between Harry and his English family that he held on to, surely an indication of the letter's significance for him. It abounds in the traditional language of simple evangelical piety: "[S]he is safe. And tho it is hard to those left behind it is 'gain' to her." It was signed "Your loving Father, H. Ward."[6]

Harry's own health continued to be a problem. Utah's high altitude put a strain on his scarred heart, and he suffered some degree of emotional agony as well, for his mother's death brought not only grief but loneliness. This loneliness was still evident four years later: "[S]ince she died, I have wandered around and not cared to go home, where I would always be reminded of my loss."[7] Perhaps one of the reasons Harry felt that his mother's "life still lingers with a benediction"[8] was the consolation she had always provided as he coped with his physical limitations. She understood. Her own poor health and partial blindness may have created a special empathy between Fanny Ward and her firstborn son.[9] She knew that God's people are seldom without adversity.

Harry had aspired to attend Northwestern University ever since meeting two impressive alumni in Salt Lake City, but his poor health would not allow it. His body needed a warmer climate than windy Chicago offered. His doctor recommended the sunny clime of southern California, and so in the fall of 1893 Harry began his college education in Los Angeles at the University of Southern California, a new Methodist institution. Soon after arriving there, he learned that he had missed the opportunity of studying with a brilliant Methodist professor, George Albert Coe, who had left two years earlier to take a post at Northwestern University. Northwestern again!

USC in those days was rough and tumble, and it struggled to attain financial solvency.[10] Harry's entering class was a rowdy bunch, more interested in parties and pranks than in study. Harry joined in the fun and joined a fraternity. Surviving photographs of the group attest to this light-hearted spirit. One beautiful June day Harry's fraternity hired a professional photographer to capture their good times together. They dressed up for the occasion in suits, vests, bow ties, and dapper straw hats.

In each group photograph one young man's attire causes him to stand out. Clad in the same suit he wore when posing for a studio photograph in London several years earlier, Harry is not so finely dressed as his friends. His trousers and coat are obviously worn, and they are less well tailored than the suits worn by his chums. Unlike the others, Harry wears no vest, and his bow tie is different. Instead of a dashing young man's neat, black bow tie, Harry wears a floppy piece of wide, white sash tied in a large bow. His long, unruly locks contrast with his fraternity brothers' stylishly trimmed hair. One wonders what Harry thought when he looked in the mirror those days, for he was a sensitive soul, self-conscious about his social limitations.

He had to work hard to pay for his expenses at USC since his savings were small. He stoked furnaces and mowed lawns for several families in the area. He may have also done some preaching, for he joined the local Methodist Conference on probationary status.

In order to be accredited as a minister in the Methodist Church, he was required to read designated books and then satisfactorily pass an examination in several subject areas. One book on that reading list would change his life—a life already full of changes. More precisely, the book dramatically altered his understanding of Christianity and thereby his basic assumptions about what is important in life. According to Harry's recollections, Richard T. Ely's *The Social Aspect of Christianity* led him to take seriously for the first time the social responsibility incumbent upon Christian believers.[11]

Ely's ideas gave new meaning to Harry's earlier experiences, for the author vividly depicted the alienation of working people from the church. Harry had seen that alienation in London, where his mission band was often regarded with curiosity and even contempt by working-class onlookers. No doubt he had wondered why more of these people did not respond positively to the gospel he preached so passionately. Now he saw himself as one of those persons Ely described as having "strange conceptions" of "the simple gospel of Christ" (23). Ely provided a broader significance to Harry's evangelical assumptions: "Christianity is primarily concerned with this world, and it is the mission of Christianity to bring to pass here a kingdom of righteousness and to rescue from the evil one and redeem all our social relations" (53). Harry's street sermons of earlier years seemed ineffectual in the light of Ely's thundering accusation: "Salvation means infinitely more than the proclamation of glittering generalizations and the utterance of sweet sentimentalities. Salvation means righteousness, positive righteousness, in all the earth" (73). Ely's subsequent phrase connected Harry to his own tradition: to establish this righteousness, said Ely, "means hard warfare." Thus Ely called the teenage lay preacher Harry Ward to a holy combat not only against personal vices like drinking, gambling, infidelity, and dancing, but also against the social forces that encourage people to take up these sinful ways.

Ely provided a new key for Harry to appreciate his religious heritage, for this key fit the Methodist emphasis on a holy life. As Ely put it, "It is a truly religious work to pass good laws, as it is to preach sermons; as holy a work to lead a crusade against filth, vice, and disease in slums of cities, and to seek the abolition of disgraceful tenement-houses of American cities, as it is to send missionaries to the heathen" (73).

This social interpretation of Harry's evangelical heritage not only opened a new door for his religious understanding, it also offered a resolution to a built-in conflict in his own life experience. The challenges of limitation—physical, social, and economic—and his Methodist work-ethic perfectionism contained the potential for conflict. What if hard work did not yield the results one sought, especially in this new land? Frustrated potential, no matter how vigorously or virtuously pursued, could lead to cynical rejection of religion as it had among many Victorian working-class folk.

These contradictions had become more personal for this young man with the death of his mother. Harry's sense of isolation from his family was exacerbated when he perceived that his brother Hugh was taking on not only his job in the family business but also (from Harry's perspective) the role of elder son. In a rare moment of self-revelation, he writes of his relationship to his father, "I have been away so long, he does not miss me now as he did at first, especially as my younger brother has to some extent taken my place."[12]

Yet despite the grief and loneliness created by these circumstances, the changes may have also engendered some much needed independence for this young adult. Though many miles separated him from his family, his mother's physical presence would always stand in silent but nevertheless compelling judgment of his shifts in religious understanding. Her death and his increasing sense of emotional distance from his father gave

Harry permission to explore new ideas. He was at a stage in a young adult's life when such shifts are natural, and his mother's death was yet another experience that would reinforce his independence from his heritage.

This is no insignificant point, for Harry had every opportunity in England to be challenged by the social message of Christianity. Richard Ely's book was not his first exposure to a version of Christianity that emphasized social responsibility. On Harry's home turf in the Second London District, a Methodist minister named Hugh Price Hughes came to great fame in Harry's youth. Hughes had also written a book calling Christians to social responsibility, *Social Christianity*, published two years before Harry's immigration to America. Furthermore, Hughes was often invited to speak at Wesleyan mission band meetings. His stature exceeded Ely's, yet it was the American, not the Englishman, who altered Harry Ward's perspective.

Why was Ely, not Hughes, the catalyst? Probably because Harry was not ready when Hughes's call first rang out. His English world was his parents', and while he might question particulars of their world, his challenges remained within ideological and organizational boundaries. In the New World, however, as a young adult developing a personal identity, the time was ripe for evaluating old views and entertaining new ones. His mother's death represented one significant break, and his movement away from home, family, and even country manifested a time of radical change in his ideology. Now everything fit together in a way he was unable to see before: the passions of the London dock strikers, the derision of working-class folk toward his mission band's sincere efforts, and the anger of the pickets outside his father's shop. Ely's book was like a pair of new spectacles through which he could see these experiences clearly.

Harry was also at a stage in his life when trust in compelling individuals provides the foundation for values and decisions. Though young people may rebel against traditional authority figures, at the same time they will often embrace new authorities based on their "feelings" about these individuals. As a result, allegiances shift. Just as one first emulates the values of one's parents, the young adult, by transferring fidelity to another person, can assume the values of that new authority with the same degree of loyalty previously exhibited for parental values. Within a year Harry would discover two inspiring professors who would make Ely's approach come alive.

Harry's transfer to Northwestern University in the fall of 1894 provided a fresh start and a rigorous academic climate in which he would flourish. Though he joined a fraternity at Northwestern, he left behind him the frivolity of his USC days. A few years later he referred to that first college experience as a time of "thoughtlessness" and "foolishness."[13] But he brought more than an academic commitment to Northwestern. Ely's book had altered his perception of the world, and he needed to integrate this new perspective into his cherished religious tradition. Therefore he resolved "to go back to Christ and learn from Him."[14]

Northwestern University offered Harry Ward religious nurture as well as excellent academic training. Active religious organizations such as the Young Women's Christian Association (YWCA), the Young Men's Christian Association (YMCA), and the Northwestern Settlement House offered opportunities for Christian service. Students' religious problems received careful attention from the dynamic young professor George Albert Coe. He and his charming wife, Sadie Knowland Coe, an accomplished musician and professor of music at Northwestern, hosted Sunday afternoon conversaziones for Northwestern students in their home, where professor and students discussed religious topics of common interest.[15] Within two years the meetings in the Coe home became so popular they were moved to a campus setting, where each Sunday afternoon students would listen to well-known speakers.[16] Coe's mentorship became a prominent feature in the religious and intellectual awakening of many Northwestern students, including a twenty-one-year-old English immigrant. Indeed, Harry may have been a bit goggle-eyed at first; with his move to Chicago, his world suddenly became much bigger and more complex.

It did not take him long to prove himself in one arena, for by the spring of that first year Harry was one of two students representing Northwestern in prestigious debates against the University of Michigan. In 1895 he was one of three debaters selected to represent Northwestern in intercollegiate competition. Though large audiences were nothing new to the former mission band street preacher, these debates drew a different sort of audience: United States "Ex-Vice-President Adlai E. Stevenson presided. The judges were men of national reputation."[17] On this occasion, Harry's team triumphed, though certain peculiar circumstances placed additional pressure on the Northwestern debaters.

As they prepared for the debate, Harry and one of his teammates went looking for a very rare book that addressed the debate question; they discovered that it had been removed from the Law Institute of Chicago and could not be located. Just two days before the debate, the book was found, prompting another, disturbing discovery: their third team member's speech had been plagiarized from that missing book. A hasty midnight meeting was arranged with President Rogers, and a painful discussion ensued.

A plan was concocted that would neither subject the plagiarist to unnecessary public humiliation nor allow him to represent the university. The teammate would feign a sudden illness and send a telegram about it to the two other Northwestern debaters. After Harry and his teammate received the telegram, both teams agreed that the two Northwestern speakers would divide the missing teammate's time between them. And Harry and his colleague went on to win the debate.[18]

How did Harry regard this deception to which he was an accomplice? No written record or family oral tradition describes this dramatic event. Does Harry's absence from the debate team the following year reflect a protest or self-imposed penance? We do not know.

The following year Wisconsin triumphed over a Northwestern debate team that did not include Harry Ward. However, he represented Northwestern at the Northern Oratorical League contest to which each member school sent one representative. Competing against debaters from the University of Michigan, Oberlin College, the University of Wisconsin, Iowa State University, and the University of Chicago, Harry came away with a second-place prize. In 1897, his senior year, he rejoined the debate team, and the young men returned the collegiate trophy to Northwestern by defeating the University of Wisconsin.[19]

Public speaking was one thing, but finding a social niche in this new place was another. Harry was still an immigrant and perhaps not so polished socially as to make him feel comfortable in all settings. He joined one of the new and therefore not prestigious fraternities. He was still not running with the in-crowd.[20] He also found a niche in Northwestern's athletic world. In Harry's junior year he was chosen to be one of six student members on the athletics committee. As business manager of the tennis association he was involved not only with the team but also with helping develop the sport and its facilities at Northwestern. Having grown up in an enthusiastic tennis community—except for Wimbledon, Chiswick's tennis tournament was the most prestigious in greater London—Harry was well prepared for this activity.

A studio photograph of him in tennis garb provides an interesting contrast with another photograph, where he is dressed for a debate. The young man with tousled hair and tennis duds does not look like much of an athlete; indeed, his shoulders appear to be no wider than his hips, and he looks small and stiff. The large hands of the butcher's son grip the racket, but rolled-up sleeves reveal rather narrow wrists. His dark leather shoes appear worn, certainly not the look associated with the upper-crust tennis crowd. By contrast, in the debater's picture his eyes sparkle with confidence. His dark three-piece suit fits him well. His hands are in his trouser pockets, with each thumb lapped over the bottom of his vest. His chestnut hair is thick, fashionably parted down the middle, and carefully brushed. He even looks comfortable in the starched, high collar of the time. This photograph represents the world of logical argument and rhetorical flourish—the world where Harry could shine.

He certainly shone as a student, not only through good grades but also by personally engaging the new ideas encountered in studies with George Coe and John Gray. One cannot overestimate the impact of Coe, whom Harry found not only intellectually compelling but relationally significant. Beyond his encounters with students in classes and office appointments, Coe opened his home to them as well. He respected their independence and questioning of authority, and he did not want to discourage it, especially in the name of religion. "Every student . . . should be taught that his doubts are common ones, and that his process of intellectual fermentation does not shut him out from the heartiest fellowship with Christians."[21] His students responded enthusiastically to this openness. One student reporter judged that "No one has felt afraid to voice his sentiments."[22] A Northwestern University history reports that "Chapel conduct improved, with the moral awakening which began in 1895 with Professor Coe's lectures on student religious problems."[23]

These recollections remind us that George Coe sought to interpret traditional Methodist faith in modern terms without abandoning the heartfelt piety which had nourished that faith tradition. Not only was his

Harry F. Ward at Northwestern University in 1897. Family history holds that Harry was captain of the men's tennis team, that Daisy played on the women's team, and that they met on the tennis courts. (Photo and family story courtesy of Nanda Ward and Robin Ward Savage)

personality and style winsome, his modernist interpretation of Methodism was evangelistic in tone. Coe promoted a campus "religious life" that was "robust, open-eyed, sympathetic, aggressive, and extremely practical. It ought to be the most sociable part of college life, and as far as possible removed from everything that hints of a 'pious clique.'"[24] As Harry Ward recalled, "Professor Coe was opening up a new approach to religion, and deeper meanings for it, in the day when Methodists were just beginning to feel the impact of Darwin and the scientific method."[25]

Coe's own personal spiritual struggle helped him connect with the Northwestern students. He was only nine years Harry Ward's senior, and like Ward and other Methodist students, he wrestled with the appar-

Award-winning debater Harry F. Ward at Northwestern University in 1897. (Courtesy of Nanda Ward and Robin Ward Savage)

ent conflicts between modernity and traditional Christian beliefs. What he would later describe as "the most significant point in my life, religiously considered" was a shift "away from dogmatic method to scientific method. Devotion to truth ascertained by scientific method became the feature of my personal religion."[26] However, this scientific method did not lead him to an adversarial or agnostic relationship with religion but to an appreciation for the common foundation of all truth.

Coe's notion of the "scientific method" did not abandon the heart in favor of the head; it brought them together. Appealing to his fellow Methodists' appreciation for religious experience, Coe argued that good science, like healthy Methodist religion, is based on the experiential, not the dogmatic. Certainly science and religion represent different kinds of experience, but they share in common a sense of humble openness to truth, insisted Coe.[27] What is most fundamental about reality is the personal, not ideas, he claimed; therefore what we experience is consciousness of a larger whole of which we are a part.[28]

This sort of logic appealed to Harry's way of comprehending life around him as well as to his Methodist sensibilities. He had grown up learning his world primarily through his basic senses. Working with livestock is a tactile experience. Many hours of the day are defined in terms of what one handles, whether holding reins, grooming, patting, and feeding the horses or hanging, cutting, and packaging meat. For most of his life Harry's body had constituted a challenge. From childhood onward he suffered from a leaky heart valve, so he never took physical strength for granted. Furthermore, his love of the New Forest was nurtured by sight, smell, sound, and touch. Thus Coe's sensory theory of knowing seemed reasonable to Harry both in his mind *and* in his body. Together with his Methodist appreciation for vital religious experience, Harry's life experience made him a likely convert to this new way of knowing and to the ideological agenda Coe attached to it.

Coe's perspective is set forth in *The Religion of a Mature Mind*, a popular book based on his conversations with students. In particular, he listened to and took seriously his students' concerns about the conflicts they perceived between religion and modern science. The intellectually rigorous Coe argued against a division between the interests of religion and science; they "must be so related," he said, "that they can live together in harmony in the same individual."[29] *The Religion of a Mature Mind*, like Coe's teaching, appealed to students to recognize that the true meaning of their religion could only be enhanced, not hurt, by modernity. The Methodist emphasis on experience need not be abandoned; instead it would be enriched by including all ways of knowing. Hence it was not inconsistent to preface philosophical discussions at the conversaziones with the singing of traditional hymns of Methodist piety, for the scientific method helps restore Christianity to its true purpose. Christianity is not escapist but rather a means through which the human community can attain "self-realization."[30] Empirical data, personal experience, and Scripture all converge to affirm basic truths, such as the importance of service to fellow human beings. Evolution finds its parallel in the belief that the Kingdom of God—that is, the well being of all humanity—can develop on this earth. In Coe's hands the traditional catechism received an evolutionary twist: "[L]et us ask ourselves what is the chief end of man. Is it to glorify God? Yes; but glorifying God consists in uniting ourselves with him in heart and work, to produce an ideal human race . . . a community of finite souls progressively realizing their union with one another and with the eternal life of God."[31]

Thus students like Harry Ward need not abandon their religion in the face of modern science, or sociology, or anything similar. The point is to hold on to the kernel of truth in one's religious tradition and not be troubled by its unusable trappings. How could the sincere student do this? Go back to Jesus, said Coe. As did most Protestant liberals of his day, Coe reminded his students that Jesus emphasized the Kingdom of God, service, and love for God and neighbor.[32] It was crucial that the first of these—the Kingdom of God—be understood carefully. It meant that at its root, Christianity was committed to the value of community, for kingdom is a social category, not an individualistic or otherworldly one. "The Christian conception of life is all contained in that of the kingdom of God. . . . There is no purely private good. In short, I am to measure all things from the standpoint of the social whole of which I am simply one of its many members."[33]

Harry seems to have been particularly influenced by this interpretation of religious experience as a social phenomenon. It was not just that the goal of Christianity is social: there are social threads in the very fabric of reality. Coe's brand of personalism insisted that religious experience is necessarily triadic, involving God, the individual, and one's fellow human beings. Since reality is corporate at its essence, so religion is corporate by nature, not individualistic as Harry had been instructed in his home and in the Wesleyan mission band. The evangelical concern for conversion and the dynamic, holy life remained, but now it had a communal overlay. As Coe said to his students, "We must realize that the real world is a world of persons, God, my neighbor, and myself, and that real living can be completed only in communion of all three."[34]

John Gray, Harry's economics teacher, offered other sharp challenges to his traditional perceptions of the world. At least from the time of his reading Ely, Harry believed that economics should be moral. During his study under Gray this notion became deeply embedded in his way of thinking. Gray's style of moral economics offered an alternative to capitalism's profit motive and its self-serving individualism. Though there were some obvious points of contact between the views of Gray and Ely, there were vast differences as well, especially in their methods of doing away with the injustices of the economic system.[35] Ely was a mild reformer, whereas Gray, like Coe, called attention to society's corporate dimensions. It would be some time, however, before Harry appreciated all the implications of Ely's, Coe's, and Gray's ways of thinking.

Harry's excellent academic record led to a Harvard scholarship for graduate work. The recommendations of his mentors say a great deal about the esteem with which he was held by Northwestern's academic sector. Harry had majored in philosophy under Coe, who wrote to Harvard that he had "never known an undergraduate who possessed greater logical acumen."[36] John Gray also provided a glowing recommendation. Comparing him with other students, Gray wrote that "In many respects the quality of his mind is the most remarkable I have met. . . . He is exceptionally clear, distinct and direct in his thinking." He described a young man who functioned according to the convictions of hardworking perfectionism: he "never thinks that he has wasted anything until he has actually gone to the bottom of it. Both his general range of knowledge and his powers of acquisition are great."[37] As Harry himself later recorded, in addition to his rigorous studies and active extracurricular life, he carved out enough time to make "an analysis of all the sayings of Jesus that had any bearing on the social problems of the day."[38]

Young Ward had made several important decisions at Northwestern. For one, he became committed to a vocation of service. "I remember how I wrote it down one day in college—our obligation to help those who had not our opportunities."[39] He was already thinking about an appropriate strategy for helping the needy. According to recollections much later in life, Harry decided as a college student never to join a political party, for he believed such affiliations would prevent him from being sufficiently critical.[40] The other major decision was much more personal. He had fallen in love with Daisy Kendall, who had come to Northwestern from Kansas City, Missouri, the daughter of an affluent family with pioneer grit and a heavy dose of Methodist moralism. Her father, William Wirt Kendall, made a fortune selling boots and shoes in Kan-

Harry F. Ward and Harriet "Daisy" Kendall on their wedding day in April 1899 in Kansas City, Missouri. (Courtesy of Nanda Ward and Robin Ward Savage)

sas City following the American Civil War. Though the Kendalls may have moved in prominent social circles, they adhered to the strict moral prohibitions of traditional Methodism: no dancing, no drinking, no profanity, and strict Sabbath observance.

According to Ward family tradition, Daisy and Harry met on the Northwestern tennis courts. There were other occasions for interaction, however, for Harry and Daisy were heavily involved in the YMCA and YWCA. They also shared common religious convictions and moral code. She, too, was a leader, becoming president of the YWCA in her sophomore year. And both were good students.

Harry was very conscious of his social limitations, so his relationship with the Kendall family was not without its awkward moments. For example, when he journeyed to Kansas City for his wedding in 1899, he was too shy to attend the party planned for the couple before the ceremony, so Daisy went by herself. Such moments of self-doubt never undermined Harry's ambition or slowed the development of his talents, however. Early on, Daisy recognized his abilities and virtues, and in November of 1895 she carefully listed them for her skeptical parents: "He is undoubtedly the smartest boy in school and is generally recognized as a leader in everything. He is chairman of the Literary committee of our Syllabus, member of the Senate, corresponding secretary of the Y.M.C.A., Business Manager of the Tennis Association, an orator, debater, preacher, and a fine scholar and strong thinker. He is of a rather sensitive nature but has good common sense. He is not overbearing as far as I know nor can he be for he has the love and spirit of Christ . . . he has in him the qualities and characteristics of the highest manhood."[41]

Just ten months earlier Daisy had written a lengthy letter to her parents describing her decision to become a medical missionary to China. During the fall term an evangelistic meeting inspired her to give her "life to God to use as He thinks best." Daisy's decision was not unusual, for many of her generation believed the "Evangelization of the World in this generation" was possible. The Students' Volunteer Movement for Foreign Missions played a key role in motivating that generation to become "converters and uplifters," as Harry put it. However, Daisy did stand apart in one way: this nineteenth-century woman decided to fulfill her missionary impulse through medicine—as a doctor, not a nurse.

For Harry the summer of 1895 was a time of religious ferment as well as new personal relations. A July letter to Daisy reveals a young man wrestling with his religious heritage. The social emphasis of Ely's book and the lectures of Professors Coe and Gray met internal resistance that summer. Perhaps Harry began to reconsider his ideological shift because he was away from campus that summer, especially away from Coe and Gray. Or maybe it was the news that some of his family were thinking about immigrating to Canada that brought to Harry's mind the cherished evangelical piety of his youth. His letter to Daisy describes "a great spiritual uplift" experienced at a YMCA camp. As a result, Harry writes, he understood how his recent efforts "had neglected to work for souls.

Our delegation is praying for a revival at Northwestern." He reports a prayer covenant with a friend: "[W]e will pray until we get the answer, if it be for years we have to wait. But it will come, it is beginning with us now. Could not you and some of the Y. W. C. A. join in this?"[42] The revival fires were burning brightly among these Northwestern students. It was probably during this period that Harry, too, felt the call to foreign mission service. Of course, it is difficult to distinguish the movements of the Spirit from hormonal surges in a young man in love.

Harry returned that fall for his senior year at Northwestern. It was a heady time, as his efforts on the debate team brought him great success. A letter from the vice-president of the United States congratulated him on the fine debate. Northwestern's President Rogers described him "as one of our ablest young men we have in our student body of three thousand."[43] Harry did so well in his philosophy classes that George Coe asked him to be his grader in logic. It was an honor, but Harry also needed the money.

During the spring of 1897 he wrote a column, "Kicks from the Kicker," for the student newspaper, expressing his renewed commitment to social reform. Harry lambasted those who practiced snobbery in their associations. His idealism was passionate: "[I]n college circles there should be a culture broad enough to despise all false standards and man made distinctions, to inaugurate the true democracy of brains and character, to recognize the qualities of true manhood and womanhood wherever they may be found."[44] This serious young man expressed indignation that nothing seemed to be sacred anymore, that among modern students no subject was beyond "levity." He criticized the loss of "the old chivalric idea of the sanctity of woman" and "the respect for all authority combined with a true reverence for all matters pertaining to the deep things of life that men everywhere have called 'religious.'" The Victorian young Englishman was convinced that these modern American young people had gone too far. "There are some subjects upon which men ought to speak with instinctive delicacy and deferential reserve, or else keep forever silent."[45] In some columns he spoke out against any matter of privilege or abuse on the campus, including transgressions by some professors "who take advantage of their position to indulge in satirical and sarcastic remarks." The "Kicker" did not mince words: "[T]o reward honest endeavor with stinging satire, to wound a sensitive spirit by the rankling barb of sarcasm is a barbarity which no gentleman would perpetrate."[46] Nothing was beyond this reform-minded young man: behavior in chapel, school spirit, nutrition, even professors taking periodicals out of the library when students needed them.

In the spring of 1897 both Harry and Daisy graduated Phi Beta Kappa from Northwestern. Harry was off to Harvard, and Daisy returned to Kansas City. She had given up her dreams of medical school, capitulating to the cultural norm that married women should not pursue a career.

Harry experienced a disappointment as well, though the context is not clear. During his senior year he held a pastorate, but his relationship with the congregation ended badly; indeed, it appears that Ward was asked to leave. The letter from his supervisor, probably a bishop, must have been difficult for the high-achieving young man to bear: "After your first Sunday I was plainly given to understand the appointment was not satisfactory. . . . I imagine that you might have overcome all its difficulties if you had had time to mingle a little with the people and thus have become personally acquainted with them."[47]

Before embarking on his Harvard studies, Harry spent the summer with Daisy and her family at their Martha's Vineyard vacation home, earning much needed money by painting the Kendalls' home. Apparently even his hard work there did not persuade Daisy's mother of his worthiness, for less than two months before the wedding in 1899, he wrote the Kendalls assuring them about his career plans, which no longer included overseas work but rather a mission field closer to home: the Northwestern Settlement House in Chicago. "I have enough of a salary for two to live on with comfort."[48]

The shift from foreign missionary to settlement work is significant, for it reflects the final triumph of a social interpretation of Christianity over his family's more personal, revivalistic views. Moreover, his Harvard studies reinforced the modernist perspective of his mentor Coe. After his year at Harvard, Harry Ward would never turn away from this social interpretation of his religion. Intellectual changes were still ahead, but this basic ideological shift would never be abandoned.

Harry Ward enrolled at Harvard well prepared for the rigors of philosophy. He had studied hard and been coached well by his mentors, John Gray and George Coe, who would also become his lifelong friends. The year at Harvard would help Ward come to terms with these new ideas and determine what he should do with his life.

Before describing that important year, it will be useful to identify both the changes and continuity in Harry's understanding of his world. Though he had experienced and considered so much since leaving his home country six years earlier, he was still very much the same person in terms of temperament and basic direction.

Conversions and the Practice of Holiness

Ely's book and Harry's Northwestern professors had won him over to the notion that social endeavor is not merely worthwhile, it is at the heart of the Christian mission. While this represented a dramatic shift in focus, it was not really a new direction. That direction remained focused on conversion from one way of life to another. Ward still believed that conversions and pursuit of holiness made a difference, only now his range of application was broader: society, too, needed to be converted so that it would act in accordance with the way of holiness.

Holy Warfare

Harry's commitment to conversion and holiness remained intense and inevitably led to conflict with the dominant culture. As his Northwestern "Kicks from the Kicker" column amply illustrates, a holy warfare mind-set was alive and well in this educated young man. The larger Northwestern culture was corrupt, and he meant to attack and change it. Of course, muscular Christianity was part of his mind-set, so it is no wonder that his column persistently called for behavior befitting a gentleman. Even if no opponent in this holy warfare was readily apparent, one must always be ready. Less than two months after arriving at Harvard, Harry wrote Daisy that "if one rests or plays, it is not merely for the sake of enjoyment, it is that one's body may be prepared to renew the fight and the very play becomes sanctified and yields a double measure of gladness."[49] Here is muscular Christianity girded for the battle.

PRIORITY OF RELIGIOUS EXPERIENCE

George Coe helped Harry gain a new perspective on the nature of religious experience, for religious experience remained central to his understanding of himself and his religion. Despite his very logical mind, he continued to show little interest in either theology or aesthetics. Doctrine and liturgy left him just as cold as they had when he was a member of his parents' Wesleyan mission band. But Coe had helped him understand that the full range of his sensory and intellectual experience would provide access to truth.

Ward followed the lead of Coe, who understood that there is a path of duty all human beings should follow and that there must be some content for that duty. A person must rely on experience for this moral content; no supernatural authorities, like a voice from heaven or a mystical vision, will provide the answer. Jesus' life and teachings point the way. As Coe told his Northwestern students, Jesus' personality is "contagious."[50] In Jesus one discovers the content of one's duty as the man from Nazareth concretizes each person's ideal.[51] The inspiring influence of Jesus as the Christ of experience is a "practical certainty" by which humans can live, because this experience of Christ interprets life more fully than any other alternative.[52]

PRACTICAL, HARDWORKING PERFECTIONISM

The emphases on religious experience and practical religion appear to be natural companions, and so it is no surprise that both remained fundamental to Harry's understanding. His father shifted the family to the mission band not because he was an anti-liturgical purist but because more formal liturgy got in the way of what really mattered: preaching to the unredeemed. What was important was changing the sinner's heart and encouraging believers to develop in holiness. Erudite sermons consisting of sophisticated theological discourse or learned biblical exegesis would never warm the heart of the hearer. Now, under the influence of Ely, Coe, and Gray, Ward's practical religion-seeking-holiness found a social focus. The work ethic and a muscular Christian temperament remained, but with a broader field of application.

Like many of his day, Ward had come to embrace the liberal Protestant view of the human creature: Human beings and human history are malleable to development, even progress. The primary human problem is ignorance, and hope leads one to believe that human reason and the civilizing influences of the West will produce progress. Theologically the Methodist belief in perfection under the sanctifying grace of God became translated into confidence in human possibility, both for individuals and for society. Thus the faithful should work hard to develop human beings and institutions for the progressive society that God intended, what the New Testament calls "the Kingdom of God."

What had really occurred since Ward's 1891 immigration was a new, holistic perception of life and the cosmos. Coe helped Ward understand that he no longer had to choose between heart and intellect, religion and science, individual and social, God and the world. These were all part of one reality that was moving toward a divine goal. Ward's year at Harvard, especially his work with William James, provided some important nuances to his understanding of reality and thereby of his own endeavors.

Harvard must have been overwhelming at times, though Harry gave no hint of this in his letters to Daisy. He attacked the academic challenge with his perfectionist work ethic. In mid-October he provided Daisy with a copy of his daily schedule. He awakened himself at 6:15 A.M. for his bath and for prayers. Breakfast was at 7 A.M., followed by an hour in a philosophy seminar or, as Harry described it, "a siege with Lotze, who is one of my plagues." The remainder of his schedule was devoted to reading and to attending lectures and seminars.[53]

Harry had flourished as a philosophy major at Northwestern, but reading intricately developed arguments of German philosophers like Lotze was like wandering in a labyrinth. After four years of Coe's charismatic teaching style, friendship, and practical bent, the theoretical wasteland Harvard seemed to represent was not what Harry had bargained for. Still, he did not lose his sense of humor, describing to Daisy the ordeal of plowing through a seminar on Lotze with William James, who regarded Lotze as "the most exquisite of contemporary minds":[54] "I wonder why those German brains are built on such a plan that you have to organize a search party before you can find out what they mean."[55] According to one of his biographers, William James "bought, read, and annotated virtually all" of Lotze's works.[56] Apparently neither James's passion nor his magnetic way with students dissuaded Harry from his first impressions of Lotze, for in a letter to Daisy four months later he wrote: "Philosophy doesn't hold my head all the time and it doesn't hold my heart at all."[57] The study of philosophy would not be his life's passion.

James was one of the main attractions that led Harry to attend Harvard, and later in life he would tell his children that James was an important influence on his thinking. Certainly Harry found James's brand of pragmatism attractive, for it had much in common with the ideas he had absorbed from Coe. Similar to Coe, James advocated a pragmatism that was richer than sheer utilitarianism, that is, choosing religion simply to get things done. Rather one ought to hold to one's religion because "in really *believing* that through a certain point or part of you you coalesce and are identical with the Eternal."[58] James argued fervently for the power of religious belief (the "live hypothesis") and religious experience as valuable resources for productive human living. As he put the matter to his Harvard colleague Francis Peabody, "You will class me as a Methodist, *minus* a Saviour."[59]

Just one year before Harry entered Harvard, William James became fascinated by the writings of Rudyard Kipling, admiring in particular Kipling's ability "to get under the heartstrings of his personages."[60] Harry may very well have been exposed to Kipling earlier, but under James's influence he came to share his mentor's fervor. Kipling appealed to the heroic in Harry's generation. Perhaps more importantly, Kipling's interest in common folk and manliness as well as his sensitivity to what William James called "human entrails"[61] connected with Harry Ward's earthy way of understanding the world. Two years after leaving Harvard, Harry published an article titled "The Religion of Kipling."[62] James's philosophers may not have captured Harry Ward's heart, but Kipling certainly had.

Harry recognized the dangerous militarism and nationalism in Kipling's work but argued that his more fundamental message overrode these excesses. Kipling's characters were real people, ordinary people who saw life as it is. These rough-and-tumble characters embodied for Harry the heart of Victorian manliness without its genteel overlay. In tune with Ward's Methodist shopkeeper heritage, Kipling's heroes worked tirelessly for that to which they were committed. They experienced life through the tactile senses, a perspective shared by Harry, the butcher's son. They were realists even as they stood by their principles. For Harry this "religion of the strenuous life" (263) was more consistent with biblical tradition, especially the Hebrew prophets and Jesus himself, who "preferred the publican to the Pharisee, and Kipling's men, sinners or not, are at least genuine" (264).

Harry's education had taken him far from his boyhood roots while at the same time encouraging him to reexamine those roots. His family's tradition fundamentally separated religion from economic life. Personal spirituality and the pursuit of holiness intersected with everyday life, but primarily in terms of virtues like fairness, honesty, kindness, and so on. The Ward family's English, sectarian Methodism learned what was true through an insulated religious experience and then applied their religious commitment to everyday life in appropriate behavior. Now Harry's religious epistemology had changed. One knows the real not in some limited spiritual sphere but by opening one's eyes to everyday life. There one finds the real. Concern for needy people is no longer grounded in the practical application of personal piety but in finding compassion based on one's observation of their needs. Personal morality is driven by a heart open to everyday experience not by mores belonging to a private religious sphere. Coe had convinced Ward that there is no separate religious sphere; Kipling's writings helped him understand that the real is not in the generic experiences of middle-class educated folk but in the raw side of life.

Of course, Kipling's writings were not the only factor influencing Harry. As an undergraduate he had observed the seamy side of life while doing some volunteer work at one of Chicago's settlement houses. He knew that he needed broader experience, that knowledge from books was not enough. From Harvard he wrote Daisy of his desire "to charge my whole nature with the living fire of sympathy," using citations from Kipling to justify this impulse. Harry wished to travel around the world for three years in order "to cultivate the sympathetic side of my nature. . . . I do know that I long to feel the pulse beat of humanity in order to be able to minister to its needs."[63]

Harry's interest in the ethics of Jesus found a ready teacher in Harvard's Francis G. Peabody, Plummer Professor in Christian Morals. During Harry's year at Harvard he assisted Peabody in preparing materials for the 1898 William Belden Noble lecture, which Peabody titled "The Message of Christ to Human Society." Since Peabody's book, *Jesus Christ and the Social Question* (published in 1900), grew out of that lecture, it is an excellent resource for understanding this other part of Ward's Harvard training. In fact, Ward once stated that this book represented his own views at the time.[64]

Like Ely's, Peabody's interpretation was amenable to the basic religious assumption of Harry's boyhood religion: Christianity changes society by changing individuals; a more moral social order requires a larger quantity of moral individuals within it. Peabody denounced Social Gospel adherents who tried to read a social program into the teachings of Jesus, but he shared with them an evolutionary metaphysic that assumed the reality of moral progress.[65]

Though Harry Ward continued to be a very serious person and a disciplined student, his letters to Daisy reveal a young man whose world has become larger and who is skating near the edge of some traditional taboos of his Methodist upbringing. He wrote her about attending a play with a Princeton student, "a nice fellow who uses strange and fearful language, yet swears by Kipling and hence is a blood brother to me." Harry and his new friend enjoyed the play and laughed at its satirical treatment of some aspects of traditional Christianity, yet Harry was uneasy about the experience, especially when his Princeton chum cursed pious audience members who did not understand the satire. While Harry delighted in the formal education that allowed him to understand the play, he was unsettled by his distance from these ordinary folk: "they feel; we reason."[66] In a letter in which he is quite full of himself and his various kinds of expertise, Harry recognizes that something cherished may be lost in the process of acquiring this sophisticated education. Earlier in the letter he comments on the huge leap in knowledge between his undergraduate experience at Northwestern and his current studies at Harvard, but here again he realizes that there is more to the pursuit of knowledge than the grand libraries and renowned professors. "This I am sure of, men learn many things here, but few of them learn to read the books of life, and fewer still can understand the pages of death."[67] Harry was all too familiar with the pages of death; he continued to grieve the loss of his mother.

After Harvard he did not travel to foreign lands to be a missionary as he had planned earlier; there were mission opportunities closer to home with needs just as great. Nor did he accept a teaching post at Northwestern extended by John Gray. Instead Harry Ward returned to life among people of common toil. He had become excited by the institutional church movement and wanted to work in such a setting in Chicago ("institutional church" was the term used for congregations with an emphasis on social ministries in blighted neighborhoods). Although there were no such opportunities in Chicago at that time, with the help of a Methodist bishop and the wife of Northwestern's president, Harry secured a job with similar responsibilities: the head resident of the Northwestern Settlement. He intended to make a difference and to do so guided by the Ely-Coe-Peabody social interpretation of Christianity.

Perhaps his desire to live and work among the forgotten and abused was stimulated by his own sense of social inadequacy at Harvard. A poem, "The Awkward Squad," published at the end of that year says a great deal about his sense of solidarity with the heroic common men of Kipling's world. "The Awkward Squad" reveals not only his disgust with unjust social arrangements but also his long-held pride in a tradition that regarded hard work and courage as real measures of worth. Published in the *Evanston Press,* this sing-song poem is one of the few clear windows into the true feelings of this young man during this time of transition. The crowning success he enjoyed at Northwestern may have been diminished at Harvard. Harvard academic competition was stiff, and he did not easily rise to the top. Family background and social standing mattered to some people at Harvard, and Harry's youthful feelings of social inadequacy resurfaced.

The poem begins with a toast "to the awkward squad."

They're not very much in the social swim,
    They don't attend Pan-Hell;
They haven't the pile, nor yet the style,
    To ever be quite dead swell.
But here's to the awkward squad,
    The fellows without a wad;
At the first of the race they set no pace,
But power's in their steady plod.

They're a kind of heterogeneous gang,
    with a mixed and mingled garb.

There's some of 'em rough
  and there's none of 'em tough
So they're most of 'em cut for a barb.
  Then here's to the motley throng,
  The fellows who scrape along;
They don't look gay, but they've sand to stay
  And some will finish strong.[68]

One suspects that he is thinking of himself and his ilk. Given his financial limitations he certainly qualified as one of "the motley throng," one who wore "mixed and mingled garb," though now he was returning to Chicago in triumph, with his Harvard M.A. and an appointment as head resident of the Northwestern Settlement House. He was painfully aware that the road to achievement for his sort comes only through hard work—not romanticized views of labor and certainly not by being well connected.

Though Harry realized success and was on good terms with several professors during his Northwestern years, perhaps after a year at Harvard there is more than empathy for awkward undergraduates in the last two lines of the verse. The relationships he enjoyed with Northwestern professors were not matched at Harvard, and it hurt to be a social outsider. It had hurt in England, and it hurt, still, in America.

They're not on colloquial terms with the profs,
  They never make much of a show;
But here's to the bunch in the rear,
  The fellows who get no cheer;
It hurts like sin, but they keep it in,
  And they smile and cover a tear.[69]

Harry was practiced at keeping it in and perhaps even more practiced in pushing ahead with determination. The final stanza reveals that Harry had come to understand that some individuals might not be able to sustain the struggle—a remarkable admission for a person who had been thoroughly indoctrinated with a Protestant work ethic based on the conviction that righteous, hardworking folk will prevail. Perhaps his mother's still painful death (and her life) contradicted simplistic assumptions about righteousness inevitably yielding reward.

Ward was headed now for a life outside academia. His experiences with the affluent Kendalls demonstrated more starkly to him the class-conscious student culture at Northwestern. He had known the pain of class limitation in his native England, and though his family's financial success had alleviated some of the problems, he was again reminded in America—especially by the Harvard ethos—of his own humble origins. The United States itself had a class problem.

3

Discovering the Battle Lines
1898–1911

There is a kind of virtue which passes into one from the humble people who in harsh circumstances manage to live with dignity. . . . Those who saw that this world was the subject of redemption did not always forget that the world is made up of people. Certainly not if they served an apprenticeship with Jane Addams, Mary McDowell and Graham Taylor.
—Harry F. Ward, "Why I Have Found Life Worth Living"

BACK IN CHICAGO and no longer a student, Harry took up the job of head resident at the Northwestern University Settlement in 1898. His marriage to Daisy Kendall was still on hold, probably so that he could accumulate sufficient funds to support them. He was taking care of business, including his new American citizenship, which he received 10 October 1898 in Cook County Court House.

Harry was pursuing his missionary work among foreigners, though on American soil. The Northwestern Settlement was located in the middle of thousands of non-English-speaking immigrants near Chicago's Polish quarter. This settlement house was one of several islands of personal care, education, and social reform serving immigrant workers living in poverty-stricken neighborhoods.

Northwestern University Settlement was neither Chicago's first nor its best known settlement house. In 1889 Jane Addams and Ellen Gates Starr had founded Hull House. Northwestern Settlement opened its doors two years later, and others soon followed. In 1894 Graham Taylor established the Chicago Commons, and under the energetic leadership of Mary McDowell, a veteran of Hull House, the University of Chicago Settlement was established nearby. By 1911 more than a third of all settlement houses in the United States were in Chicago.

Settlements were only one manifestation of what became known as "the Progressive Era," a period when reform-minded Americans sought to address the human carnage of the Industrial Revolution. The Chicago settlements focused on the problems facing their neighbors—the many immigrants for whom the "American Dream" had become a nightmare of low wages, dangerous working conditions, filthy, crowded tenements, and corrupt political and legal systems. Settlement houses addressed these problems with an interpersonal strategy that employed a favorite American moral framework—the family. Idealistic, hardworking, educated reformers occupied residences in struggling urban neighborhoods, and from these homes they offered friendship and a variety of aid to their immigrant neighbors. As the Northwestern Settlement newsletter described its mission during Harry's second year as head resident, the settlement is "an experiment in neighborliness." Settlements did not consider themselves schools or missions but collections of residents "living here as ordinary citizens. Being here, we would place our house and our help at the disposal of our friends."[1] Jane Addams described Hull House in very similar language: settlement house residents "must be content to live quietly side by side with their neighbors, until they grow into a sense of relationship and mutual interests."[2]

In hindsight we can discern that the settlement movement was sometimes politically naive, often prone to imposing Protestant moralism on a heavily Catholic immigrant population, and frequently patronizing in its relationships with the uneducated. Without question settlements gave too little attention to citizens of color. It is easy for subsequent generations to scoff at these late-nineteenth-century idealists, yet in fact their efforts were sincere and energetic. They genuinely cared for and helped these people even though they sometimes related to them clumsily. However one may judge the settlement workers' programs and attitudes, their fundamental virtuousness is indisputable. However privileged, Protestant, and white these people may have been, their moral sensibilities were outraged by the ravaged human lives that had become acceptable casualties of American industrial development, and their compassion drove them to do something about this monstrous evil. As Ward reflected on that situation thirty years later: "From people we got back to conditions. Dirt, disease, ignorance, injustice, oppression—these things challenged us; and we became reformers."[3] Even for someone like Harry Ward, who was familiar with London's poor working-class neighborhoods, the filth and human degradation of Chicago's back-of-the-yards district must have been shocking. Only by recognizing the emotional and physical effects this place had on Harry's religious commitments can one understand the radical ideological and strategic shifts that became a permanent part of his understanding.

Ward's health faltered after nine years in this atmosphere, if for no other reason than the poisonous air. As observer Upton Sinclair declared, "You could literally taste it, as well as smell it."[4] For many workers, living conditions were intolerable. Over 35,000 people were crammed into the square mile known as Packingtown. Poorly lit and inadequately ventilated, two-story frame houses and four-story brick tenements were jammed with immigrant families; frequently several families shared a single room. There was no such thing as privacy when six to fourteen boarders occupied one small space. Often the rooms' furnishings consisted of no more than mattresses (or whatever bedding was available) lined up on the floor, with a stove the only other fixture. It was not unknown for landlords to rent a bed to one man on the morning shift and the same bed to another man on the evening shift. And there were no indoor plumbing facilities.

Shortly after taking up his job at the Northwestern University Settlement, Harry was appointed to the sort of parish for which he had longed. Chicago's Wabash Avenue Methodist Episcopal Church near Northwestern Settlement had fallen on hard times after most of its original members migrated to Chicago's more affluent suburbs. With the underwriting of a Chicago shirt manufacturer, Wabash Avenue became an "institutional church," and Ward and another Northwestern alumnus became co-pastors. Very quickly Harry also began to assert himself in larger church affairs, becoming secretary of Chicago's Open and Institutional Church League.

In February 1900 Harry delivered a sermon that became a standard in his preaching repertoire. "The Dreamers" was based on Genesis 37:19: "And they said one to another, 'Behold this dreamer cometh.'" Perhaps Harry heard in this sibling accusation against Joseph the criticism of his ministerial brothers who questioned his social focus. The sermon describes how the business world and even the church scoff at dreams of a better world. But this energetic young preacher insisted that "History is controlled not by physical and economic facts but by spiritual forces, by ideas, truth, righteousness." This way of thinking is rooted in God, for "The power of seeing ourselves better than we are, is one of the forces of our nature that God has given us to call us unto him." Christians learn how to respond to this call by modeling their lives on Jesus: "He comes to deliver us from the lower [materialistic way of life] to make the dreamer rule, the better self the master."[5]

Along with his duties as co-pastor, Harry continued to carry out the tasks required of the head resident of the Northwestern Settlement. As he anticipated having children of his own, he must have grieved at the plight of the neighborhood youngsters, who were dirty, hungry, and poorly clothed. He would never forget their wretched lives, especially on the back-of-the-yards' western boundary—the open garbage dump where "[s]ometimes visitors would stand by and debate as to whether the children were eating the food they got, or merely collecting it for the chickens at home."[6]

It is no wonder that articles appeared regularly in the settlement's newsletter, the *Neighbor,* addressing the needs of these children. The Northwestern University Settlement was the first Chicago institution to ensure that children in their neighborhood received a commodity that was rare during the summer: sterilized milk. This was a significant undertaking, because the deaths of one-third of the children under five who died in Chicago during July and August 1894 were attributed to the effects of unsterilized milk. In 1900 the *Neighbor* observed that in the city ward in which the Northwestern Settlement was located there had been a 9 percent decrease in infant deaths since the settlement began its milk distribution program.[7]

The *Neighbor* also printed an article titled "The Neglected Boy," which pointed out the immense needs of the neighborhood children. The settlement ran thirteen clubs for boys that year, with an average weekly attendance of 130. Approximately 8,000 boys lived in that city ward, and to help meet the needs of this population the newsletter appealed for donations toward a gymnasium. With Harry's love of nature and his fond memories of regaining health in the countryside, it is not surprising that the *Neighbor* also asked rural people to open up their homes to one or two of these children for a couple of weeks each year. The writer, perhaps Ward himself, contrasted the fresh country air with the back-of-the-yards environment in which children "are stifled and depressed by the closeness, the dust and heat and dirtiness of an overcrowded district."[8]

In addition to boys' and girls' clubs the settlement also offered a kindergarten and day nursery. Harry and his fellow workers encouraged the children to acquire public library cards and use them. Education was a prominent focus of settlement houses. Classes offered immigrants opportunities for learning to speak and read English. Jane Addams recalled one neighborhood person who remarked that Hull House was "the first house I had ever been in where books and magazines just lay around as if there were plenty of them in the world."[9]

The settlement house was also a place for the free exchange of ideas. Given the interests of the residents and neighborhood concerns, forums often addressed the economic issues of the day, with speakers advocating a wide range of solutions to the problems. It is not surprising therefore that some observers regarded the settlements as seedbeds of anarchy and radicalism, for indeed these viewpoints were represented. Neither is it surprising that settlement residents, including Harry Ward, were often sympathetic to union organizing and union causes.

Working conditions in the meatpacking industry were horrid, and many children were part of the labor force. Without their children's contributions to the family income, many families could not survive. Survival was a constant concern, even on the job. Ward must have been appalled by the conditions under which many of the workers labored. Upton Sinclair described it vividly:

> Let a man so much as scrape his finger pushing a truck in the pickle rooms, and he might have a sore that would put him out of the world; all the joints in his fingers might be eaten by the acid, one by one. Of the butchers and floorsmen, the beef boners and trimmers, and all those who used knives, you could scarcely find a person who had the use of his thumb; time and time again the base of it had been slashed, till it was a mere lump of flesh against which the man pressed the knife to hold it. . . . There were wool pluckers, whose hands went to pieces even sooner than the hands of the pickle men; for the pelts of the sheep had to be painted with acid to loosen the wool, and then the pluckers had to pull out this wool with their bare hands, till the acid had eaten their fingers off.[10]

Jane Addams observed the same kinds of conditions, especially among those who were part of the "sweating system," in which piecework was contracted out at ridiculously low rates. Women and children performed this work in settings unfit for human well-being. As Addams observed, "An unscrupulous contractor regards no basement too dark, no stable loft too foul, no rear shanty too provisional, no tenement room too small for his workroom, as these conditions imply low rental."[11]

In April 1900, the *Neighbor* published information about a current strike, counseling sympathy for it and trying to clarify the charges leveled against the strike's leaders. "There is no excuse for the ignorance and prejudice of the men who pose as educated members of society, and who, at a recent dinner of a certain club in this city, branded all unions as conspiracies."[12]

Harry Ward understood that shared experiences with the working poor provided a key part of one's education. Writing "A Personal Appeal" in the university newspaper, he called for students to work at the Northwestern Settlement House in order to gain the kind of knowledge that begins "face to face and . . . engenders understanding, fellow feeling, forbearance."[13] Harry had learned at the settlement what he could not grasp as a teenager during the London dock strike or from the shop assistants' petitions to his father: one must have an experiential foundation before joining the moral struggle. Or, as he stated the matter so eloquently in his appeal to the college students: "There can be no sympathy without acquaintance. Ignorance is always the fertile mother of prejudice."[14]

Harry's work at the settlement ended unhappily. Other members of the settlement's governing council did not care for his style of leadership. They fired an employee without consulting Ward, the head resident. Nor were they happy with his management of the settlement's finances and the way he related to people in the neighborhood—what the council committee called "a lack of temperamental adaptability to settlement work." Given the nature of such disagreements, one suspects that personality clashes were part of the turmoil as well; Harry certainly could be independent-minded, even stubborn. He attempted to refute these charges and argued that he was not satisfied with being a "mere employee" of the council. He asked that his fellow residents consider how firing him would hurt his career. When it became clear that termination was inevitable, Harry chose to resign effective the end of July 1900.[15]

Harry was right to be concerned about the effect this trouble would have on his career. Perhaps, too, the wound from the earlier difficulty in his student parish remained unhealed. He must have wondered what the Kendalls thought about this development. Surely this was a step backward. Following his forced resignation from the Northwestern Settlement, Harry and Daisy visited Kansas City, and Harry preached to the Kendalls' congregation. The sermon he gave was "The Dreamers." Was Harry trying to justify himself in his in-laws' eyes, if not in his own heart, with the worthiness of his dreams for himself, Daisy, and the larger society?

Meanwhile, back in his Wabash Avenue congregation, he called for a "revolutionary" approach to "Christian politics," one in which "expediency is gone. Compromise is unknown. It is to fight for principle, win or lose. Better to be eternal minorities than to compromise." Ward called on his congregation to purify political life so that it might be an "expression of the divine ideal, working out the dreams of the prophets, bringing in the Kingdom of God, establishing a true theocracy, a democracy led by God in the shape of the teachings of His Son."[16] He would preach this same sermon on at least two other occasions in his Chicago parishes, for he recognized that Chicago politics represented a significant obstacle to reform.

Harry had learned a great deal about Chicago politics from other settlement leaders like Mary McDowell and Graham Taylor, as well as from Jane Addams, who dubbed Harry "my little preacher." The settlements were engaged not only in what they called "personal work"—that is, the personally interactive experiences of clubs, reading groups, milk distribution, and literacy efforts—but also direct political action. With its intricate webs of corruption winding through political and economic communities, Chicago was challenging turf. A newspaper clipping from this period in Ward's files describes the coalition of aldermen and criminal elements that controlled liquor, prostitution, drug, and gambling interests.

Harry's work continued unabated with his next pastoral appointment in October of 1900: the 47th Street Methodist Episcopal Church, a back-of-the-yards congregation located in the Eastern European immigrant area. And he continued to be frustrated by the absence of working men from the congregation's activities. Women and children came but the men did not, despite his best efforts. Then one evening Harry Ward learned why.[17] He overheard a laborer, trudging home from work, say: "Well, we worked for the church again tonight, didn't we?" Ward soon came to understand what the fellow meant: unskilled workers were paid hourly overtime wages only if they worked beyond forty-five minutes of each hour. Watching the clock carefully, foremen routinely worked their men right up to the forty-five minute limit and then dismissed them. When workers discovered that business owners gave regularly and generously to Chicago churches, they became cynical about the financial underpinnings of local churches. Some consequences of exploitation were even more dramatic. Ward recalled talking with a young woman who became fed up with her working conditions and turned to prostitution: "She belonged to the church and attended the settlement, but both of them together were unable to prevent the moral disaster which was the inevitable consequence of such an attitude. Unchristian industrial conditions had proved stronger than organized Christianity."[18]

After his tenure of service at the 47th Street Methodist Episcopal Church Harry F. Ward would never be the same. The scales had fallen from his eyes. Absolutely committed to following the teachings of Jesus,

Ward was struck by the challenge of doing so in a Chicago parish. Apprehending his world best through his sight, sound, and touch, he felt his direction was unmistakable. The reformist notions of Richard Ely and Francis Peabody were ineffectual, and he must look elsewhere for clues. Painful Chicago experiences, together with George Coe's view of human beings as social creatures, had helped Ward understand that Christianity must be about the business of social change, but now he understood that the strategy for achieving this goal must focus on removing the unjust conditions that inhibited the Kingdom of God. Changing individual hearts was not enough.

There were more mundane things to change as well. When Harry first entered the 47th Street Church, his eyes were immediately drawn to the outrageous pulpit chairs. Made from rough cowhide with arms of curving longhorns, these gaudy chairs screamed the congregation's primary identity—the meatpacking industry. In short order Harry clandestinely removed the chairs, blunt symbols of the owners' point of view. The workers did not need these icons of cruel power looming behind the pulpit each week.

Harry threw himself into his work, joining the packinghouse workers' union and helping persuade the United Ministerial Association of Chicago to support a strike by garment workers. He encouraged fellow ministers to invite these workers, most of them immigrant girls, to speak to their congregations.[19] He joined the Civic Club of Chicago and chaired its Committee on Labor Conditions. He also chaired the Commission on Church and Labor. Years later, he reflected on those days: "Every man in my little church except a dentist was a stockyard worker. And as my successor was to tell me later, 'One couldn't preach in that church if he didn't believe in the union.'"[20] Ward's sermon titles reflect his commitment to his parishioners' economic needs: "Humanizing the Machine," "Abolition of Poverty," "The Rights of Property," "Economics of the Kingdom," "Sunday for the Workers," "Out of Work," and "Jesus' Call to the Working World."

These sermons were not lectures on politics and sociology. Like many Protestant ministers who were part of what came to be called "the Social Gospel," Harry spoke with evangelical fervor and based his appeals on Scripture and church tradition. As is typical of traditional evangelical piety, Ward's preaching emphasized Jesus, but Jesus was far more than a personal redeemer. Jesus was also the one who brought the Kingdom of God, which was not only a state of being in the believer's heart but also—as the image of "kingdom" implies—the corporate redemption of humanity. When this understanding was married to the popular liberal assumption that humanity is steadily progressing toward an ideal state, Jesus became the prototype of human development. The last Sunday in May 1902, Harry Ward assured his 47th Street congregation that Jesus "takes his place at the head of the marching millions of humanity that press . . . forward into the great destiny. . . . He alone can head the race to its goal."[21]

The following week Harry made preparations for a period of reflection. He and Daisy were off to enjoy the honeymoon they did not have immediately following their wedding. It was about time to start a family, so opportunities were running out for long trips like this one: a summer's journey in Harry's native England. He had not been back since leaving home more than a decade earlier. His father was remarried, to a woman named Florence who had been a cashier in the Wards' London shops. The family home would have been the logical first stop after their arrival, but Harry and Daisy headed elsewhere—to the place most dear in the stockyards preacher's heart, the New Forest.

As they hiked and bicycled the forest paths, Harry recounted for Daisy the stories of the New Forest folk and pointed out various kinds of trees and flowers. They traveled to the New Forest villages, where Harry introduced his relatives to Daisy. He took her to Boldre parish church, high on a hill overlooking New Forest pastureland, and pointed out the graves of his great-grandparents. Harry and Daisy worshiped with the Anglican congregation and found the liturgy to be "very high," an assessment that suggests Harry had not completely abandoned the religious orientation bequeathed to him by his parents. The last Sunday of the month they "heard a very good sermon"[22] at a Nonconformist church in Lyndhurst, the New Forest town where young Harry Ward had regained his health.

They still had two months free, so they visited London and did the sorts of things they never had time or money for in Chicago: a play, art galleries, the British Museum, the Houses of Parliament, and the London Zoo. Harry took Daisy to Covent Garden, pointing out the flowers, fruits, and vegetables, and perhaps sharing stories of youthful days driving the family cart in from Chiswick. One Sunday they attended the West London Mission, the church where Hugh Price Hughes preached and developed groundbreaking social ministries. The young minister from inner-city Chicago had a new-found appreciation of this leader of Christian social action. Of course, they also spent time with family members. Harry and Daisy toured the English countryside by themselves, visiting castles and the standard tourist sites, but they also traveled to Ireland with Harry's father. Nearly two months into their journeys, they finally visited Fanny Jeffrey Ward's grave site in London's Ealing Cemetery. No other family members were buried there, so it stood alone, its physical isolation a metaphor for Harry's life during his early years in America.

As they headed south to the port of Southampton for their return voyage, another stop in Lyndhurst was in order. The comments in Harry's trip diary are invariably concise, but the few words he wrote for August 28 and 29 reveal what he cherished about this place.

Aug. 28 Lyndhurst Rd. Forest beautiful with heath and trees turning.
Aug. 29 Fine trees. Beautiful lights.[23]

"Beautiful lights"—Harry must have stayed out late on that August night, letting his eyes savor that place of health and happiness. He and Daisy sailed from Southampton the next day, perhaps with thoughts of the unrelenting challenges waiting for them when they returned to life in the back-of-the-yards.

On 10 October 1902 Harry Ward received his preaching certificate from Rock River Conference, for he had passed the examination for preachers without seminary training. Two days later he was ordained an elder in the Methodist Church,[24] and he was becoming known in Methodist circles. He continued to push himself and his 47th Street congregation to address the social needs of Chicago and the larger world. With his move to Union Avenue Church in the spring of 1903, Harry Ward gained a congregation of predominately white-collar workers in the stockyard industry.

During his five-year pastorate at Union Avenue, Ward tried to communicate to his parishioners the oppressive conditions he knew so well.

His views of ministry, particularly with regard to the function of evangelism, had changed. The evangelistic religion of his youth had focused on personal salvation, calling individuals from a life of sin to a life of redemption through a personal relationship with God in Christ. Ely, Coe, and Peabody broadened evangelism to include works of social reform. Still, at Wabash Avenue "evangelistic preaching" was given "the pre-eminent place" in the congregation's mission: Sunday evening services were devoted to preaching to "the unsaved." Of course, given the social dimension of redemption, this could not be a private salvation for the individual; Ward preached a "gospel of salvation of the individual from sin to righteousness, of a gospel which covers every department of life and redeems it."[25] But by 1905 he was telling his Union Avenue congregation that the next revival in this country would be a "revival of ethics and social relations."[26] The young minister who led the Wabash Avenue congregation to "give two-thirds of its time and energy . . . to preach the gospel to those who have it not" and the other third to social work now emphasized corporate redemption through drastic social change.[27]

His passionate solidarity with the needs of laboring folk required some explanation, for his Union Avenue parishioners were worried about the increasingly violent aspect of labor struggles. For Chicagoans the virulence of the Haymarket Riot of 1886 and the Pullman strike of 1894 could not be easily forgotten. Then on 6 September 1901 President William McKinley was assassinated in Buffalo, New York, by an anarchist. Two days later Chicago police rounded up hundreds of persons whom they regarded as radicals. The following Sunday, when the mortally wounded President McKinley died, Ward spoke to his parishioners' anger and fears. He argued that instead of focusing on anarchist tendencies ascribed to immigrants such as the man who assassinated the president, they should be concerned about the economic depravation that breeds such violence: "[T]o let Mammon control, to let the rich man run church and state, is surely to breed the anarchist tribe and spirit."[28]

Ward tried to open the eyes and hearts of the white-collar workers at Union Avenue Church so they would see the situation as he saw it. On the occasion of Lincoln's birthday in 1904 he held up the former president as a model of empathy for the common people."[29] (Just two years earlier, when Harry was still pastor of the 47th Street congregation, he reminded that congregation of Lincoln's empathy for black people—perhaps a dicey topic in this pro-union congregation, since company bosses often used African Americans as strikebreakers.) Harry reminded his Union Avenue congregation of Lincoln's ordinary appearance, his "homely face and the sad eyes. . . . The spirit of Lincoln says this: the lot of the man who will fight for righteousness shall be full of pain."[30]

During the summer of 1904 stockyard workers went on strike and some 27,000 walked off the job. Harry had joined the packinghouse workers' union, and he tried to keep his parishioners aware of the workers' legitimate complaints. It may have been on this occasion when he received some information from a fellow English immigrant, a worker who had taken note not only of Harry's accent but also his sympathy with the workers. Pulling Harry aside, the worker warned him, "You'd better watch yourself. They are watching you." "They" meant the spies of Swift and Company, the principal firm in Chicago's giant meat packing industry. Later in life, Ward could chuckle, "That was my first experience with industrial espionage,"[31] though it is highly unlikely that Harry was laughing about the incident in 1904. More and more he was coming to understand just how power worked in a capitalist system.

The pressures and unrelenting hard work in his parish as well as with social agencies took their toll on Harry's fragile body. His doctor strongly urged him to get some rest, and so from the end of June until late September 1904 he set aside all professional responsibilities. During this period he traveled to Canada to purchase some land on which he could build a summer refuge for his overworked body. He found a beautiful, remote spot on a two-and-a-half-mile-long body of water labeled Meredith Lake on the maps but called Lonely Lake by an earlier settler. The figure-eight-shaped lake was surrounded by dense forests of evergreen, maple, and birch. It brought to mind England's New Forest, and so Harry named his camp "Boldrewood" for Boldre, the home of his New Forest Ward ancestors.

Harry desperately needed this Canadian refuge. In itself the Chicago environment was enough to undermine Ward's physical and emotional well-being, especially given his history of heart trouble. And now Daisy was expecting another child. Two years earlier, on 27 June 1903, their first child, Gordon Hugh Ward, was born. Harry's fascination with Victorian manliness was evidently unabated, for he named his firstborn after General George Gordon, the hero of Khartoum. When the second son was born in June of 1905, Harry chose a very different name for the child—Lynd Kendall Ward. "Lynd" was derived from Lyndhurst, that memorable place of health and nurture in Harry's boyhood. Given Ward's present state of health and the balm he anticipated from his newly purchased land in the Canadian wilderness, this choice is no surprise.

The two boys' names offer a helpful pair of metaphors for what might be regarded as the yin and yang of Harry Ward's life. He was forever committed to a "manly" way of living in the Victorian sense: fighting courageously for the right cause, living with vigor, overcoming challenges, and delighting in self-reliant physical and moral strength. On the other hand, Ward also reveled in the quiet solitude accessible in nature's wilds, where he found renewal and health, even communion with the divine.

Though Lynd was born healthy, the hot summer air in the back-of-the-yards was poison to his infant's body, and he contracted tuberculosis in his neck glands. The doctor lanced the infected area but the baby's health did not improve. Lynd continued to lose weight and cried night after night; Daisy and Harry feared the worst. Harry did the only thing that seemed reasonable to him: he took his family to the Canadian wilderness late that summer, hoping that his infant son would find there the same healing he himself had experienced in the New Forest.

It must have been a difficult journey—first the long train ride from Chicago to a remote rail station in the Canadian wilderness and then a trek on a farmer's wagon to the lake. Since there were no roads into the camp, a leaky rowboat took them the final leg of the journey to the far end of the lake. All this accompanied by a toddler and a very sick infant! The Wards looked forward to blue skies and emerging autumn colors, but instead they were blanketed with an early snow. Rather than finishing the cabin floor as planned, Harry had to cut and split wood for the kitchen stove to keep the family—especially the frail Lynd—warm. Twice a week Harry rowed down the lake, the quickest access to supplies, and then walked another half mile to get milk from a farmer's springhouse. Ever resourceful, he tied a trolling line to his leg on the return journey in order to catch trout. While the rigors of the Canadian wilderness must have proved very stressful, this was the sort of challenge that appealed to Harry's sense of Victorian manhood. He was the father protector, and he would overcome any obstacle.

The Canadian wilderness environment worked its magic. The little child named for Lyndhurst got well, and the Wards returned to Chicago by mid-September. Not surprisingly, Harry's first sermon back from Canada was titled "The Great Physician."

But Harry's own health continued to be a problem, and so he negotiated a year off from his pastorate. What had happened? The sheer physical neediness of the hordes of people he encountered every day was overwhelming. Viewing this need against the backdrop of the massive corruption of city government and the opulent way in which some Chicagoans lived, anyone who knows his world by means of his physical senses would become flooded by empathy for the needy and anger against their oppressors. Add to this a workaholic warrior's temperament, and the result was a man obsessed. Harry devoted all the energy he possessed to social reformation. Lynd's severe illness and the tragic death of George Coe's wife, Sadie, that summer added personal elements to the burden of Ward's professional responsibilities.

It is unclear what Harry did during his sabbatical year, though there is credible evidence that, among other things, he read Karl Marx for the first time. However, he did not need Marx to inform him about the class struggle or the fundamental rottenness of the present social order. From Ward's vantage point the system was hopelessly corrupt and would never work unless it were overhauled. Furthermore the system was at odds with the values he associated with Christianity. But Ward's experiences in Chicago primed him for an appreciation of Marxism, which offered labels for and an interpretation of what he knew firsthand. Indeed, Marxism provided a theoretical framework for his indefatigable social passion. As Henry Sloan Coffin later assessed this period in Ward's life: "The wretched plight of the underprivileged in this land of plenty had entered into his soul."[32] Ward's troubled soul could tolerate neither indifference nor inactivity. The old Methodist evangelical-perfectionist juices flowed. There had to be change; the battle must be won.

In the fall of 1906 Ward returned to work from his year-long break, ready once again to take up the battle for change. During his first two months back, several of his sermons held out an idealistic hope. His sermon "Achieving the Impossible" used the biblical text, "I can do all things through Christ that strengtheneth me." This was not the proclamation of a sentimental optimist, however, for Ward noted the destructive forces of nature, death, ignorance, and "the assaults of evil" that undermine utopian hope for natural human progress. The only hope resides in cooperation between the human spirit and God's spirit. When these wills are merged, said Ward, "the sons of God have their limitations removed [and] the impossible becomes possible."[33]

Ward's time in Chicago was a period of enormous personal growth, both in his understanding and in his public stature. One Methodist journalist observed that Ward's move out of the back-of-the-yards parishes to Union Avenue Church would give this "coming man in Methodism in Chicago" a congregation "of thinking people who will appreciate his scholarly attainments and his unusual pulpit ability."[34] The writer was correct. Despite his career setback at the Northwestern settlement and his ongoing physical difficulties, Harry was hitting his stride professionally. He was one of several like-minded Methodist clergy contacted by Frank Mason North, a prominent Methodist Social Gospel leader, about the possibility of establishing a social service organization for Methodists.

Together with three prominent Methodist ministers in Ohio—Herbert Welch, E. Robb Zaring, and Worth M. Tippy—and a couple of denominational leaders, Ward called a national conference in Washington, D.C., for the purpose of creating a "Methodist League for Social Service." The conference had specific goals: "to stimulate a wide study of social questions by the church, side by side with practical social service, and to bring the church into touch with neglected social groups." The invitation to the conference made it clear that the organization would be ideologically broad; as William McGuire King has astutely observed, the fledgling organization would be more "a promotional agency than a social service organization in the strict sense."[35] Hence the new name— Methodist *Federation* for Social Service (MFSS)—was entirely appropriate, for it could encompass a range of programs and supporters.

The conference's organizational meeting on 3 December 1907 was promising. Harry Ward was one of the speakers, and he offered a number of practical suggestions for publications and education that would develop better training for social workers and greater knowledge of so-

cial conditions and programs among ordinary church folk. He chaired
the committee on programs, which suggested an ambitious set of undertakings for the organization. It was all very practical and tactical: getting
the new organization's message out through tracts and speakers; providing help in organizing local chapters; promoting "social study" among
young people's church groups, women's missionary societies, and more
formally at Methodist colleges and universities; and coordinating local
efforts with national undertakings.[36]

Following the conference, the vice-president of the United States,
Charles Fairbanks, who had attended the sessions, escorted the group to
the White House for a reception with President Theodore Roosevelt.
Certainly the president had been an outspoken advocate for Progressive
Era legislation, but the meeting also emphasized the broad coalition that
had come together to found the Methodist Federation for Social Service.
Among the officers, Harry F. Ward, pastor of the Union Avenue M. E.
Church, had been elected second vice-president, giving him membership
on the executive committee.

The business at hand was to gain recognition of the federation by the
General Conference of the Methodist Episcopal Church, which would
meet in May 1908. A principal concern was to retain a "wholly unofficial
[status] in its relation to the General Conference, and to the other
official societies of Methodism,"[37] even as the federation used its formal
recognition by the General Conference as a means of becoming the
major player in the denomination's social efforts. Harry led the charge
in hammering out a document, "The Church and Social Problems," to
be presented to the General Conference. One paragraph in the document laid out in plain language the Methodist Church's commitments
to industrial problems. Though the statement emerged through a group
effort, it was primarily Ward's handiwork.[38] The passion and clarity of
what would come to be known as the "Social Creed of the Churches"
was vintage Harry Ward.

> The Methodist Episcopal Church stands:
> For equal rights and complete justice for all men in all stations of life.
> For the principles of conciliation and arbitration in industrial
> dissensions.
> For the protection of the workers from dangerous machinery,

occupational diseases, injuries, and mortality.

For the abolition of child labor.

For such regulation of the conditions of labor for women as shall safeguard the physical and moral health of the community.

For the suppression of the "sweating system."

For the gradual and reasonable reduction of the hours of labor to the lowest practical point, with work for all; and for that degree of leisure for all which is the condition of the highest human life.

For the release from employment one day in seven.

For a living wage in every industry.

For the highest wage that each industry can afford, and for the most equitable division of the products of industry that can ultimately be devised.

For the recognition of the Golden Rule, and the mind of Christ as the supreme law of society and the sure remedy for all social life.[39]

The General Conference endorsed the document, for the "Social Creed" fit the temper of the Progressive Era. That same year the newly organized ecumenical body, the Federal Council of Churches, also adopted the "Social Creed." Harry Ward's influence was rippling wider and wider.

Ward was also assuming leadership in Chicago to address some of the specific needs in his own backyard. Since his days as a settlement worker, he had known firsthand the political corruption and economic exploitation that contributed to the city's malaise. A series of sermons in the spring of 1907 focused on specific problems in that city, including "Vice and Crime" and "Neglected Children of Chicago."

Harry's own children were beginning to experience another sort of neglect that would characterize most of their childhood: Harry was far too busy to spend much time with them. Though they would remember him as an affectionate father, they also would recall with some resentment his frequent absences from the household.

The year 1907 seems to have been a particularly difficult year for Daisy and her young children, as her brief notations in a calendar indicate. Apparently Lynd's mastoid infection returned, for the doctor lanced the eighteen-month-old boy's neck again in January. In mid-February Daisy gave birth to a little girl, and they named her Muriel.

Ward family photograph, 1907. Harry, Daisy, Gordon Hugh (four years old), Lynd Kendall (two years old), and Muriel (eight months old). (Courtesy of Nanda Ward and Robin Ward Savage)

The next day Mrs. Kendall arrived to help. Ten days later Daisy got out of bed for the first time, and on March 23 she ventured outdoors. That same week Harry's father, his wife, and their daughter Phyllis arrived from England. Mid-April saw Gordon with tonsillitis and Lynd with the "croup." Throughout the year Daisy recorded the various achievements of her children: Lynd's first step, and Muriel's first smile and first audible laugh. Only two entries mention her husband. On August 7 Daisy wrote "Harry went camping," and at month's end she recorded "Harry and Mr. Coe—pleasant." Harry loved his children, but child care was never an important part of his life. In this respect, he was unfortunately not so different from most American fathers.

His limited family life was not the result of sloth, however, for Harry was a very busy man that year. In addition to parish duties and related church work, he was a popular public speaker. In June 1907 he presented a lecture in Chicago on "Christian Socialism," which was published by summer's end.[40] The lecture reveals that Ward was hardly persuaded by Marxist theory,[41] though he called for his audience to take it seriously, and he was beginning to see his Chicago experiences through socialist lens. Since his college days, Ward had been searching for a moral form of economics—or, more precisely, an economic system— that was consistent with the values of Jesus and the Hebrew prophets. He had found it in socialism, though, he argued, socialism had "unconsciously" come to this convergence. Socialism, like the teachings of Jesus, did not concede that selfishness must reign over human economic life. In fact, socialism on paper and in action had "come very near to the position of Jesus in his relation of the individual to society and of the society to the individual." While the "Church cannot ally itself with any political body, or with any class or faction of the body politic," Ward argued, the church must nevertheless attend to socialism seriously, for socialism's ideas could be traced to the New Testament.[42]

Ward's interest in Christian Socialism was not unusual among liberal Protestants of his day, though most of them preferred a reformist approach to social change. Ward, on the other hand, was one of those Social Gospel advocates who advocated social reconstruction. At this time people were reading and talking about Walter Rauschenbusch's *Christianity and the Social Crisis,* which was published in 1907. Like Rauschenbusch, Harry Ward had come to his position not only intellectually but also through many years of firsthand observation of the workers' plight. Rauschenbusch's sensual knowledge had come through his pastorate in New York City's Hell's Kitchen; for Ward, it was through Chicago's back-of-the-yards. And in 1907 Ward believed that Christian Socialism was the way out of this morass of social and political evils.

Given the biases of many Christians against anything with a socialist bent, even in the days before the Russian Revolution, Ward knew that he had to present an airtight case for socialism. The old debater met head-on the most prominent accusations against it. For those who regarded socialism as equivalent to Marxism, Ward insisted that socialism was still developing. The movement began with Marx's teachings, but that was "the dogmatic, creed-making period," a period that was passing.[43] Is there anything unchristian in socialism's economics? asked Ward. While acknowledging the limits of Marxist analysis, he argued that the issue for Christians must be that socialism offers "an economics that recognizes human values, which has at the heart of it a cry for justice" in contrast to the immoral foundation of laissez-faire economics.[44] Indeed,

Christianity owes socialism a great debt. The practicality of Marxian economics remained to be proved, yet it certainly ought to have a better claim on Christian sympathy than capitalism.

Ward did not hesitate to draw on the resources of the Bible and Christian tradition to make his case. He reminded his audience that throughout most of its history the church regarded private property as a sin; therefore capitalism is at odds with the larger Christian tradition. He also appealed to Jesus and the Hebrew prophets, especially their call to speak out for and work on behalf of the needy. In Ward's judgment the whole Christian mission was on the line, and so he preached the message like an evangelist, seeking to convert sinners and calling wayward Christians back to their commitments.

> But if you say that some must always roll in luxury and some must starve in squalor, I refuse to believe it, because I believe in a God of justice who has called himself the God of the poor. When men tell me a thing cannot be done I like to quote that good old Methodist verse about a faith that cries "it shall be done." . . . The human spirit has set itself to many tasks that men have deemed impossible. Never in history has it set itself to the conscious organization of society on the principles of brotherhood, and never have the economic conditions been more favorable, never has there been the necessary social background until this time. And now it can be done.[45]

He ended with a call to holy battle. The rhetoric includes some apocalyptic flourishes: "The Day of Armageddon is upon us. We must quit ourselves like men. . . . To raise one's voice in behalf of the suffering and oppressed, to set one's hand to the overthrow of all social injustice and iniquity."[46]

In this good work socialism and Christianity could be partners, for both criticize the existing order, both express faith in a new social order, and both share an ethic of a cooperative society.[47] Ward admitted that no economic system could alter humanity, "yet one economic system may encourage and develop the lower and selfish instincts, while another will develop and express unselfish and humanitarian instincts."[48] Only a Christianized social order would do. Ward was no thoroughgoing

Marxist, but he had discovered an analytical tool and a promising social movement that could lay the foundation for a Christianized economy. Here was a way out even for those desperate people in the back-of-the-yards.

Not surprisingly, Ward's sermons now began to include more than words of encouragement and challenges to action. There were words of accusation as well. Playing off the Genesis text in which God queries the murderer Cain, Ward's sermon "Where Is Your Brother?" laid out the personal side of the industrial crisis in blunt terms to his congregation. Surely some parishioners squirmed as their pastor asked them the same question God asked the fratricidal Cain: "Where is your brother? He is trying to keep the cold out of his room. Trying to forget the pangs of hunger. Tomorrow he will [be] walking the streets with holes in his shoes and a thin and worn overcoat. And he is your brother. And you don't care. . . . As long as one man can walk these streets and not get work, we have not become Christian[,] to say nothing of our civilization, the reproach of God is upon us. Where is thy brother?"[49]

The level of intensity here is new in Ward's challenge to his parishioners. The sermon is dated just a few weeks after the initial Methodist Federation gathering. But it was probably more than a sense of euphoria from that meeting that evoked Ward's harsh words. His health was in danger again, and perhaps for all his efforts he felt as if time was running out. Despite extended breaks from his pastorate, he could not maintain such a pace without serious physical consequences. His manly sense of self was at risk, and so another leave of absence was necessary. His final Sunday before the hiatus he preached on "The Parable of the Steam Engine." Like the little engine, he had reached his breaking point and could only hope that with enough will ("I think I can, I think I can") and rest he would be able to return to the battle.

Just as he was set to begin yet another extended period of convalescence, Harry was offered a trip around the world with a Chicago Methodist leader, who had already discussed the matter with Daisy. She believed it would be good for her exhausted husband to settle into a leisurely routine. Harry felt bad about leaving her with three small children, but Daisy reassured him, saying that she would manage just fine by taking the children to stay with her mother in California.

Harry relented and in 1908 set out on a journey to places he had only imagined he would ever see. In some ways he was realizing a longing from Harvard days, when he dreamed of taking time to study different peoples and cultures and thereby cultivate his sympathy, though his sympathy had been cultivated, even stretched, in the "foreign" cultures of Chicago. Yet Harry still had much to learn, and during these days of travel and convalescence his eyes and ears helped him discern even more. This trip solidified a perspective molded in Chicago, a perspective that would grow increasingly global and radical as world events took some drastic turns.

Harry's correspondence with Daisy during that year of world travel provides a rare opportunity to eavesdrop on the private man few people knew intimately. He was just weeks away from his thirty-fifth birthday when he embarked on this trip. He was married to a strong, supportive woman with whom he shared three young children. He was well educated and had demonstrated ability as a church leader, speaker, and writer. After a rough start, his career had recently begun to show promise, even on the national level. But his health was terrible. A family photograph taken just before the trip shows Daisy and the children well groomed and well dressed; their eyes sparkle. The fifth figure in the photograph almost fades into the shadows. His tie is askew, his face gaunt. He does not seem to fit in with the other persons in the picture. Harry Ward was exhausted.

In his first letter to Daisy, written just before sailing, he reminds her that the trip is for his health; otherwise he would not leave her for so long. Repeatedly during the trip Harry writes that he is concerned about Daisy working so hard. His concern for his wife reveals some of that old self-doubt, as he speculates about what Mrs. Kendall thought of her son-in-law now.[50] Daisy and the children were living in style in Mrs. Kendall's large Pasadena residence, which was in sharp contrast to the modest Chicago home provided by Daisy's sickly husband. In several postcards he reassures his mother-in-law that he is "feeling fine."

Harry's self-doubt extended to other relationships as well. He felt awkward in the company of some of the ship's passengers, a group he described as "pretty sporting." He overheard a critical remark about the blue shirt he wore for dinner. Embarrassed, the butcher's son confessed to his wife, "On the whole I think second class on this boat is good enough for the likes of me."[51] Nevertheless he retained his sense of humor. Early on, he encountered among the ship's passengers a young Presbyterian missionary, who tried to persuade Harry and his party to join a "prayer meeting, bible study, etc." The young man persisted "until a merciful attack of sea-sickness tempered his zeal, and saved us."[52]

Thanks to the fresh air and leisurely pace of the excursion, Ward's health was restored. He knew the source of his problem: the relentless stress of the work in Chicago. His first letter after departure declares that the "Pain [has] almost entirely disappeared—chiefly due to the fact that I have nothing at all to bother my head about."[53] He was playing shuffleboard and writing poetry, he reports, but still he worked. As second vice-president and editorial secretary of the MFSS, he was responsible for several publications, especially its *Handbook for Social Service*. Throughout the trip he continued to supervise this project by correspondence.

The poetry he composed during the voyage includes "The Call of Lonely Lake," which muses on the nurturing environment of his Canadian camp.

> There is a call come down from the North today
> With the whirr of the wild goose wing;
> It whispered softly at my desk
> On the street I heard it sing.
> Who calls? The cabin on the hill,
> Whose great logs stand with folded arms
> To guard my sleep.
> The wide hearth in the twilight, reaching hand
> Of light and cheer across the shadow deep.
> The hills along the shore—those wondrous greens!
> Who laid them clear to far horizon, shade on shade.
> Come away, come away.
> Who calls? The rhythm of the dripping oar, the pull
> Of the straining sail.
> The ease of the pack, well-hung, the joy of the new made trail.
> The plunge in the deep cool tide, the ring of the axe swung true
> The lure of the distant lake, the glide of the lithe canoe
> The calm and gentle converse of the trees,
> Making plain to man the ancient mysteries

They're all a calling. Loud they say
Fling far the worry and care
Come and play in the open air,
Come away, come away.[54]

The poem is not a sirens' call to escapism. Rather it expresses delight in the physical and spiritual nourishment to be found in the wilderness. The poem may be the most representative example of Ward's religion at middle age and indeed for the rest of his life. It reflects the wholeness that Ward found in the natural world and confirms his increasing alienation from things ecclesiastical. Of course, his own family legacy emphasized personal experience to the virtual exclusion of traditional ritual and theology, but Harry's reason-oriented education and negative experiences with the church during his back-of-the-yards years had burned away his evangelical inclinations. The institutional church remained only *functionally* valuable. Ward's spirituality was now rooted in the natural world, for there he repeatedly found healing for his frail body and balm for his troubled soul.

As Ward observed organized Christianity in the lands of its origins, his experiences in Chicago were reinforced. He disliked the "florid" ornamentation of St. Peter's and found the Catholic mass disagreeable. When he had his fill of Rome's sights, Harry set out for the nearby mountains.[55] In biblical lands he found organized Christianity a fraud. His Nonconformist iconoclasm showed: "The Greeks and Catholics have everything so plastered up with tinsel and pictures and altars and candles and incense that a plain man gets sick at the stomach."[56] The atmosphere of Jerusalem in particular was repulsive to a person, like Harry, who valued the simple ways of the teacher of Nazareth. "We have shaken the dust of Jerusalem from our feet and do not regret it." Yet despite his disgust, Harry's dry sense of humor remained as he opined that the author of "O Little Town of Bethlehem" probably had Jerusalem in mind when he wrote "How still we see thee *lie*."[57] The man who would come to prefer "the religion of Jesus" to the designation "Christianity" nevertheless relished tracing Jesus' route from Nazareth through Samaria.[58] He also enjoyed reporting to Daisy about various sites associated with great biblical events.

The trip that was intended to provide him with a leave of absence from clerical duties became an opportunity for him to reassess the church. On the whole the picture he saw was not pretty. Shallowness and self-serving authority were evident even in the "Holy Land." Ward believed in the basic moral claims of Jesus' teaching, and he found solace and hope in the cosmic presence and power human beings called "God." He understood that the church could be a valuable tool in social regeneration, and he firmly believed that science and other tools of human progress needed to be imbued with the message of Jesus and the prophets to realize humanity's true goals. But that was about the extent of the church's function, and so Harry wrote his wife even before his Holy Land sojourn: "Daisy, I would prefer you told them [the children] Bible stories to sending them to Sunday School."[59]

Ward observed foreign places and populations carefully, frequently describing in letters home the climate, plants, smells, food, customs, and people in each country. He was surprised by some experiences—for example, a Hindu temple with a sign forbidding entry to "Europeans" and Muslims. Harry recognized that the social oppression he observed in Chicago was not a purely American phenomenon; it was both global and historical. The Egyptian pyramids "impressed me chiefly with the waste of labor, and the uselessness of the task."[60] A rickshaw ride in Singapore was unsettling for Ward as he realized that the one "who pulls you is doing something that you ought not permit another human being to do for you."[61]

The encounters with other cultures forced him to come to terms with his prejudices and to take more seriously his cherished commitments. He was surprised by the affection that existed among extended family members in polygamous cultures.[62] He struggled with his own patronizing attitudes toward the native folk: "Unconsciously one adopts a superior attitude towards the lower classes. . . . [Y]ou feel that you are one of the dominant race and perhaps are proud of it."[63]

Still, common stereotypes of other religions and cultures appear in his letters. This orderly man did not take kindly to the disorder he found in foreign cultures, though he was not without a sense of humor about some situations. The pushing and shoving among the locals as the voyagers disembarked at Constantinople brought this tongue-in-cheek remark: "They needed about four Irish policemen from Chicago. . . . I thought of recommending a squad of Irish to the Sultan as a solution to his trouble but he did not grant me a private audience."[64] Though he enjoyed much of his stay in Egypt, he mused that "When Moses put the plague of flies on this land, he did not do a good job in lifting his magic."[65]

In other settings Ward was less kind about Islamic cultures. He found Damascus to be "a very fanatical city" and relayed to Daisy some unpleasant experiences there, including a confrontation precipitated by a "sheikh from Algiers" who "jumped on us for not taking off our shoes" in the Arabic library. Harry longed to be in Galilee, the home of Jesus and a place where "fanatical Moslems will not be so much in evidence."[66]

It was truly a trip around the world. By the time he returned Harry had traveled not only across the Mediterranean world to India but also to a number of other Asian countries, including Burma, Singapore, and major cities in China and Japan. However, his thoughts were never far from home. It was very difficult to be away from his family at Christmas, and his encounters with children during the trip made him terribly homesick for his three little ones.

Near the end of his journey Harry's confidence in the benefits of a more even-keeled pace is evident. "I've had *enough*. I want only to sit down in peace with my family and not move until I have to in October." But demands on his time and energy remained: "Everybody seems to want me to do something else."[67]

A week later he wrote Daisy on the occasion of their tenth wedding anniversary. Given his own family's reserve in such matters, it was difficult for him to express his emotions. "I believe that sometimes you wish I were a little more demonstrative, but . . . the chances are that if I were with you today I should not find many words to express my feelings and on paper I shall find fewer." Actually his prose is strikingly straightforward: "I never cease to thank God that you have come into my life. . . . I have put heavy burdens on you the last ten years and the way in which you have borne them has added unlimited measure to my admiration and to my love." He concludes by expressing his gratitude to Daisy for being mother to his children "but far more for the companionship of spirit that is the richest glory of married life. I love you much for practical counsel." In this letter Harry expresses above all his thanks to Daisy for her support.[68]

Harry Ward needed that support, for he was a driven man, what some today would label a "workaholic." Eventually he came to understand the value of the rhythms between his professional life and his summers in Canada, but he was seldom one to sit idle. He maintained a busy schedule whether at work or at rest. When he returned from his year-long journey, he made a beeline for Canada, not even waiting for the family he had not seen in nine months to join him. There was work to do at the camp.

Come October, there was work to do in Chicago as well. The Methodist hierarchy placed Ward in a parish more conducive to his health needs: the suburban Euclid Avenue Methodist Episcopal Church in Oak Park, Illinois. Now he found time to play golf on Mondays with three fellow ministers. And he enjoyed gardening and instructing six-year-old Gordon in the proper methods of planting and pruning.

Though Harry and Daisy had distanced themselves from the doctrinal orthodoxy of their Methodist parents, they sustained a Methodist moral orthodoxy in their own family. Like her parents, Daisy did not serve caffeinated beverages to the children, and early on she admonished them about the dangers of drinking and smoking. The children were not only instructed in the personal virtues, honesty in particular, but also in proper observance of the Sabbath. Gordon, Lynd, and Muriel attended Sunday school and worship, and unless an early bedtime was called for, they also attended Sunday evening services at the church. The Sunday routine applied to other activities as well. Vigorous recreation such as baseball was prohibited on that day, as was the reading of the Sunday comics. Instead the parents encouraged serious reading or drawing on the Sabbath. This observance represented more than puritanical tradition; it expressed solidarity with all people's need for rest from their labor. Like many reformers, Harry had argued for a decade that workers deserved a weekly opportunity for rest and recreation with their families and friends.

Though his new parish load in Oak Park was less stressful, there was still Harry's work on behalf of the Methodist Federation. Ward was miffed to discover, during his nine-month trip, that better known Methodist leaders were receiving credit for "The Social Creed of the Churches." Its authorship was ascribed to Frank Mason North, though North had added only "a few generalizations," according to Ward. Harry's pain at this misattribution is evident: "I am waiting to see whether he acknowledges any credit to anyone else. I suppose a man ought to be satisfied to do the thing and let other fellows get the credit."

Yet his ambition was not crushed, for he concludes that "if I'm spared I hope to show those fellows something yet."[69]

Ward's reference to being "spared" reveals another dimension of his frustrated ambition. His health had repeatedly cracked, and so his prospects for many productive years seemed questionable. He was now thirty-five years old, and it was time to make his mark. He did show them something, for by 1913 he had been asked to write a book for the Federal Council of Churches on the implications of each statement in "The Social Creed." Ironically there is no evidence that the Federal Council understood that it had asked the real author to explicate the meaning of "The Social Creed" for American churches.

Ward's first sermon to his new congregation in Oak Park was "The Gift of Spiritual Vision," and within the first three months he preached again his powerful sermons calling for development of the God-given power for progress, including "Achieving the Impossible" and, of course, "The Dreamers." True to form, Ward did more than appeal to his parishioners' best side. He also challenged them. Even "well fed, well dressed scions of society"—some, no doubt, members of Ward's suburban church—may live by the "greed and lust" associated with the savage. He reminded his congregation that photographs of lynchings often caught "good citizens . . . grinning at a burning negro."[70]

Increasingly Ward was stating the case for social justice more pointedly. In particular he was leading the charge for the church to take sides in the labor struggle. It was no longer enough simply to encourage better personal relations between the church and labor. Churches must now "uphold certain standards . . . , to insist upon them with the authority of a Divine imperative, to apply them to actual conditions with a trained intelligence, to work for their practical realization with unflagging zeal." The time had come to move beyond social reform to a strategy that "does not stop short of the reconstruction of society."[71]

Ward was determined to make his contribution to this social reconstruction. His work as the MFSS editorial secretary had impressed Methodist leaders. He had completed *The Handbook for Social Service* and also initiated several useful pamphlets, including a series on great leaders who contributed to the meaning of Christian social service. He took the lead in establishing a press service for the MFSS in order to disseminate information on the MFSS and other socially minded organizations. Always concerned with the nuts and bolts of social change, Ward recommended continuation of the "What to Do" series, with new pamphlets on "The Church and Public Health." He was also concerned that church people receive accurate information about key social developments of the day, and so he proposed "a series of industrial pamphlets of a purely expository nature on Trade Unions, Profit-Sharing, Cooperation, and Socialism."[72] Reading the MFSS minutes it becomes clear who was the catalyst for these new initiatives. Harry Ward had returned from his nine-month journey revived, and it was he who encouraged other MFSS members to adopt a more aggressive posture.

Some of the other executive committee members became discouraged with the slow progress of the MFSS, especially in the organization of local social service efforts. William Balch followed Worth Tippy as MFSS secretary, but Balch resigned in December of 1910, lamenting that "Little or nothing has been carried to full completion. No one has had time, and funds have been short."[73] One day soon after that, the executive committee met all day and late into the evening, working on a fund-raising strategy that would ultimately provide a salary for the federation's energetic new secretary, Harry F. Ward.

In 1911 the first issue of the *Social Service Bulletin* was published, signaling a shift in the identity and maturation of the MFSS. In his history of the MFSS, Milton John Huber notes that prior to 1911 it had "focused its program of social service for the local churches on the pastors, district superintendents, and departmental officers of the church." The goal was to educate these individuals and thereby make an impact on the larger Christian body. But in 1911 the *Social Service Bulletin* assumed the role of disseminating information and program ideas for all Methodists. The second issue reported that the MFSS could no longer function adequately with volunteer help and that the situation called for a headquarters with "a salaried executive secretary whose training, experience, and acquaintance peculiarly fitted him to carry out its program."[74] With limited funds the MFSS could only afford a part-time executive secretary, but there was no doubt who this would be. The October issue of the *Bulletin* included an announcement by MFSS President Herbert Welch that Harry F. Ward, pastor of the Euclid Avenue Methodist Episcopal Church, Oak Park, Illinois, had assumed the role.

4

The Increasing Price of Battle
1912–1917

The purpose of missions is not simply to put the flag of Jesus on the last frontier, not simply to carry the gospel to the rim of the earth, but to put it at the center of human life. It seeks to make the gospel the inspiring force and power of the whole social organism.
—Harry F. Ward, *The Gospel for a Working World*

IN 1912 THE Methodist Federation for Social Service came of age. Bishop Welch, the founding president of the MFSS, stepped down, and a young, rising Methodist leader, Francis J. McConnell, who had just been elected bishop that year, replaced him. With McConnell and Ward offering energetic leadership, the 1912 General Conference allotted the MFSS special standing as "the authorized agency in the Methodist Episcopal Church for the purpose of raising before the church the question of the social implications of the gospel of Jesus."[1] With this mandate from the church and the professional opportunities now open to Harry Ward, he, too, came of age.

The Social Gospel also gained prominence that year, with the publication of Walter Rauschenbusch's *Christianizing the Social Order*. Like

Rauschenbusch, the standard-bearer for what later historians would call the "radical Social Gospel," Ward had come to believe that the basic structure of dominant social systems, including the economic sector, must be democratized. Merely tinkering with a corrupt system, as reformers proposed, failed to address fundamental problems. An economic system based on competition and selfishness can never be socially useful, for it drags humanity down. Only a system promoting cooperation and service would benefit humanity.

Rauschenbusch argued that the American institutions of government, education, church, and family had been "Christianized." Democratic government still had many flaws, but there was hope, for it was at least fundamentally altered to promote equality and justice. Public education had its ups and downs, but it was available to all persons and thereby democratized. As a Protestant, Rauschenbusch believed that although the Reformation had not cured all of institutional Christianity's ills, at least it had broken the hierarchical stranglehold of Catholicism.[2] According to Rauschenbusch the West had also democratized the institution of the family by promoting an egalitarian arrangement versus an abusive patriarchal structure.[3] Rauschenbusch did not claim that these institutions of government, education, church, and family were now perfect, but, he asserted, like the Christian convert, each had fundamentally altered its foundational commitments. And this is what he meant by "Christianizing the social order."

Rauschenbusch believed that although a Christian existence is not guaranteed within a Christianized social order, altered social structures can encourage corrupt persons to do good things. Likewise, an unchristian environment tempts good persons to do bad things, and such was the problem with the last remaining social system to be Christianized: the economic sector. By its very arrangement capitalism promotes attitudes and behaviors inconsistent with Christianity: competition and selfishness, which in turn promote greed and exploitation. Reforms of capitalism were not sufficient; the economic order must be converted. No wonder that Harry Ward informed Rauschenbusch that "[w]hen a man asks me what to read, your books always come first."[4] Ward had become increasingly suspicious of Ely and Peabody's overly tame reformism. Only a Christianized or democratized social order would suffice. Like

Rauschenbusch, Harry Ward arrived at this position not only through his head but also through many years of firsthand observation of the workers' plight, especially in Chicago.

Though Chicago was still his home, Ward did not spend much time there now. He reported to the MFSS executive board that during 1912–1913 he "addressed 347 meetings and conducted 36 group conferences in 17 states."[5] In fact, that year he spent the better part of three months on the West Coast, in addition to stopovers in the industrialized Midwest. Newspaper accounts of his appearances provide a useful window into the spirit of the time as well as a confirmation of Harry Ward's celebrity status as a Social Gospel evangelist.

His was a message of social salvation. He identified the nature and sources of social sins, described what must be done for society to be redeemed from its ills, and appealed for real changes in attitude and behavior. This was the old Methodist message of sin, conversion, and holiness set within a social framework, and Harry was brilliant in communicating this gospel.

On his swing through western states Ward presented a compelling message that captured the imagination of church people, laboring folk, women's groups, and students. The first two months were an extraordinary undertaking for Ward; during that period alone he visited thirty-seven cities and towns, addressed 118 meetings, and led eighteen conferences. His experiences and leadership activities in the previous decade had established his credibility. Newspapers variously described him as a "noted clergyman," "one of the most interesting men in church circles in the country," "one of the acknowledged authorities on this line of Christian work," "noted lecturer," "leader in the social service movement," "noted pastor and sociologist," and "one of the founders of the social service movement."[6] As a representative of not only the MFSS but also the Federal Council of Churches (which he served as an associate secretary by virtue of his MFSS position), Ward in effect represented thirty denominations and seventeen million Protestants.

High praise came from all quarters. "[I]n the unanimous opinion of those present, [Ward's presentation was] the most clear, forceful, vigorous putting of practical Christianity that they had ever heard. Dr. Ward did not attempt any flights of oratory, but his simple, temperate utterances were eloquent."[7] From San Francisco came the report that a ministers' meeting was "deeply stirred" by Ward's address.[8] Harry knew how to communicate the severity of problems in concrete terms. For example, in an address on the "Relation of Christianity to the Labor Movement," he urged his audience to trace the path of the production of their fine clothing. That path included "long lanes of white-sheeted cots," a reference to the death and mutilation of laborers in unsafe working conditions. "The time has come," argued Ward, "for the people to refuse to take the products of industry at the cost of the life of the working class."[9] After interviewing Ward, one reporter concluded, "Mr. Ward is enthusiastic and earnest as a boy . . . even though he is old enough to have graduated from Harvard and to have associated for the last ten years with Jane Addams."[10]

Harry must have been euphoric when he saw the positive response from workers, especially the sort who felt alienated from his Chicago congregations. Still, there were major problems. Given the vested economic interests of most denominations, many laboring folk were suspicious of church leaders. The San Francisco Building and Trades Council initially refused Ward an audience because the local Methodist newspaper was published in a nonunion shop. After the publisher promised to negotiate with the unions, Ward was allowed to speak. In most other instances labor halls were filled to overflowing with people eager to hear the former back-of-the-yards pastor speak about the common interests of labor and church folk. According to reports, even some of the most jaded union men responded positively to Harry's simple message. Drawing on his years of firsthand observation in Chicago, Ward described straightforwardly the abuses of the present industrial system. Since Christianity stood for social justice, all true Christians must regard these abuses as intolerable. Christianity "must stand behind the struggle of the working class. The church and labor should unite to wreck this exploitation."[11]

Surely Harry's pulse rate surged when a Spokane labor newspaper described him as one who "knows the game of the exploiter and also the fight that has been made by organized labor to loose the hands of that parasitic class from the throats of the working people." Harry had won over some of the skeptics with his no-nonsense appeal. "Brother Ward wasted no time on 'bunk' and piffle and maudlin sentiment, but dug into the very vitals of the economic and social question like a steam shovel chewing away at a bank of sand."[12] The president of an Indiana brewery workers' union told a reporter: "You put this dope in just the way I give it to you. I say that I want every brewery worker in town to attend these meetings."[13] Before Ward arrived in Colorado that March, he received an unsolicited invitation to speak at the Denver Trades Assembly.

He spoke not only to labor groups but also to ministerial alliances, churches, high school assemblies, college chapels, women's groups, and YMCA-sponsored gatherings. His standard fare to these varied audiences included speeches on "The Religious Aspect of the Labor Movement," "The Social Creed," "The Challenge of Socialism to Christianity," "The Relation of Christianity to the Labor Movement," and "Social Waste." In the last of these, which was frequently offered to women's groups, Ward decried the horrible abuse of women and children by the present industrial order.

The response in Denver was particularly noteworthy. Nine major women's organizations, ranging from religious and temperance groups to the Grade Teachers Association, sponsored a mass meeting addressed by Ward. Prior to his address, the Denver newspaper promised "Women to Hear Hot Talk" and "[Ward] Promises to Conceal None of Known Evils of Smart Set, nor to Spare Members' Feelings."[14] Ward focused on the relationship between low wages and poor working conditions and the lure of prostitution for young women. As the newspaper account put it, Ward so fervently "stirred the great company" of women with his descriptions "of the loss through poverty, disease, and vice" that they resolved to "require of all candidates for commissioner . . . in the coming election a statement of their position on the vice problem."[15]

Though Harry Ward was very much a man of his patriarchal culture, relatively speaking he was a strong advocate of women taking control of their lives. This may seem a bit surprising given his Victorian background, but then again he had regularly interacted with strong women: Daisy Kendall, Jane Addams, Mary McDowell, and, of course, his mother, Fanny Jeffrey Ward. When asked by a Denver reporter, "What about women in this work of [social] redemption?" Ward responded: "The finest thing today is the way women are being given the franchise in the Western states. . . . They'll win everywhere. That is inevitable, and men are only showing themselves short-sighted by opposing their claims to political equality."[16]

During his year's travels on behalf of the MFSS, Harry Ward regularly delivered an address that was sure to catch the public's attention: "The Challenge of Socialism to Christianity." Though Americans generally regard socialism with suspicion, prior to the Russian Revolution and the First World War various socialist ideas and strategies were often the subject of public discussion. In 1912 Eugene Debs, the Socialist Party candidate for U.S. president, garnered 6 percent of the popular vote, nearly 900,000 votes. In 1910 socialists were elected to Congress, and socialist mayors ran city halls in Milwaukee and Schenectady. By 1914 Socialist Party members held thirty legislative seats in twelve states, and the party counted more than a thousand of its members holding municipal offices across the nation.[17]

On many occasions, Ward delivered the address "Religion of Christ and Philosophy of Marx Not Antagonistic," not only to inform church members about an important and even promising social movement, but also to draw socialists into conversation and common cause with Christian institutions. What was at stake for Ward was the very nature of the present economic system and the abuses associated with it. His Northwestern University professor John Gray and others had taught him that as with all areas of human experience, economics should be moral. Yet how could a system be moral when it rewarded competition, promoted greed, and placed a higher value on property than on human life? By contrast, socialism promoted "an economics that recognizes human values, an economics that has at the heart of it a cry for justice."[18]

Ward identified four socialist challenges to Christianity, all of which called religion back to its true nature. First, as a worldwide political movement of the proletariat, socialism continued the tradition of Moses' protest to Pharaoh and Jesus' conflict with the money changers. "God is always in sympathy with the weak and the oppressed."[19] Second, Marxist economic theory challenged Christianity to embrace again economics as a moral science. Third, though Christians should reject extreme forms of economic determinism and the necessity of class warfare, these theories challenged Christians to recognize the importance of economics in human affairs. Ward implored his listeners to witness real class struggle in places like New York: witness the beautiful homes and luxury stores of "the idle rich" and the "monopolist," then visit the "warrens of tenements and see the brutal misery, the filth, the squalor, the poverty and the disease in which the toilers are forced to exist."[20] Christians must stand with those who seek democracy in all human relationships; neutrality is not an option. "Christianity must throw all its strength into the struggle of the working class to secure justice. . . . For this is God's movement."[21] Finally, socialism's desire for collectivism challenges Christians to recommit themselves to the realization of the cooperative commonwealth, what Jesus called "the Kingdom of God." In Boston Ward's responses to the audience's questions demonstrated his no-nonsense style. When asked if he considered Jesus a socialist, Ward retorted, "He never had a chance to be." When pressed on the similarity between Christianity and socialism, Ward argued that their ethics are identical. In fact, he suggested, socialism had arisen because Christianity had lost sight of its mission.[22]

In late October a Methodist paper reported that Ward's social service campaign in New York brought "together under the same roof" church leaders, laborers, and socialists, thereby creating "a better understanding between them." On at least one occasion Ward won over some skeptical socialists, for one of them said after the meeting: "This is the first time I have been in a church for eighteen years. I would go regularly if I could hear such sermons as I heard tonight."[23]

In Des Moines, Iowa, Harry endeared himself to a socialist audience with his "large sympathies, consecrated earnestness, masterful logic and wide knowledge of his subject and men."[24] Still, he did not hesitate to criticize socialists, especially for their unwarranted bias against all religious folk. He insisted that it was time for socialists to stop misrepresenting Christianity just as it was time for Christians to stop misrepresenting socialism.

Ward won over his labor audiences by asserting that "a business that is unable to pay a living wage has no right to exist. It is a parasite on society."[25] On one occasion, he addressed a socialist crowd that, on the basis of their experience with church leaders, expected a verbal assault from Ward. According to a newspaper report, they were "primed with questions ready to be hurled at the speaker, [but] remained instead to shake his hand and congratulate him on the 'best Socialist talk they ever heard.'"[26]

Of course, Ward's primary audience remained church people, and despite his harsh indictment of the capitalist economic system and his emphasis on the shortcomings of Christianity, on most occasions they were receptive listeners. His strategy was not only to awaken their sensitivities but to move them to action. In each city he helped them identify a social service project to which they could immediately apply their new enthusiasm. Ward cleverly appealed to the basic religious convictions of even the naysayers: "Is this a dream? Well, the dreams of the Carpenter of Nazareth have a way of coming true."[27] He would also issue his challenges bluntly. In Toledo he asked Methodists how many of them had ever done anything to alleviate the situation "of the widowed mothers and girls" in factories and stores, women who were "robbed of the ordinary joys of life." "Your answer is the test of your Christianity," asserted Ward.[28]

Speaking to his own Methodist conference in Chicago, Harry "received one of the finest and most spontaneous ovations ever given a speaker before that body." He must have been very gratified, perhaps even more so when a reporter described his address "as having been delivered in Dr. Ward's straightforward and manly way."[29] The weakling whose physical strength was insufficient to cope with the back-of-the-yards parishes and who had admitted self-doubt and anxiety about his future was now publicly recognized for his forceful, even manly leadership. Perhaps Harry was no longer concerned that many folk did not know about his primary authorship of the "Social Creed." What mattered is that he distributed fifteen thousand copies of it in 1912–1913, and church people and union members consistently lauded its merits. One Methodist publication noted that "Harry F. Ward has a stubborn notion that the social creed is not a set of smug platitudes, but a working program, to be carried out literally and in detail."[30]

Within a year, however, Harry's "stubborn notion" came to irritate more than a few Methodists. The Methodist Church's own business enterprise was suspect from the union point of view because of an ongoing conflict between the International Typographical Union and the Western Book Concern, a Methodist publishing house in Cincinnati which had refused to negotiate with organized labor. Ward asserted to his fellow Methodists that this was "a time of crisis in the labor world," and for Methodism "it is the day of our opportunity." Unless the matter of the Methodist Book Concern was addressed appropriately, unions would continue to harbor suspicion of the churches' social evangelism, and a great opportunity would be lost. "[I]t is obvious that this issue must be met,"[31] argued Ward, and he was not one to wait for others to act. He wrote to a Book Concern executive[32] and placed the case before the MFSS board in his annual report, reminding them that the Book Concern's antiunion policy had led to rebuffs in both Chicago and San Francisco.

Despite the enthusiasm for social service among many Methodists, their financial support was not enough to keep the MFSS budget from being stretched thin. The situation improved somewhat when Bishop McConnell intervened. Through his connections at the Boston University School of Theology,[33] McConnell secured a half-time teaching position there for Ward so that a portion of his MFSS salary could be devoted to other needs. Ward's appointment as the first chair in social service at an American seminary was hailed as an excellent choice by the Methodist press. The *Christian Advocate* characterized his MFSS work as "remarkable both for the quality of his public lectures and his extraordinary power to bring into more sympathetic relations the labor forces and the Church. He has kept the evangelistic temper and spirit that marked his work in the pastorate and is probably without a superior as an industrial evangelist."[34]

In the summer of 1913 the Wards packed their belongings and shipped them to Boston. They moved into a large frame home in Newton Center on the outskirts of Boston. Gordon, Lynd, and Muriel were now all of school age. Harry and Daisy had struggled financially during some of their time in Chicago, but the future looked much brighter. Harry was almost forty years old, and he was now focusing his energies on that which he obviously did very well: writing and speaking on behalf of social causes for the church. Methodists knew the name and acknowledged the influence of Harry F. Ward.

Perhaps if Daisy had foreseen all that lay ahead, she would have discouraged this move. Harry would indeed find fulfillment and success, but he was away from home so much of the time that Gordon, Lynd, and Muriel rarely had significant contact with their father during the critical years of their childhood development. The only surviving informal snapshot of Harry in Boston shows him about to toss a ball to one of his sons, but he is not dressed for play; attired in a business suit, he is probably leaving for or just arriving home from work. That was the typical pattern. Many years later Lynd alluded to "the tragic gulf between a man's professional success and the reality of his family life."[35] Though the Ward family enjoyed good times together, Harry's extended absences and the attendant frustrations for Daisy cast a pall over the children's lives, especially the older son's; Gordon struggled to meet the increasingly high expectations set by his absent father, whose extended absences exacerbated the situation.

A record of the kinds of duties that drew Harry Ward away from his family is contained in his 1914 report to the MFSS. During that year he addressed 254 meetings and seventeen conferences. He also taught two courses at Boston University, prepared two books and four pamphlets, provided monthly press service to Methodist publications, and wrote social service materials for the Methodist adult Sunday School lessons. However, in November of 1914 his MFSS office load was lightened considerably with the hiring of an office secretary, Grace Scribner.[36]

Despite this frenetic pace, Harry and Daisy continued the established family tradition of spending summers at Lonely Lake. Here Muriel and the two boys could be with their father, though work was still at the heart of the camp routine. As homesteaders in this isolated part of Ontario, the Wards were obliged to clear, fence, and cultivate at least 5 percent of their land. Harry paid a local resident to plow and plant their huge vegetable garden in May so that the Wards could live off the land during their summer stay. There was always plenty of work at Lonely Lake, and Harry relished it. Each day followed a careful schedule so that all the tasks were done properly and in order. During their first summer in Canada after moving to Boston, Harry helped Gordon and Lynd construct a softball diamond near the lakeshore. The result was a creative adaptation to the hilly terrain and limited open space. Both Daisy and Harry joined in the games. On Sunday evenings the Lonely Lake families would assemble for food and conversation at "Picnic Rock" or around the fire at George Coe's campsite, which was adjacent to the Wards' property and occupied by Coe virtually every summer.

Refreshed by these summers of outdoor work and play, Harry Ward returned home each fall ready for the battle once again. His time in Canada was not a removal from his other world, for while he was at the lake he continued to analyze and strategize for social change, especially in lengthy conversations with his good friend Coe. For Harry there was nothing quite like spending time with Coe in the Canadian wilderness.

In March of 1914 Ward received a letter from George Coe[37] encouraging increased pressure against the Methodist Book Concern to force it to stop using nonunion labor. The organization must be brought into line with the public statements of Methodism. But the Book Concern did not budge. With the regular quadrennial meeting of the Methodist General Conference on the horizon the following year, Ward turned up the heat. Apparently in early January of 1915 he ripped into the Methodist Book Concern during a Boston Methodist Preachers' meeting, and management responded by firing off a blunt letter to Ward, questioning his motives.[38] It may be that his remarks to his fellow ministers played off his lectures on "The Labor Movement" given that same month at Boston's Ford Hall Forum. There he had painted a very positive picture of organized labor's efforts toward constructive social change. He tried to take seriously the noble intentions of both sides, labor and management alike, but he hammered away at the all too common exploitation of labor and the militaristic tactics of American capital—which included the use of spies, thugs, and government—and the deliberate misrepresentation of progressive forces for change. Some of Ward's charges were based on firsthand experience, including "the honour of being reported upon by the spies that are maintained in certain industrial corporations."[39] He even appealed to management's pragmatism: "You get back from men the same attitude with which you face them. If you try to skin them, they will try to skin you, and if you try to treat them with justice and appreciation, they will respond in the same spirit to you."[40] Ward encouraged an Illinois pastor to hold the line against the antiunion Methodists: "Good work. Do not let them bluff you. Handle them easy but stand firm. . . . We have got to get at these men individually and change their point of view."[41]

Despite evidence of a backlash and despite growing resistance to the concept of social justice, Ward would not back off. In early 1916 he solicited letters from labor leaders from around the nation, especially those who were church members, in hopes that their responses would persuade Methodists to change the Book Concern's antiunion policy. The letters poured in. One enthusiastic union leader was baffled that church folk could fail to see the consistency between union values and Christian values: "Christ was a Carpenter and the greatest organizer of men. He advocated trade union principles."[42] Some letters were lengthy discourses laying out the case; others were short handwritten pieces that got right to the point: "[T]he open shop policy in Church enterprises estranges union workers."[43]

Ward and his MFSS allies marshaled their forces and appealed to their fellow Methodists for help at the denomination's 1916 General Conference. An old ally, William Balch, was not confident: "The General Conference will pay no more attention to the labor issue in the Book Concern than it would to a personal visit by Jesus of Nazareth." Still, the task was not completely impossible: "There is just one hope—it is that you, Ward, go there in the power of a prophet and that the Holy Ghost compels them to hear you. For this I pray."[44]

Ward and his MFSS colleagues produced a report to the 1916 General Conference calling for the "same application of the teachings of Jesus" to industry as to the state. Industry must be democratized, and the first step in that process is collective bargaining, "the only means by which the individual worker can protect himself against the power of concentrated capital."[45] The conference debate went on for two days. Ward thundered like a prophet, echoing the words of St. Paul: "If we permit our words of brotherhood and sympathy [for laboring folk] to become mere sounding brass and tinkling cymbals, it will mean that our souls will become as hollow and empty as our words."[46] In the end conference delegates worked out a compromise. Though it fell short of what he had hoped for, Ward thought he could find a way to make it work.

On the whole the General Conference was remarkably successful from the perspective of the MFSS. The report of the Committee on the State of the Church hailed the MFSS's contributions to Methodist life through both literature and aid in organizing social service endeavors. No doubt Ward was delighted that leaders sympathetic to the MFSS agenda occupied key positions throughout the denomination. But the best moment of that General Conference for Harry must have come during the address of Charles Macfarland, general secretary of the Federal Council of Churches, who hailed "the man regarded by the denominations of the Federal Council as the greatest prophet today, in our Christian churches, of our social order, Harry F. Ward."[47]

He had made it. Harry F. Ward was now generally recognized as a leader among mainstream American Protestants. Despite the fact that some of his views continued to make the Methodist hierarchy uncom-

Harry F. Ward. (Cour-
tesy of Nanda Ward and
Robin Ward Savage)

fortable and some lay people downright angry, Ward had found a recog-
nizable niche in American Protestantism. His reputation as prophet
was based on more than his organizational and speaking skills. Though
he had published a number of articles and edited some useful books
over the years, he now began to write books himself, including *Social
Evangelism*, which was published in 1915. Thus Harry Ward increasingly found himself at the forefront of what was known as "the Social
Gospel."

Too often the American Social Gospel has been defined in terms of
ideas, regarded as simply a religious version of popular late-nineteenth-
and early-twentieth-century assumptions about human social progress.
To be sure, such ideas were in the air, but they were being used by persons
with a variety of ideological commitments and social agendas. For in-

stance, strong-willed industrialists embraced the idea of the survival-of-the-fittest and advocated an unregulated marketplace so that the strongest capitalists would succeed, in accordance with the natural scheme of things. Even among Protestant liberals there was no unanimous understanding of the prospects for human progress. Some believed that human moral progress was all but inevitable if ignorance could be stamped out and replaced by good will. Others argued that the social and economic system itself required reformation. Still others called for replacing the system of greed (capitalism) with a system of service (usually some form of socialism). Clearly it is wrong to regard the Social Gospel as a Protestant version of the ideology of the Progressive Era, for no such unified version existed.

The Social Gospel was rooted less in ideas than in experiences—the experiences of certain reform-minded ministers and lay people with the victimized underclasses of the turn-of-the-century industrial expansion. In volume after volume of the Social Gospel literature many pages are devoted to descriptions of the horrid conditions under which the working class suffered. Harry Ward's *Social Creed of the Churches,* a commentary on "The Social Creed," is a prime example. Here he details the difficult life faced by working-class men, women, and children—especially new American immigrants. Unless one recognizes the first-hand experiences on which such descriptions are based, one cannot appreciate or explain the passion of Social Gospel writers. These advocates knew that the problems of American immigrants were more than cuts and scrapes on the skin of the rising industrial order; they were oozing, gaping wounds that threatened the moral fabric of American society. Thus the authors describe in detail the illness and symptoms of that society. Their experiences with the suffering workers remained etched in their souls even after they moved on to more comfortable stations like the university or seminary. Their concrete experiences with the victimized workers, not abstract ideas about progress, represented the driving force behind the Social Gospel.

And the Social Gospel was usually communicated in very personal, practical terms. Social Gospelers sought to capture the imagination of ordinary church folk, so their books read like tracts; they are written in plain language, use vivid illustrations, and seek to inspire concern and action. Ward stood firmly in this tradition, gearing most of his writings to popular audiences. He was less interested in developing sophisticated arguments and more concerned with mobilizing religious bodies to act for change. Indeed, few theological treatises were produced by Social Gospel advocates. Their theology was simple, practical, and plain spoken. Walter Rauschenbusch's 1917 *A Theology for the Social Gospel,* perhaps the most theologically sophisticated book by a Social Gospel advocate, is unusual both for him and for the movement. His *Christianity and the Social Crisis* (1907) and *Christianizing the Social Order* (1912) are much more typical; they are passionate and filled with examples taken directly from observation of American society.

To fully appreciate the excitement of the Social Gospel, it is necessary to understand the headiness of the times. Real changes were taking place in the industrial order. The Progressive Era led to workplace regulation and social reform, and real changes in the lives of the working class could be documented year by year. Reformist efforts were making a visible difference! While Social Gospelers differed in their levels of optimism, most were convinced that the trajectory was moving upward—though they recognized that the progression would be neither easy nor without setbacks. Ward insisted that "As one of our prophets has reminded us, he who works for social progress must learn to think with the geologist and with God—in eons, not centuries."[48]

Most Social Gospel advocates spoke the language of traditional evangelical Christianity—salvation, sin, conversion, holiness, and so on—and applied it to the social order as well as to individual experience. Ward himself employed this vocabulary, especially in his *Social Evangelism,* where he insists that people must understand the existence of social sins: transgressions for which all persons are responsible and in the face of which they must demonstrate social repentance and social righteousness. In an article from the same period as *Social Evangelism,* Ward insists that the church must be in the vanguard of economic change. It must exercise responsibility on several fronts, including putting its own economic house in order. Since the church's business ought to reflect the principles of Jesus' teaching, the church must reject the values of the prevailing economic system.[49]

Such statements did not endear Harry Ward to the protectors of capitalism, including those who managed the Methodist Book Concern.

Despite the progress on this dispute at the 1916 Methodist General Conference, some folk continued to be discouraged by the situation. A union brother and member of Ward's Euclid Avenue congregation in Chicago commended him for his efforts, but lamented the Methodists' decision. Harry must have shaken his head as he read the man's statement: "[I]n my opinion our grand old church has thrown out its hand and it has returned a mailed fist."[50] Charles Sumner, a union leader and MFSS member, initially construed the situation more hopefully. "I really haven't felt so kindly toward the church in years. . . . I put myself at your service in this matter so far as my time and talents will permit."[51] But Sumner's optimism faded in subsequent months as the Book Concern played a clever delaying game, insisting that it had fulfilled the intent of the General Conference's instructions. Sumner was livid, and in a letter to the Book Committee he wrote: "If I were dealing with non-Christians I might be prepared to expect this. . . . I am certainly becoming awakened."[52]

Other union folk were getting restless too. Ward received a letter from James Kline, a Chicago union president and Methodist who was in contact with Charles Sumner, in which Kline groused about the "double-crossers" in the church and the big money that was trying to keep workers in their place.[53] Ward was appreciative and sympathetic, but he encouraged Kline not to give up. The real gains of the last four years must not be overlooked, and the hard work might yet pay off at the next General Conference. Then came some straight talk: "You must not forget that the other crowd has been in control a long time, and we have been at this job only a little while. Now is the time we need more effort than ever, because we have a chance to do something now, and a backing we never had before. I realize just as much as you do, I think, the size of the job that is ahead of us, but this is no time to quit!"[54]

When the fall of 1917 rolled around, there was still no resolution of the issue in sight. That year Ward published a book, *The Labor Movement from the Standpoint of Religious Values*, in which he did not mince words. Like all institutions with commercial aspects, he asserted, the church is obligated to deal fairly with labor and demonstrate its willingness to be involved in collective bargaining. At year's end Ward wrote to Sumner, apologizing for not having been able to pursue the Book Concern issue more vigorously in recent months. He was exhausted, and the American public was consumed with the rumblings of war. "I do not see that we can get anywhere just now by a campaign of publicity chiefly because we cannot get an adequate hearing for it while the war fever is so high."[55]

5

War without End
1917–1920

[I]t is good for a man to find out early in life how many will be missing from roll call on the day of battle. Then he will discover in time that the few who will stand are sufficient.
—Harry F. Ward, "Why I Have Found Life Worth Living"

ALTHOUGH THE RUMBLINGS of the European war may have seemed distant to most Americans, the German torpedo that exploded into the *Lusitania* on 1 May 1915 certainly caught their attention. Nearly twelve hundred passengers died—among them American women, men, and children—as the ship sank in eighteen minutes. American attention was increasingly diverted away from progressive domestic policy toward the European war and the attendant debate over how the United States should respond.

Like his parents, Harry Ward was never one to alter his commitments in the face of changing cultural values or even the dominant church climate. He had set his face to Christianizing the industrial order, and so he continued to wage the battle for social change. He was determined not to be moved, and he opposed the growing sentiment for war. His 1915 poem "Not Peace, But a Sword," written as a prayer, brooked no compromise; curiously enough, it was a call for Christians to maintain a holy war mentality against the advocates of war.

> To such conflict thou callest us,
>   To bitter struggle of soul.
> Help us to stand firm against
>   those who stand against thee!
> Save us then from softness of soul,
>   lest we cry Peace, Peace, when there is no peace.
> Keep us, thou Steadfast One, from making terms
>   with Death or compromise with Hell.

The poem's language and tone reflect a siege mentality throughout. It contains a lengthy description of being hardened for any challenge, even "the lonely task of standing out against our friends." Everything was at stake, and Ward called for uncompromising commitment to the righteous cause of social justice: "[G]rant us, we pray Thee, the utter abandon to the battle spirit. / So help us joyously to risk our all for thee and thine Eternal Cause."[1]

Ward recognized full well that America's entry into the European war would divert energy away from social reconstruction. He realized that American industrialists could restore their reputations by making important contributions to the war effort. In fact, he understood far better than most progressives how the war would make social change far more difficult.

When he addressed these concerns, Harry spoke not from a theoretical perspective but from an experiential one. The Methodist Book Concern issue continued to be unresolved, in part because war fever had created a hysterical reaction to serious social change. Ward's standing at Boston University suffered because of his antiwar and pro-labor attitudes. In early 1917 L. J. Birney, the dean of the School of Theology, admonished him to show more balance in his critique of industrial conflict. In Birney's judgment, Ward was not giving sufficient credit to Christian employers' efforts on behalf of working folk.[2] (No doubt some of those employers had been complaining to the school, and Birney felt compelled to take action.) He suggested not too subtly that Ward was being exploited: "I find a very distinct impression as I go about that you are under the control of labor, and are therefore afraid to utter those strictures. . . . I have never heard you say anything in chastisement for the sins of labor."[3] This was not the last time Ward would be accused of taking sides unfairly.

Ward's position on the war created tension in other areas of his life as well. There is no evidence that he was ever a wholehearted pacifist, but his revulsion to war had deep roots. A boyhood experience was forever seared into his memory: line upon line of riderless horses returning home to England from the Boer War with the dead soldiers' boots upside down on the sea of empty saddles. Now a new war promised to do what he had feared: shift human energies away from social reconstruction to war preparation and thereby allow capitalist barons to tighten their grip on power. Like many folk sympathetic to socialism, Harry Ward remained wary of the class divisions perpetuated by militarism.

There were differences of opinion about the war within the MFSS, and thus the organization took no formal position on the conflict. MFSS heavyweights such as Frank Mason North and Worth Tippy worked hand in glove with the War Department. Ward himself lectured across the country on behalf of the Federal Council of Churches General War-time Commission. Ward had an MFSS ally in his assistant Grace Scribner, and the two of them would not be silenced. As the United States entered the war, they warned *Social Service Bulletin* readers that churches ought "to keep down the spirit of vengeance, hatred and unjust suspicion." Just as importantly, the church must help protect the rights of free speech and even of conscientious objection, which, they argued, should not be limited to religious pacifists but should extend to any and all who had moral scruples about the war.[4]

With the United States now committed to an all-out war effort, most Americans did not want to hear such cautionary words, much less the kind of antiwar sentiments Ward voiced when he addressed college students. As a result, some of his scheduled lectures in the Midwest were canceled. In June 1917 a New York newspaper linked Ward with Emma Goldman's No Conscription League and the American Union Against Militarism. (Goldman was a well-known figure of the American left, notorious among most church folk for her views on anarchism, free love, and birth control.) Boston University's president sent a copy of the newspaper story to Dean Birney at the School of Theology. Ward's

MFSS associate Grace Scribner reported that Birney stormed into the office, "shaking with emotion" over the newspaper article and demanding to know whether Ward was, in fact, connected with these groups. According to Scribner, the dean "exploded" and insisted that the School of Theology would not employ anyone with such connections. Ward was out of town, but Scribner assured the dean that the story was not true. Birney fired off a telegram to Ward, in which he informed him of the news story and assured him that the university doubted its veracity, yet called on him to make a clear statement on the matter: "President asks me to learn your relation or sympathy with such organization. Please send night letter."[5] The university meant to deal with the matter quickly. Given the nature of the crisis, Ward's reply was extraordinarily terse: "No connection with organization or movement described."[6]

In his William Penn Lectures in May of 1918 Ward made his concerns about war explicit, echoing some of the sentiments he expressed in his *The Christian Demand for Social Reconstruction*. In that book Ward argued that militarism and capitalist industrialism are inextricably linked, and that both are enemies of Christianity. Militarism and capitalism "both seek special power and privilege for few."[7] Civilization stands at the crossroads between progress and destruction, and Christianity offers the resources to encourage a turn toward progress. Christianity can provide both a goal—the supremacy of human personality—and an organizing principle—mutual service, and together this goal and this principle can deter human conflicts, whether they derive from capitalism or from militaristic nations. However, conflict will prevail if the gods of Mammon and Mars continue to reign supreme. Ward insisted that the global war left no doubt about capitalism's true colors: the system that fed off the acquisitive instinct had brought on the war. Yet there was still hope, the social evangelist argued, for Christianity can regenerate the world through its goal and its principle.

Perhaps Ward realized that his tenure at Boston University was coming to an end. In any event, he had been cultivating another academic opportunity since 1916, when he began lecturing on a part-time basis at New York's Union Theological Seminary. And in 1918, Union—the most prestigious American Protestant seminary of that era—called Ward to fill a vacancy in Christian ethics. Boston University's president wished him well, remarking that they had been through "some trying experiences" together.[8] Boston theological students were sad to see Ward leave; as one of them later recalled, Professor Ward "inspired me to think for myself and ask questions about everything."[9] Another sad farewell came from a promising young student named Bromley Oxnam, who graded papers for Ward and occasionally minded the Ward children while Daisy and Harry went out for an evening together. Oxnam would miss his mentor; Ward had inspired him and illuminated his thinking. In his diary he recorded Ward's impact on an audience at the Ford Hall Forum lectures in 1916: "Students and religious workers attending the sessions claimed to have experienced a revival of their flagging reform zeal."[10]

In light of the events at Union that led to the vacancy in Christian ethics, Ward's appointment may have seemed an odd choice: his predecessor was axed for his antiwar views,[11] and Harry was perhaps headed for the same fate. His friend George Coe, a professor at Union, had warned him back in March about rumors linking him with Norman Thomas's pacifism.[12] Indeed, as a representative of the American Union Against Militarism, Ward engaged in serious conversations with Thomas about the defense of conscientious objectors.[13]

Since their early days in Chicago, Harry's friend Coe had told him that he would never be able to express himself fully until he had the opportunity to teach. Now Harry had his chance, as a full-time professor at Union. Over the course of the following decade, a torrent of articles and major books flowed from Ward's pen. And what a bonus to work alongside his friend Coe, who had been teaching at Union since 1909.

Once again the Wards relocated, moving to a home in Englewood, New Jersey, across the Hudson River from the seminary, which was located on Manhattan's upper west side, just a few blocks north of Columbia University. New Jersey seemed a curious choice, for Union faculty typically lived in or around the seminary compound. But Harry needed open spaces for his walks and sufficient ground to plant a garden.

The anticipated move to New Jersey is probably the backdrop for the only surviving private reflection by Daisy, who wrote it in March, just weeks after Union's announcement of Harry's appointment, and poured out her heart on the back page of a travel book. During their nearly twenty years of marriage, Daisy had made many sacrifices for Harry. She relinquished her dream of a career as a medical missionary; she gave up a life of wealth and privilege to live in the slums of Chicago; and she virtually raised the children by herself. She repeatedly helped Harry cope with physical illness, and she stood by him when he was caught up in controversy. Now, instead of moving to socially vibrant New York City, they were buying a home in the hinterlands of New Jersey. Feeling terribly alone, she wrote to herself: "The older Harry grows, the more the outside work of gardening will appeal to him, and the less he will want to go out evenings or to social affairs. . . . I love the outdoors, the trees, birds and flowers, but I also need friends."[14]

The Wards' life in a new environment was not easy. Shell bursts of antagonism directed against Harry began shortly after his arrival at Union. It might seem this would be a period of relative calm, for the armistice that ended the war was announced just months after the Wards moved. But Harry knew what lay ahead. He understood all too well the damage inflicted on labor's endeavors by wartime conditions. In *The Gospel for a Working World*—written before war's end and published in 1918 by the Missionary Education Movement of the United States and Canada—he predicted that during the postwar era the United States would undergo "the greatest period of labor conflict it has ever experienced" (102). In 1918 Ward was only five years removed from his days in Chicago pastorates, and despite all that had happened to him during that time those experiences remained vivid in his mind. In *Gospel for a Working World* he cites them repeatedly or draws on the experiences of others to illustrate the dilemmas of working folk in the violent conflict between producers and owners.

The book's first chapter, entitled "A Right to Live," describes in words and photographs the horrible working and living conditions faced by many American laborers, contrasting these with "Jesus' teaching concerning the worth of every human life" (10). This dichotomy had become a key moral problem for Christianity, and Ward generously illustrates the moral case using biblical texts. He insists that missionary efforts, especially among immigrant workers, will continue to fail unless Christians take their side in the labor struggle. With compelling logic, he appeals to the idealist as well as the pragmatist: "If low income is a source of delinquency, if it leads to the breakdown of morals, the religious forces must be interested in the questions" (84). Though Ward never mentions the Methodist Book Concern or any other religious publisher by name here, he characterizes the church's antiunion behavior as "still another count in labor's bill of grievances against the church" (136).

Ward also counsels his readers to understand the warlike nature of industrial conflict, and he does not mince words: "Only those who read the press of the labor world know how constantly the battle rages. There is no peace in the process of production. The goods necessary for life are made in the constant atmosphere of war" (101). He takes great pains to portray this war's grim conditions, including the vicious, violent methods employed by owners against labor. And Ward does not hesitate to examine the radical and sometimes violent wing of the labor movement, the Industrial Workers of the World (IWW). Though there is much antagonism toward the church in their ranks, the radicals must not be discounted, he argues, for there is religious hunger among these folk, and many are open to Jesus even if they are fed up with the church. "The people at the bottom feel that the changes which Jesus demanded in human society are the changes which their interest requires" (151). To realize these changes will require taking a stand. Should the church support strikes? Using the principles of the "Social Creed" as their standard, churches ought to "give support to the side that accepts those principles and is trying to carry them out" (157). Critical moments in history call for making common cause with like-minded folk: "There is no other propaganda for social reconstruction which goes so far or demands such thoroughgoing change as the propaganda of Jesus. There, then is a point of contact between the churches and the social radicals" (149).

As Ward readied himself during the summer of 1918 for his transition to full-time professor at Union Theological Seminary that fall, he received word that Walter Rauschenbusch, the great Social Gospel prophet, had died. Harry's note to the widow, Pauline Rauschenbusch, expresses his admiration and affection for her husband and his determination to continue Rauschenbusch's work: "[T]he banner he so gallantly lifted will not fall. It will be carried forward by many of those whom he has taught by word and pen."[15]

Ward's inaugural address at Union reveals that he understood the importance of socially active Christianity in a postwar environment: "In a desperate military situation, oftentimes the only possible defense is a vigorous offensive. This is now the case with the ethical teaching and practice of Christianity. We cannot merely hold the ground gained in twenty centuries of development. If we do not advance, then we retreat. . . . It is a task of creation that awaits us. A new world is to be made."[16] This fellow assuming his first full-time teaching position was no young man. Harry Ward was forty-five years old, and he had a wealth of experience. Nor were the thoughts he expressed on this occasion new to him. He had described these challenges earlier, particularly in two books published that same year: *The Christian Demand for Social Reconstruction* and *The Gospel for a Working World.*

As his inaugural addressed trumpeted, Ward's agenda for the church was not limited to the American scene, as important as this was. He had been keeping an eye on a development on the other side of the world, a development that made many Westerners nervous: the Bolshevik Revolution in Russia. The Bolsheviks seized power less than a year before Ward began teaching full-time at Union. As Ward's most recent writings indicated, he was committed to changing the economic order that exploited so many all over the world for the benefit of a privileged few. At this time he was also working on his first major book, *The New Social Order: Principles and Programs.* As the subtitle indicates, Ward was endeavoring to maintain his allegiance to the nonnegotiable ideals of Christianity (the principles) and correlate these with workable programs.

The New Social Order was released in 1919, a time when sobriety and even cynicism had replaced the optimism associated with victory in "the war to end all wars," "the war to make the world safe for democracy." When the war ended, progressives—many of whom had enthusiastically supported the war effort because it seemed consistent with their ideals of human progress—were ready to continue their good work. Greater successes seemed likely, but the American public was weary of change. Furthermore, Americans found it difficult to shake off the wartime mentality that focused on absolute loyalty and intense animosity toward nonconformity.

The postwar period was also a time of great labor unrest. Unions were now ready to achieve the goals they had patriotically set aside during the war. Management, on the other hand, was feeling its oats. The war's success had polished big business's image; American industry had demonstrated its capacity to supply materials for the victorious Allied effort. Aggressive management would not capitulate to aggressive labor, and thus confrontation between them was inevitable. During that first year after the Armistice there were many strikes: 175 in March, 248 in April, 358 in May, 303 in June, 360 in July, and 373 in August.

The large number of strikes was more than just an inconvenience for normal commerce. The nation longed for normalcy and on the whole despised the chaos created by union unrest. The outbreak of strikes represented a threat to the American way of life, for in the public mind they were part of an international socialist conspiracy. By the end of 1919 more than four million American laborers had been out on strike at some point during that calendar year. To many Americans it looked like revolution in the making, and they did not develop this perception by themselves: they had a great deal of help from a sensationalist press, opportunistic politicians, and the public posturing of some socialists themselves.

Socialist behavior during the First World War did not help their cause. In general, American socialists argued against the war, and few Americans were saddened when Eugene Debs, the standard-bearer for American socialists, was imprisoned in the Atlanta Penitentiary for repeatedly speaking out against the war effort, a violation of the wartime Espionage Act. Debs was not alone; during the war virtually every major socialist figure was indicted for similar violations.[17]

Even worse for the socialist cause was the perceived betrayal by Bolshevik-controlled Russia, which negotiated a peace treaty with Germany eight months before the armistice. And if that were not enough, the Bolsheviks then encouraged workers around the world to revolt against their capitalist governments. In the minds of many folk, "Bolshevik" had become a synonym for "traitor." The American popular press threw kerosene on the fire with sensational descriptions of terrible atrocities committed by the Bolsheviks.

Harry Ward was well aware of the obstacles to social change in this hostile environment. He recognized that the war might well represent a turning point for humanity, but a turn in the wrong direction. His little book, *The Opportunity for Religion in the Present World Situation*, describes the choice facing civilization: a philosophy motivated by conflict or a philosophy motivated by good will. Grounded in greed and conquest, the philosophy of conflict inevitably leads the world into war.

Thus it is incumbent upon religion to effect a change in the human will in order to follow the alternative philosophy. Religion must call for disarmament and a cooperative form of economics.

This sense of a critical historical moment brought great urgency to Ward's efforts. Unlike many progressives, he did not believe that progress was inevitable. The opportunity for change may be real, but should humanity choose the path of selfishness, apocalyptic descriptions become appropriate. Ward was not only trying to steer between the Charybdis of naive progressivism and the Scylla of jaded cynicism and hedonism brought on by the war and its aftermath, but also between the increasingly dominant thirst for "normalcy" and its attendant passivity and suspicion of change.

Ward's sense that he was living at a time when a spiritual dynamic was moving through the human race is clearly evident in his massive work, *The New Social Order*, published in 1919. In this book he carefully, even exhaustively delineates the principles that ought to govern the construction of the new social order: equality, universal service, efficiency, supremacy of personality (the value of persons over things), and solidarity. Devoting a chapter to each principle, Ward seeks to demonstrate that each is a practical necessity for the new social order and that each fulfills an ideal for which humanity has longed. Thus the practical and the ideal coincide. Moreover, he analyzes some contemporary programs that were trying to achieve the new social order: the British Labour Party, the Russian Soviet Republic, the League of Nations, the churches, and such progressive movements in the United States as the Socialist Party and labor organizations. Though some of these efforts appeared more promising than others, the author was not completely satisfied with any of them.

One reviewer of *The New Social Order* described it as "one of the most important books for the citizen of this generation to read thoughtfully,"[18] yet this remark fell mainly on the deaf ears of frightened Americans. In 1919 the American public was reacting hysterically to the threat of "domestic bolshevism."[19] On February 3 national attention focused on Seattle, where a general strike was announced. Three days later some 60,000 Seattle workers walked off the job, and newspaper headlines across the nation screamed, "REDS DIRECTING SEATTLE STRIKE—TO TEST CHANCE FOR REVOLUTION."[20] Public officials throughout the country jumped on the bandwagon, and Seattle's mayor became a hero when he personally directed the placement of federal troops that broke the strike on February 10. His cause was aided immensely by the refusal of the American Federation of Labor to support the strike; though sympathetic to the strategy of work stoppages, the AFL was wary of general strikes, for these were socialist tactics. Previously, Samuel Gompers and AFL officials had carefully distanced themselves from the violent reputation of the Industrial Workers of the World and rejected the antiwar sentiments of socialists. The AFL wanted to be part of the American mainstream, and therefore it avoided any association with radicalism and socialism. (Nevertheless, most of the 1919 strikes were AFL-supported, and they were regarded by many Americans as Red-inspired.)

Everything seemed to be coming apart. The inroads that Ward and his MFSS colleagues had worked so hard to establish were cluttered with "Red Scare" debris. The secretary-treasurer of an organization defending the Seattle strikers wrote a harsh letter to the Methodist Department of Evangelism condemning the denomination's inconsistencies. Having received a copy of Ward's *The Gospel for a Working World*, the letter writer expressed delight that the book "shows conclusively that there is a class war, and the reason why we must decide on which side of the fence we stand." And yet, observed the correspondent, a prominent Seattle Methodist pastor and the ministerial alliance applauded the authoritarian tactics of their city's mayor and police chief. "Even though you gave away ten thousand of your books in Seattle, how could you expect to Evangelize one single working man, when he sees just where the 'Headers of the Flocks' stand?" This must have been an encouraging yet painful letter for Ward to read, for it verified his own assessment of the church's corrupt position.[21]

On February 20, ten days after the Seattle general strike ended, the "Red Scare" got a new dose of adrenaline with the news that French leader Clemenceau had been wounded by a "bolshevik agent." Newspapers announced on February 24 that four "Wobblies" (IWW members) had been arrested in New York for their violent tactics. That same week, and also in New York, the Methodist Federation for Social Service published the January–February issue of the *Social Questions Bulletin*, which included an analysis of the Russian Revolution by Harry Ward. Many

Methodists could hardly believe what they read there: "[T]he aim of the Bolsheviks is clearly the creation of a state composed entirely of producers and controlled by producers. This is manifestly a Scriptural aim."[22] Ward admonished readers to wait and see if these new Russian leaders took account of and pursued "the rest of the Christian ideal."[23] Ward's article set off a firestorm of controversy. Already unnerved by postwar labor violence in America, many Methodists reacted angrily to Ward's wait-and-see attitude toward the Russian Revolution. Of course, the issue was not limited to what was happening halfway around the world; there seemed to be parallel events occurring in the United States.

Harry was never one to back down from a confrontation. His parents taught him to stand by his principles. Yet this situation was about more than principle. There was a warrior temperament coursing through Harry's body. Confident in himself and his judgments, he was rarely inclined to compromise in such situations. With his keenly logical mind, he spotted weaknesses in his opponents' arguments and responded with a quick jab of his sharp tongue. He generally respected those who disagreed with him, but in this instance it was not a friendly fight.

The *New York Christian Advocate,* "a leading organ of [American] Methodism,"[24] denounced Ward and the MFSS in the harshest terms. It accused Ward of having "surrendered his mind and heart to the fundamental idea of Bolshevism" to the degree that he could not be trusted to present a reasoned view of the Russian upheaval.[25] Now, after several years of frustrating confrontations with Ward and the MFSS, the Methodist Book Concern had its revenge. Ward was a marked man, and few Methodists would object if the Book Concern ceased printing his *The Bible and Social Living,* which was part of its popular Sunday school series. In what may have been a kind of ritual exorcism, the Book Concern declared dramatically that it would burn the plates of the book.

The MFSS found itself in a terrible quandary. In just a single decade, the organization had managed to acquire a measure of influence among Methodists, but now this all seemed in danger. Harry's friends were concerned as well. On March 24 MFSS leaders and advisers met in New York to address the controversial issue of the *Social Questions Bulletin.* Among those present were George Coe and two MFSS founders, Worth Tippy and Harry Ward. Reactions were mixed. Some asserted, especially Tippy, that Ward's analysis of the Russian Revolution was too one-sided, that it seemed to condone Bolshevism. Others argued along the lines of George Coe: "It is impossible to find anyone who will handle any question in a vital manner and not handle it a little partially." However, all agreed that the Methodist Book Concern had overreacted and that the *Christian Advocate* had been "unfair" in its editorial against Ward.[26]

Prominent Methodist leaders—including George Coe, Halford Luccock, Ralph Sockman, and Worth Tippy—tried to bring sanity to the controversy by asking Ward to clarify his "personal attitude toward the movement known as Bolshevism."[27] The *Christian Advocate* published Ward's reply. His statement may have quieted the minds of some, but many were still incensed by his unwillingness to issue a blanket condemnation of Bolshevism. His statement did offer three negative judgments of the Russian Bolsheviks: their theory of the dictatorship of the proletariat, their vindictive policy that meted out new injustices for past injustices, and their prohibitions against teaching religious doctrine. He called attention to the complexities of each of these issues, especially to the history of corrupt, brutal, and autocratic rule by the czars.

Ward was unwilling to give up on this new regime. He argued that the "agnostic materialism" of these Russian revolutionary leaders was "nearly always accompanied by an idealistic passion for human brotherhood which could be led to co-operate with a socialized religion."[28] These revolutionaries were advocating a society consistent with an ideal for which Christians also longed, and therefore Christians ought to watch carefully this "first blundering attempt" to organize society on the basis of this common ideal. Though he disagreed with "the Russian definition of this ideal," Ward argued that "no matter how blundering it may be, it flings a thundering challenge to our churches. Where are they going to stand in relation to this great Christian ideal that is now dimly moving the common peoples of the earth?"[29]

Harry paid dearly for this controversy. His standing among Methodists would continue to be influential, but now many people regarded him as a suspicious character. How could they trust someone who would not renounce atheistic revolutionaries? Moreover, this was not the first trouble Ward ran into that year. His antiwar position had created problems far beyond Boston University. His name—and particularly his association with three prominent antiwar groups—had come to the attention of the U.S. Senate Committee Investigating German Propaganda. In a response to the Senate committee Ward not only clarified his relationship with the three organizations, he went straight to the heart of the matter. The issue was not his affiliations, he wrote, but his fundamental position on militarism: "I was against militarism before the war; I was against it during the war; and if there is any of it left after a large part of the world has been trying to destroy it, I am still against it."[30] As he was preparing this letter, he also wrote a poem for himself. Entitled "Consolation," it reveals his sense of alienation from the mainstream. Each stanza begins with a negative assessment of human efforts, e.g., "When there's no profit in the words of men." Ward's refuge was the wonders of nature, not just its beauty but in the communion it offered.

. . . .
I will take counsel of the silent stars.
I will hold converse with the friendly trees.
. . . .
I hail the welcome of the joyous flowers.
I greet the laughter of the genial earth.
. . . .
I seek the solace of the abiding sea.
I hail the comfort of the unvarying hills.[31]

Lonely Lake called again, but it was not yet summer.

For the present, comfort came from a few supporters. With all the hate mail Ward received in reaction to his antiwar views and his analysis of the Russian Revolution, how he must have treasured a letter from the recently widowed Pauline Rauschenbusch, with whom he had conversed during numerous stopovers in the Rauschenbusch home. It is a warm and cordial letter. Noting the recent attacks on Ward, Pauline Rauschenbusch offers not just consolation but the highest compliment: "[Y]ou well now know . . . that you are a prophet." She reminds Ward of her husband Walter's difficulties with reactionary social forces following the release of his 1907 *Christianity and the Social Crisis.* "Walter has gone on, and is out of this phase of the strife and so I'm doubly glad you are still here."[32] The prophet's mantle had been passed on, and Pauline Rauschenbusch did not want this new prophet to lose heart.

Another letter arrived within a day or two of the Rauschenbusch one, but this was not so encouraging. The results of Harry's extensive physical examination at New York's Life Extension Institute were not good. His body was failing him again. It must have been humiliating to see himself described as "markedly underweight, hav[ing] faulty posture and show[ing] lack of general muscular development"; this is hardly a flattering description of one who prided himself on physical achievement. The report also identified problems with Harry's circulation and his kidneys, and there was mention of headaches. The prescription was a familiar one by now: the patient needs "relief from occupational strain."[33]

Ward may have been discouraged by this news, but his aggressive commitment to social change did not slacken. By month's end he was sending out letters as MFSS secretary calling for members' assessment of which areas required most urgent attention. The letter's first sentence testifies to Ward's unfaltering combative spirit: "[T]here is a need of a much more aggressive program for Christianizing industrial relations and conditions than the church has yet adopted."[34]

Before these letters reached their destinations, another powder keg exploded. On April 28 a mail bomb was sent to the Seattle mayor who had broken the general strike, but the bomb did not detonate. On the following day another mail bomb exploded, in the Atlanta home of a former U.S. senator, and his maid lost both her hands. On April 30, the same day Ward mailed his letters to MFSS members, an alert New York City postal worker led authorities to sixteen suspicious packages that turned out to be mail bombs intended for public officials. Eighteen more were subsequently discovered, all addressed to prominent public authorities. In some American cities—including Boston, Cleveland, and New York—May Day celebrations turned into riots. The nation was in a state of panic. Was there a revolution in the making?

Within a week many World War I veterans met in St. Louis to organize a new group devoted to promoting "100% Americanism" against the onslaughts of anarchists, Bolsheviks, and the Wobblies. The veterans called themselves "the American Legion," and by September they numbered 650,000. In this atmosphere it is no wonder that not all the responses to Ward's April 30 letter were positive. He received a letter from one New York Methodist district superintendent calling for a focus on personal evangelism as the answer to "the evils—I almost said madness—of Bolshevism."[35]

The violence continued. On June 2 bombs exploded in eight American cities and resulted in two deaths. The private residences of public officials, including Attorney General Palmer, became targets. The American public was horrified. The American Federation of Labor took notice, and during its June meeting it passed a strong anti-Bolshevik resolution. Nor were these organized labor leaders sympathetic toward a planned general strike on July 4 supporting clemency for Thomas Mooney, who had been convicted of a 1916 bombing in San Francisco.

For many radicals Mooney's case became a cause célèbre in the effort to establish equal justice for the working class. Though the Independence Day strike did not materialize, over three hundred labor-related strikes took place every month during that summer. On the second day of September two American Communist parties organized, and later that month a major steel strike began. Riots followed. No doubt many Americans believed these events were connected. The prevailing atmosphere promoted little tolerance for the views of Harry Ward and his kind. In fact, there was sweeping public support of government raids against various activist groups in 1919–1920 as Attorney General Palmer led the charge against what he believed to be the sources of these public disturbances.

Years later Ward reflected on the lessons he learned in this period, and his reflections reveal much about his mind-set. "[I]t is good for a man to find out early in life how many will be missing from roll call on the day of battle. Then he will discover in time that the few who will stand are sufficient."[36] But Ward was no wild-eyed idealist, eager to swim against the current without resources for the struggle. Allies had to be sought out wherever they might be found, and in the summer of 1919 Ward received his union card from the Associated Teachers Union of New York City. But it was also a time to do more than act behind the scenes. The pen and voice of the Social Gospel prophet must not be muted.

As controversial as he was, Harry Ward was a shining star in the world of those who embraced the reconstructionist agenda of Walter Rauschenbusch's brand of Social Gospel. The *Nation*'s reviewer of Ward's first major book, *The New Social Order*, informed readers of the legacy: "The mantle of Walter Rauschenbusch seems to have fallen on the shoulders of Harry Ward."[37] Ward was very conscious of the Rauschenbuschian legacy he represented. In response to a student's request for a list of ten names of "representative 'modern radicals'" in the last hundred years, Ward distinguished Rauschenbusch as the representative in the American religious world.[38] On another occasion he identified Rauschenbusch as the one who "showed us how we might get some certainty of direction."[39]

Like the best of the Social Gospelers, Ward wanted to communicate this direction clearly to all sorts of folk; his books were meant to be read, not line the shelves of admiring students and scholars. He continued to publish widely in books and journals, but his regular access to church lay people was coming to an end because of the controversy over the Bolshevik Revolution. The liberal Protestant journal, the *Churchman,* invited Ward to contribute, on a weekly basis, plainly written essays that would be published under the column heading "Some Studies in Christian Fellowship."[40] Thematically there is nothing new in these pieces. Their language is straightforward, with few rhetorical flourishes: the church "is the champion of the forces that unite and increase the life of mankind against the forces that divide and destroy it."[41]

But this series of articles represented more than a retread of old ideas. Here Ward addresses the needs of the hour, especially the mood and issues of the immediate postwar period. He faces head-on the "paralyzing and cynical distrust" wrought by the war on the agents of social change, especially on those who read the advances of the Progressive Era as evidence of inevitable historical progress: "[T]here can be no sudden exorcism of the competitive spirit."[42] Ward made his best moral case for the church to take sides in this moral struggle: "To keep silence is to throw the weight of its tacit consent behind the existing order and to leave that order to control and consequent destruction by the forces that are un-Christian."[43]

Despite his disappointment with the church in recent years, Harry Ward was convinced that it served three important functions: "the teacher of the principles of conduct," "the voice of moral judgment," and "the herald of a new order."[44] The church had demonstrated its will and power in other national social reform endeavors, especially abolitionism and the temperance movement; now it was time to bring the same passion and knowledge to bear on the economic realm.

6

A Pragmatic Holy Warrior
in the Making
1920–1929

I have seen the settlement movement stereotyped; the socialist party
blown to pieces by the war and the Russian revolution; . . . the churches
formally adopt the social service movement without understanding the
revolutionary nature of the religion of Jesus; and I am more convinced
than ever that this religion of Jesus can become the transforming force
in all human affairs.
—Harry F. Ward, "Why I Have Found Life Worth Living"

ON THE SURFACE Harry Ward's ideas seemed to change very
little between the "Red Scare" of 1919 and the beginning of the Great
Depression in 1929. He began and ended the 1920s calling the church
to serious social action, defending civil liberties, fighting capitalism's
vices, and advocating a socialist economy as the true realization of the
religion of Jesus for the social order. In fact, these basic social commitments changed very little for the rest of his long life. Yet the 1920s were
an unsettling period for Ward's basic convictions. During this decade he
wrestled with some difficult social and personal issues and reached some
workable conclusions about how to sustain resilient hope in the face of
persistent obstacles. The epigraph above expresses his sentiments well.

The year 1920 began with Harry assuming a significant role in a new organization formed to address the postwar world of public fear and increasing government suppression of leftist organizations and free speech. On the twelfth day of that year the American Civil Liberties Union hung out its shingle, with Roger Baldwin and Albert DeSilver serving as directors and Harry F. Ward chairing the board, which included such notable activists and public intellectuals as Jane Addams, John Haynes Holmes, James Weldon Johnson, Jeanette Rankin, Scott Nearing, Helen Keller, Felix Frankfurter, William Z. Foster, Elizabeth Gurley Flynn, and Norman Thomas. Thomas had walked into Ward's Union Seminary office and asked him to shoulder this important responsibility for a fledgling organization that promised to play an essential role in the difficult days ahead. Ward had been a key ally of Thomas and Baldwin in their efforts on behalf of conscientious objectors during the war. When Thomas and Baldwin were frustrated by limited cooperation from the leadership of the Federal Council of Churches during the war, they pursued one promising FCC contact: "[O]ur best hope is through Prof. Ward."[1] Ward was pleased to help in 1917, and now he was more than delighted to accede to his friends' request that he chair the ACLU board, for clearly the forces of change needed protection in the prevailing atmosphere of repression.

As the ACLU went about the difficult business of seeking amnesty for World War I political prisoners and protecting freedom of speech for union organizers and various sorts of social radicals, Ward's antagonists found one more reason to label him a troublemaker. In the context of national social unrest, the ACLU appeared to be yet another "Red" effort. Ralph Easley, head of the National Civic Foundation, informed the FBI that the ACLU was financially underwritten by communist Russia.[2] Easley also sent a report to the officers of the United States Steel Corporation asserting that Ward was part of a communist conspiracy behind the Interchurch Report on the steel strike.[3] Easley's damning evidence included a 1920 interview with Ward, who allotted his visitor twenty-five minutes before a mid-morning class. After summarizing that conversation, Easley offered his "analysis" of the Union professor by focusing on his physical appearance: "Mr. Ward has a receding chin, a nose too large for his size of face, and a low, broad, receding forehead, generally indicative of the laboring class."[4] This is a revealing statement, for the forces of reaction had more at stake than disagreements about economic theory and constitutionally guaranteed freedoms. Easley and his ilk were working against the changing face of America. For them the true America was Protestant, Anglo-Saxon, middle and upper class. Easley's description of Jerome Davis, a Union Seminary student and YMCA representative in Russia, betrays the reactionary perspective: "Pronouncedly German-Jewish type; Pronouncedly Jewish *tone* of vocalization; Neurotic."[5]

Ward did not take quietly subsequent accusations against himself, Davis, or another student, Julius Hecker, a Russian emigré. As he often did, Ward challenged his antagonists to use their evidence more carefully and to stop circulating lies about him. For example, that summer he fired off a letter to Vice-President Calvin Coolidge, who had accused Ward and the ACLU of advocating violence on behalf of social change; Ward firmly asserted that such a statement was a complete distortion of the facts.[6]

Government agencies such as the Justice Department's Bureau of Investigation (FBI) had been observing Ward's activities at least since the war. A 1922 letter from FBI Director William J. Burns demonstrates the bureau's awareness of Ward's associations and reveals its venomous antipathy toward the Union Seminary professor, whom it regarded as yet another "alien . . . who like so many of them . . . while our guest, reviles our sanctuary, pollutes the temple, and spreads from the very sanctum itself the seeds of discord, envy, and strife."[7] Burns was not the only bureau employee to display antagonism toward Harry Ward. In early 1924 Burns received a memorandum from an FBI colleague who reported a speech given by Ward to the American Sociology Association. According to the attached *Washington Herald* clipping, the ethics professor had denounced the Justice Department as a government agency "now functioning to destroy civil liberty" and specifically criticized Burns's tactics. The internal memorandum concluded with an assessment of Ward: "Of course you know the general character and standing of this creature."[8] The unsigned memorandum was dictated by "JEH," surely the initials of one J. Edgar Hoover, who shortly assumed the FBI directorship when Burns was fired for his connections with the Harding administration's financial scandals.

Ward's leadership in the ACLU was an important part of his activity in the 1920s, and this association created trouble for him in other arenas. Many Methodists were not happy to have the MFSS linked so publicly with ACLU free speech cases, especially those involving communists or other radical leftist persons or groups. In a *New Republic* essay dripping with sarcasm and righteous indignation, Ward denounced the rising tide of propaganda by American military leaders against the forces for social change. "Today the interlocking publicity machine of certain industrial propagandists, professional patriots, and the War Department" are uniting against democratic treasures such as freedom of speech.[9]

Harry had more to worry about than government surveillance or even the hard struggle for freedom and justice. In 1920 his twelve-year-old daughter Muriel contracted a disease[10] that left her legally blind, a condition the family understood to be derived from one of the diseases brought back to the States by returning American soldiers. Yet another manifestation of the evils of war! Muriel was a bright girl, but if she was going to complete her education, she would require much more of Daisy's time. The condition was noticeable—Muriel's eyelids drooped badly; even surgery would not conceal the effects, and Muriel became extremely self-conscious. Her parents, especially her mother, were alarmed by the young woman's reaction, and from this time onward, Daisy was very protective of her youngest child and only daughter.

Harry Ward never spoke publicly about Muriel's difficulties, though by the end of the decade he would write about the terrible uncertainty of the physical universe, which even the technological proficiency of modern society could do little to ameliorate. Given his own history of physical struggles and his mother's early death, Harry knew full well how one's body can thwart personal expectations: "With all our prevention of disease, still suddenly without warning, out of the darkness or at high noon, the grim Destroyer strikes and one with whom our life has been knit, falls at our side. Then the world is a lonesome place. The skies are dark, and the heavens are dumb. Against their gates of brass we beat in vain with our futile fists. There is no answer. The universe seems both irrational and cruel."[11]

Thankfully Gordon and Lynd were in good health. Following in their father's footsteps, they took up debate at their Englewood, New Jersey, high school. Round-faced and mechanically minded like his mother, Gordon became a social introvert. Unlike Lynd and Muriel, Gordon expressed little interest in social events at school. Perhaps his father's frequent absences during so much of his boyhood and now his mother's preoccupation with Muriel's physical problems nudged Gordon to retreat within himself. Examining all his surviving boyhood pictures, one looks in vain for a smile on his face. By contrast, Lynd's eyes often sparkle in his childhood photographs.

The Canadian camp continued to be the one place where their father spent significant time with his children. While they were growing up, they spent most of their summers there. Those Canadian summers continued to mean more than family time and relaxation away from the job. "Camp" also meant work. The summer of 1922 was particularly memorable for hard work; during these months Harry, his sons, and their friends rebuilt the Ward cabin. As a reward for their hard work, Harry took the teenage boys on a six-day canoe and fishing excursion. In subsequent years canoe trips became regular father-son experiences, especially for Gordon and Harry. Each person had his job: Harry, cooking and cleaning up; Gordon, repairing the canoe; Lynd, maintaining the tents. The canoe trips entailed rigorous exertion, what with heavy backpacks, long portages, and the unrelenting aggravation of mosquitoes and black flies. Harry savored every moment of these trips, for such outdoor challenges provided opportunities to demonstrate manly skill in the face of nature's challenges. Ever since his restoration to health in England's New Forest, Harry had relished the beauty of unspoiled nature. Many a summer stay at the Canadian Boldrewood camp began with Harry sighing on arrival, "I'm home." For all his determination to make the cities of the world a democratized social order, his ultimate frame of reference was the sounds, sights, smells, and tactile experiences of the forest. Here he felt whole.

The rebuilding of the cabin and the wilderness expeditions are appropriate metaphors for Harry Ward's ideological struggle during the twenties. Though he was never naively optimistic, he retained hope for social change even through the war years. But since the war the forces of progress had lost ground, and Ward had witnessed firsthand how vicious the forces of reaction could be. Americans elected a president who stood for "normalcy"—a smokescreen for the status quo. Despite the best efforts of organizations such as the ACLU, the forces of repression were

Lynd Ward's wood engraving "North of the Height of Land" depicts
Harry F. Ward and Gordon Hugh Ward on one of their wilderness camping
excursions. (Courtesy of Nanda Ward and Robin Ward Savage)

on the offensive. So much was changing for the worse, and it was not
clear to Harry how a promising future could emerge from the trials of
this period—though most observers, noting Ward's unrelenting efforts,
would never imagine that he harbored such doubts.

He continued to address the relationship between economic morality
and the religion of Jesus throughout the 1920s in spoken and written
words, especially through the Methodist Federation for Social Service.

Prospects were daunting, for the dominant American ethos was a celebration of "the good old days that never were," as John Dos Passos's
returning doughboy Charley exclaims.[12] The most popular religious
book of the decade was Bruce Barton's *The Man Nobody Knows,* in
which Jesus is portrayed as the prototypical businessman.[13] Given the
immense challenge, Ward missed no opportunity to broaden the impact
of his work, and so the *Social Questions Bulletin* became a resource for
other activist groups with which he had connections. In 1920 the ACLU
distributed to congressional representatives 1,000 copies of an issue devoted to political prisoners.[14] A series of pamphlets, "Vital Questions
Leaflets," were developed on such topics as "The Open Shop" (by
Ward), "Have You Free Speech?" (by Roger Baldwin), and "The Nature
of the Acquisitive Society" (by Ward), and these were distributed to
churches, labor unions, students, and social action groups. The pamphlets were written in everyday language and were pocket-size for
portability. They were the social version of the traditional gospel tract,
and they were widely read. For example, one thousand of them were
shipped at the request of an evangelist who wanted to hand them out at
street meetings.[15]

Ward and his colleagues knew it would take more than tracts and
speeches to alter the social climate. Institutions must be persuaded to
join the battle, and so the MFSS invested its energy in persuading
church bodies, especially its own Methodist Episcopal Church, to take
a stand on important social issues. In 1923 Ward presented "a tentative
outline of a General Conference Statement" for review. There was nothing tentative about its contents, however. The document called on the
church to embrace economic practices foreign to most of American life.
It urged the church to reject "unearned income," "repudiate the profit
motivation for our economic life," reject absentee ownership, place limits
on ownership of private property, and consider public ownership of
natural resources. The outline appeals strongly to Methodist heritage—
e.g., "We issue a call to our people to go on to perfection in the matter
of seeking the Christian social order."[16]

Despite his confidence in human reason and science, Harry retained
some reservations about the growing influence of what has been called
"the machine age," and he was not alone in this view. Many people who
had grown up in less complicated times found the increasing presence

and influence of machines quite threatening. The impact of new technology during the twenties was remarkable. For example, in that decade the number of American homes with a radio jumped from 0 to 40 percent.[17] The Ward family had enjoyed music on Mother Kendall's old gramophone since her death, but Harry did not purchase a radio and record player until 1927. In subsequent years the record player brought great pleasure to his life; he enjoyed a variety of music, especially folk songs about the labor movement and social justice. Visitors to the Ward home would later recall hearing the rich voice of Paul Robeson booming from the record player and resonating through the house. Still, three decades later, Harry would grouse, "to me machinery is something only to be endured when necessity compels."[18]

Harry was of two minds. He did not trust impersonal machines. He refused to drive an automobile (especially after a near-miss with a reckless driver), yet he endorsed whatever means human reason and science discovered to make life better. His 1925 lecture, "Ethical Aspects of Industrialism," reveals his appreciation for technology as well as his insistence that these new discoveries must be guided by proper ideals. He employed a utopian vocabulary in his arguments in defense of modern science and technology: "No map of the universe is complete that does not contain Utopia. . . . Our Utopia today is not a dream of the idealists, it is also the diagram, the chart, and the map of the scientists."[19]

Yet Harry Ward rejected any notion of theoretical utopias,[20] for he prided himself on his own manual labor. Over the years he acquired most of the skills of self-sufficiency that made the Lonely Lake camp comfortable and productive. Back home in New Jersey he enjoyed cultivating his flowers and baking bread. The butcher's son was very particular about slicing meat. Working with his hands was more than a hobby; it was part of his sense of being connected with life. He took great pride in mastering the skills required for the long canoe expeditions in the Canadian wilderness and all but sneered at tourists who were pampered by guides. It was exhilarating, asserted Ward, to combat nature and succeed. That is how human beings should employ the advances of science: to master the world for human betterment.

What mattered most for him was that science become informed by moral ideals. Though science and ideals might be naturally complementary, Ward maintained that their cooperation is not inevitable. A hard

Harry relied on his wife for many things. Here, Daisy gives Harry a trim.
(Courtesy of Nanda Ward and Robin Ward Savage)

task lay ahead: "Christian idealism must face the problem of organizing
the administration of the complex life of humanity."[21] The economic
sector remained the crucial part of this complex life, and so Ward insisted that the economic system must acquire "a human end and a spiritual purpose."[22] Increasingly Ward argued that science and religion
offered complementary critiques of capitalism. Science verified that
capitalism is not efficient, and the religion of Jesus verified that it is not
moral either. Taken together, science's superior methods and religion's

superior ideals offer humanity a real future.[23] Ward's argument for the compatibility of science and religion was an updated version of his long-standing appreciation of human reason informed by religious ideals.

Other changes were swirling around Harry Ward in the early twenties, most of them personal and even traumatic. The fallout from the "Red Scare" continued among Methodists, including previously loyal MFSS members. It did not help that the New York State Legislative Joint Committee Investigating Seditious Acts named "Union Theological Seminary of New York, where Christian Ethics are taught by Dr. Harry F. Ward" as one of "two dangerous centers of Revolutionary Socialist teaching of a university type in ecclesiastical institutions."[24] In its so-called Lusk Report, the committee also associated Ward with what it labeled "a kind of Bolshevism far worse than the Bolshevism of Russia"[25] and cited his leadership role in the ACLU. This organization received special scrutiny from the Lusk Committee, which noted in particular the ACLU's roots in the American Union Against Militarism, which had, among other things, been guilty of "encouraging naturally timid boys and discontents to register as conscientious objectors" and "assist[ing] any radical movement calculated to obstruct the prosecution of the war."[26] Among the report's supplemental pages are facsimile copies of what it considered damning correspondence, including a 1917 letter (on MFSS letterhead) from Harry F. Ward agreeing to serve with the Emergency Peace Committee, an organization promoting neutrality during the First World War.[27]

To such accusations Harry Ward developed several replies, e.g.: "As for myself, I belong to no party or economic faction. I am neither Socialist or Communist. In answer to that question, I usually say, 'I am something worse than that, I am a Christian.' That is to say, I expect to follow the teachings of Jesus wherever they may lead."[28]

The Lusk Committee was not alone in its scrutiny of Ward. Worth Tippy, one of the MFSS founding members, had been uneasy with Harry's views on the war and unhappy with Ward and Grace Scribner at least since the brouhaha over the 1919 *Social Questions Bulletin* issue on the Russian Revolution.[29] Tippy objected to what he saw as the MFSS publications' heavy reliance on materials from what he called the "radical and labor press." This, he claimed, revealed a lack of balance in the MFSS office: "They have the same extreme point of view: collectivist in conviction, intense propagandists and in the left wing of the religious social group."[30] At a November meeting of the MFSS Ward presented his vision of the organization's work. In Tippy's eyes it was a dangerous program for the MFSS, Methodists, and American society. He also contended that the Executive Committee was being reconstituted with persons who agreed with Ward's views. "Dr. Ward is just the person who needs restraint and counsel of a sympathetic opposition minority." Tippy became fed up with the situation and resigned.[31] The parting shots by this MFSS founder had a clear target: "Dr. Ward's agitation is feeding straight into the revolutionary movement, whether he designs it or not[;] . . . the total effect of his criticism of our institutions is not constructive and helpful, but demoralizing and undermining."[32]

The significance of this charge goes far beyond Tippy, for as William McGuire King's study makes very clear, the MFSS's Social Gospel coalition was unraveling. The "Federation" had intended to bring together a range of ideologies and strategies, but the war and its aftermath served to pull folks apart. The MFSS was becoming home mostly to what King labels the social reconstructionists, the radical Social Gospelers who demanded a fundamental alteration in social structures, including the capitalist economy.[33] Though Ward was on the winning side in this MFSS dispute, his soured relationships with former allies had repercussions.

Even more painful was the sudden death in 1922 of the MFSS associate secretary Grace Scribner. As she was crossing Broadway near Union Theological Seminary, she was struck down by a hit-and-run driver. Harry knew nothing about this when he arrived home very late that evening. A note by his telephone told him something was wrong, for it asked that he call some New York friends "no matter how late it is." Before he could make the call, a newspaper reporter telephoned, asking for information about Grace Scribner, and this was how Harry learned of the tragic death of his friend and co-worker. In the first moments of shock, Ward responded to the "plainly perfunctory" questions of the reporter for whom this death was just another news-gathering opportunity in "the hunt for profit."[34]

Grace Scribner possessed qualities Harry Ward had long admired: "her sheer fighting capacity, her indomitable courage, the quality of her will."[35] In many respects Grace Scribner was for Ward a female version of Kipling's heroic figures. She came from a humble background and was fiercely independent, even to the point of refusing financial assistance for a college education. At her memorial service Harry spoke fondly of these qualities: "We talk of our self made men. What about the self made woman? This woman fought her way from ignorance to where she sat at the council table with the best minds in the land. Do you understand what that means in this world that is largely a man's world?"[36]

Scribner was not the only woman at that table. At least three women were members of the MFSS Executive Council: Scribner, Mary McDowell (Harry's settlement colleague from Chicago days), and Winifred Chappell of the Chicago Training School for (Methodist) Deaconesses. Like Ward, Chappell had been heavily influenced by the teaching of George Coe at Northwestern, and she became the new MFSS assistant secretary with the understanding that she and Ward were "partners" in this endeavor.[37] And again like Ward, Chappell brought a keen mind and social passion to the job.

Coe himself was facing some difficult issues that year, though none of them was life-threatening. Strongly disagreeing with Union Seminary's failure to promote a junior colleague in his department, Coe abruptly resigned in August and became a lecturer at Columbia University's Teachers College, just a few blocks down Broadway from Union Seminary. In 1927 he retired, and his friend Harry paid him a high compliment: "Your unfailing support of every cause, movement or protest where an issue of freedom or justice arises has been and is a constant inspiration and stimulus to those who are younger."[38]

During this period, friends such as Coe were important to Harry Ward. For example, he expressed gratitude to the former Boston University student and family friend G. Bromley Oxnam for his encouraging words: "In these days of reaction, one of my constant encouragements is the knowledge that fellows like you are going to carry the cause forward."[39] Despite the war and the "Red Scare," Ward's confidence in the future was unbroken. "Christianity offers men the eternal hope; this is why it inspires them with an unwavering confidence that their vision is not a mirage."[40]

For all his public bravado, Ward's sense of hope was vulnerable. His basic convictions had become unsettled. Though he would never succumb to the pessimism or cynicism of the twenties' "Jazz Age," history and the cosmos now seemed to him less reliable than before. Perhaps it was the increasing repression by government and big business. Maybe it was the loss of solidarity among union folk, as labor leaders like Samuel Gompers and John L. Lewis distanced themselves not only from radical groups like the IWW but also from the ACLU. It may have been the ongoing personal attacks, especially those by former allies like Worth Tippy. It may have been Muriel's serious illness, the tragic death of Grace Scribner, Coe's unhappiness at Union, or the cumulative effect of all these troubles that led to Harry's more cautious confidence in the future. He commented stoically after Scribner's death: "Gone like a candle. It is one of the ways that life has."[41]

More than twenty years had passed since Harry studied philosophy with William James at Harvard, but now James's notion of reality was making more sense than ever. One strives for the right and true even if these goals prove to be unreal and unreachable. What matters is the effort of pursuing something worthwhile. Ward still called for waging war on behalf of right, but now he lacked the same degree of confidence in its outcome. "If for both [God and humanity, it is] only a mirage—never reached—yet a great adventure—to join in faith with the eternal struggle is the greatest men can do."[42]

The mid-twenties were full of changes for the Ward family. By 1924 all three children had graduated from high school. Daisy's nurturing and her daughter's persistence and sheer brilliance paid off when Muriel graduated as the valedictorian of her Englewood High School class. She entered Swarthmore that fall, and the family found some students there who would read to her the texts she could not read herself. Gordon became an undergraduate at Massachusetts Agricultural College, perhaps a reflection of the years of gardening he enjoyed with his father. Following the completion of his master's degree work at the University of Minnesota, Gordon began doctoral studies at Columbia University. Lynd pursued a major in fine arts at Teacher's College of Columbia University and studied at the Leipzig Academy of Graphic Arts.

The Ward offspring were all raised not only to value education and learning but also to follow the traditional morality of their Methodist forbears, avoiding destructive vices like tobacco and alcohol while practicing the virtues of honesty, hard work, respect for one's elders, and moderation in material expense. Yet this was no typical moralistic Methodist family, for Gordon, Lynd, and Muriel were also schooled in the traditions of radical social change. As Harry had admonished young people at a summer student conference in 1921: "Those who have taken Christianity seriously have never been comfortable citizens"; they inhabit "two worlds—the one that is and the one that ought to be."[43] During her first year in college, Harry advised Muriel that "those who try to do something worthwhile in the world will never find more than a few who really understand and with whom they can have true fellowship."[44] This outsider's view of American society created some problems during Gordon's undergraduate years, for he asked to be exempted from the college's requirement of military training. In correspondence with the college's president, Harry Ward argued his son's case in terms of his own views on war and militarism: war is "contrary to the teaching of Jesus, destructive of the aims and ideals of Christianity, and the negation of human progress."[45] Apparently local newspapers got wind of the story and stirred up "a tempest" about the college's granting such an exemption.[46]

Two years later Gordon explicitly thanked his parents for helping him become a person who could make wise judgments in the face of countervailing popular opinion. It was the occasion of Daisy and Harry's twenty-fifth wedding anniversary, and Gordon, a reserved person like his father, displayed some rare, open affection in his words of appreciation for his parents' guidance. Not only had his parents taught him to think for himself and provided him with "principles and ideals," Daisy and Harry had schooled their three children to pursue a simple but profound purpose in their lives: "leaving the world a little better to live in than I found it."[47]

Harry's world continued to become larger, especially with his first sabbatical in 1924–1925. With their daughter and sons all out of the nest, Daisy and Harry could now take advantage of opportunities to see firsthand the revolutionary changes that were becoming characteristic of this new century. Sherwood Eddy secured an invitation from the Chinese Christian Council for Harry to deliver a series of lectures entitled "The Ethical Aspects of Industrialism." Hearing of the lectures, similar organizations in India and Japan also invited Ward to speak in their countries. All these nations were experiencing social ferment, and in these times of potentially dramatic change, who better to address them?

But first Harry and Daisy wanted to see for themselves the dramatic changes in Russia they had only heard about. They would determine for themselves who was telling the truth about the historic revolution there.

As they embarked on this exciting journey, Harry penned an article for the *Christian Century*, "How Can Civilization Be Saved?"[48] Here he rehearsed the familiar radical Social Gospel argument, insisting that only Christianized social structures can bring a positive response to the title's question: "The only hope of civilization lies in the religion of Jesus" (1176). Reform had failed because the profit system still prevailed, and "until organized Christianity recognizes that capitalism is required by its own nature to limit the program of reform, its strategy will not be adequate" (1176). In contrast to his Union Seminary inaugural address just seven years earlier, Ward now concluded that the "religion of Jesus" had replaced "Christianity" as the only positive label for the Christian moral trajectory. Ward's hopes for institutional Christianity had diminished considerably, but his commitment to religiously inspired social change had not withered a fraction. How to proceed? Ward stated that society had lost its way, "trying to go forward by muddling through one experience after another without any sense of their relation to the map of the universe" (1177). The religion of Jesus offered a way with the principles of personality, fellowship, and service as road markers.

How then to implement these principles? Ward harked back to the evangelical language of conversion and regeneration; the very nature of social order must change. The "core of evil"—that is, the profit system and the modern state's "assertion of its absolute sovereignty"—must be purged (1177). How to do this? Events in Russia offered some guidelines, though the violence that took place in Russia was not to be emulated. Ward noted Trotsky's admission that "physical force is too costly a method of economic transformation" (1176). Rather, what Ward called "revolutionary reform" could chart a course of change between the instability of revolution's drastic alteration and the inadequate tinkering of reform. For starters, Christians must insist that their own institutions organize their business on the basis of cooperation, not profit. "How Can Civilization Be Saved?" concluded with a series of questions, reflecting Ward's ongoing ambivalence about the significance of hope and perseverance in such a struggle.

What does the realization of success in failure do in relating us to God? Does the present state of the world give him no sense of defeat? Is his life too an eternal, uncompleted struggle with evil, and is it in entering this struggle that we come into and keep in touch with ultimate reality? Is the essence of our religion that knowing we ourselves cannot win in our day, we should nevertheless continue to fight for what is for us unattainable? Is the victory that overcomes the world not our accomplishment but our faith as it calls into action the creative forces that continually renew life? (1178)

Now it was time for Harry and Daisy to see if such creative forces were truly at work in Russia's cooperative economy. At the beginning of their month there, they quickly discovered that it was not always easy to gain access to what they wanted to see. Each morning the Wards queued up at the Russian Bureau of Information to discover which site or person they might gain permission to visit.[49] They met with Lenin's widow Krupskaya, and Ward was impressed with her descriptions of Lenin's love for his people.[50] Venturing into the countryside, the Wards slept in hay barns and spent a weekend with a Tolstoian community just outside Moscow.[51] When Harry asked the leader how this pacifist religious group got along with the Bolshevik regime, he learned that there had been some trouble because of a few atheistic zealots, though the matter was settled through Lenin's personal intervention.[52]

This was not the only time Ward encountered reports of religious harassment, and so he devoted an entire article—"Will Religion Survive in Russia?"—to reporting on the matter, for this was a topic that concerned most American Christians, even those who were sympathetic to the goals of the Russian Revolution. In this article Ward describes the problem as a conflict between the government's stated policy of tolerance—which included a constitutional assertion of freedom of religion—and the antireligious agenda of the Communist Party, which wielded most of the governmental power. After describing in some detail the anti-religion efforts of the party, Ward calls attention to the root causes of the movement: the Orthodox Church's historical support for the status quo, and modern confrontations between science and religion.

Though Ward never makes the analogies explicit, it is clear that he wants his readers to recognize the alarming parallels with American institutional religion. Ward was convinced that communists could not destroy religion. As a Russian man put it to Ward: "[T]he soul of Russia will never be satisfied with cold science. . . . The soul of Russia will then awake and its true religion will develop." Ward believed that purging the excesses of the Orthodox Church would allow Christians and communists to unite in common social purposes.[53]

Harry was particularly concerned with the abuses of civil liberties in Russia, and his article for the *Nation* on this matter is one of the most revealing documents with regard to Ward's ambivalence about the Russian socialist endeavor.[54] Here he makes every effort to analyze the Russian situation on its own terms, taking seriously the difficulties created by a historically authoritarian nation, the different strategy for change advocated by communists, and the continuing struggle against counter-revolutionary forces. He does not hesitate to point out the parallels between Russian repression of civil liberties and postwar America's quashing of freedom of speech and assembly. Ward endeavors to take seriously the Russian claim that reforms would continue—including more careful regulation of the General Public Administration (GPA), the organization responsible for policing and incarcerating dangerous political opposition. Still, Ward was disturbed by what he saw and heard, even as he acknowledged the possibility of exaggeration and misrepresentation in what was reported. Freedom of assembly and freedom of speech were very limited. "Of freedom of the press there is none. . . . The censor is still omnipotent if not omniscient" (236). Ward clearly understood the dangers of such repression, as is evident in his discussion of the case of a woman accused of "unconscious economic espionage": "Whatever may be true of individual cases, it is historically certain that no matter what the system of government, when political repression is deemed necessary and secret or semi-secret methods are employed, miscarriage of justice, rank injustice, and oppression are bound to occur" (236). He called for a general amnesty and limitation of the powers conferred upon the Commissariat of Justice to "send away" people without the benefit of a public trial (235).

Ward concludes the article with a warning to American civil libertarians to lower their expectations of the Russian situation, especially given "the Communist system [that] requires regimentation." The best face he can put on the present situation is that "the atmosphere that makes for repression still continues, though at a lower temperature." He reminded "friends of freedom in other countries who have stood for the right of Russia to develop in her own way" that necessary reforms take time, especially given the continuing threat of counter-revolutionaries and the communists' determination to approach change more efficiently (237).

Harry and Daisy's trip to India in late September was much more than an opportunity to lecture and observe an important developing nation; it was also a chance to see firsthand the impact of Gandhi's style and strategy for social change. Harry must have been all but despondent when he was hospitalized with malaria and could not keep his much coveted appointment with Gandhi. Daisy was not to be denied, however, and she enjoyed her conversation with the Indian leader, who, like her husband, had a frail body but a strong will and intellect. After hearing of Ward's illness, Gandhi visited him in the hospital several days later, and they shared a lengthy bedside chat. Ward and Gandhi did more than talk politics; they allowed a little time to discuss "the comparative joys and values of spinning and working with the soil,"[55] for two men who valued common toil and the land could not always remain intellectually ethereal. Gandhi's visit caused quite a stir among the hospital staff, who thereafter regarded their American patient as a special guest.

Harry and Daisy enjoyed at least one other visit with Gandhi before leaving the country. The Indian reformer was impressed with what he had heard, especially from his followers who sponsored one of Professor Ward's lectures in Bombay. If it was a speech similar to the one he gave in Calcutta, "The Future of the Intellectual Class," one can understand Gandhi's enthusiasm. Ward challenged India's intellectuals to shed the sins associated with their class—"separation from toil," "the feeling of superiority," and "dogmatism"—and offer their services to the lower classes on behalf of the inevitable social changes that would occur in the modern world.[56] He warned his audience against repeating the errors of Western intellectuals who have "been afraid of losing their jobs and their social status and the future of their children, and therefore stop short in the search for justice and the search for truth under the inhibiting influence of that fear."[57]

Not everyone was pleased with Harry's remarks, and his comments were reported back to Mr. Hoover, now director of the Justice Department's Bureau of Investigation. This report described Ward's movements and speeches in Bombay and, of course, emphasized his favorable remarks about Russia. Surveillance continued as the Wards moved on to China. The American consul general in Shanghai sent a dispatch to the State Department describing "the Bolshevist proclivities of Dr. Harry F. Ward." The American consul in Nanking also fired off a confidential dispatch, decrying not only Ward's complimentary assessment of the Russians but also his negative influence on China's unstable political situation. The irate consul reported "that several of the more responsible Christian Chinese ascribe much of the pro-Soviet tendency in Nanking to Dr. Ward's remarks."[58] On at least two occasions Ward was censored. In India he was forbidden to give a speech on Russia "because the British government did not want it," and in China his lecture on "What May Be Expected from Communism" was canceled by a college chancellor because he feared it would encourage the students' communist sympathies.[59] Daisy wrote to her children that on several occasions the Wards were asked not to discuss Russia with the Chinese students, for officials believed Russian influence was already too widespread.[60]

Chinese officials did have legitimate concerns about civil order, and the Wards witnessed some of the chaos firsthand. In early May, Harry candidly observed to his children that Russian rhetoric was not helping the Chinese situation, that it provided only "too plentiful hot air about world revolution, soldiers and workers fighting together, etc."[61] By June he was reporting a very tense situation in Wuchang. His lectures were suspended due to a student strike and the administration's fear of violence. Wishing to observe the students' demonstration, Ward contemplated attending it in disguise, but, given his prominent English features, he realized such a ruse would fail: "[U]nfortunately the Lord or someone else, gave me a beak that will never pass as Chinese."[62] As feared, the demonstration turned violent, and guards were required to protect the Wards and other foreigners in the compound where they were staying. It was an unlikely picture: the wiry little leftist professor and Daisy setting forth to his lecture accompanied by "fourteen soldiers with bayonets on the end of their rifles," two officers, and eight police for protection against radical students. Never one to lose his sense of humor, even in a tense situation, Harry observed that it "looked as though we were going to jail."[63] The Wards did not laugh about the behavior of the Chinese communists, though. Both of them remarked on the contrast between the restraint and discipline of the Russian communists and the lack thereof among their Chinese counterparts.

Ward reported back to the ACLU on the Shanghai strike, during which police fired multiple rounds into an armed crowd. He noted that the strike was supported by a variety of Chinese groups: students, labor, small merchants, and even for a time by the chamber of commerce. At issue in Shanghai was foreign interference in Chinese affairs, and Ward raised serious questions about the injustice attributed to British and Americans in particular.[64]

He was struck by his own change of roles in this context: "Queer to get to a place where I may not be radical enough for them." He suspected that the real issue might be his identity with religious organizations.[65] His diagnosis proved to be correct, for there was much antagonism among progressive Chinese forces against the cultural imperialism and apolitical religion of Western Christian missionaries. After demonstrating "that we were not trying to put over any Christian propaganda," Ward reported, their reception among the leftists warmed up.[66] Daisy observed the difference: "Dad . . . is appreciated by most people since they think he is not teaching religion nor Christianity—but we feel they don't understand what either are."[67]

There was a certain personal sadness in Daisy Kendall Ward's visit to China. This was to have been the place where she practiced medicine after college. She gave up all that to marry Harry, and she expressed a measure of open regret about this choice in correspondence with her young adult children. They were now in the season of life during which she had abandoned her medical studies and career for marriage.

The tension between present security and unrealized dreams had been driven home the previous fall in Russia. Daisy was caught off guard by an inquiry from a young Russian who asked why had she given up her medical studies. "I had to explain that twenty-five years ago, girls who got married did not practice medicine. I felt I had been quite weak to give up my own career to get married. Yet I can't say I am sorry."[68] It must have been difficult for this independent, talented woman to let go of these regrets as she watched her children, especially Muriel, grow up in a society where women could now at least vote. Daisy herself voted for the first time in 1920, on the threshold of her forty-seventh birthday.

No doubt the demand for Daisy to speak regularly during the China tour provided some solace. One of her topics was "Women's Contributions to the World Peace Movement." She also proved her weight in gold as a mechanic for the automobile used during their China travels. In fact, she became something of a local legend when she wired a connection with one of her long hairpins after their driver declared that the broken-down engine was hopelessly inoperable.[69]

Harry recognized in China the same problems he observed in Russia and elsewhere: the cozy relationship between capitalism and Christianity inevitably bred hostility among the forces promoting economic equality. At the heart of the anti-Christian movement was a diagnosis of an "ethical deficiency of Christianity.[70] The time of reckoning had come for Christians. Around the world and now in Asia, workers were "challenging Christianity to decide whether it is the official religion of the capitalistic, democratic state."[71]

As the Wards traveled through China, they understood that they were observing a society in flux. This must have been an exciting prospect for Harry as he considered the possibility that he might be able to influence the outcome of this revolutionary period. It was a teachable moment, and he meant to make the most of it. His lectures in China often focused on economic issues, and, as in India, he challenged the country's intellectuals to avoid the mistakes of their Western counterparts and stay in touch with the workers. His lectures were well received. Ward reported that in Tientsin his lectures were printed in one English and two Chinese newspapers.[72] His lectures resonated with the hopes of Chinese students and leaders as he melded the rhetoric and concepts of democracy, idealism, Marxism, religious ethics, humanism, and modern science and technology. These lectures encouraged the human spirit to soar, for Ward still had confidence in the rhetoric of the Progressive Era: "There are limits to what we can do in any one generation, but if we decide what we want to do with the economic process it will increasingly yield itself to our purpose and we shall find ourselves able intelligently to guide it to ethical ends."[73]

All the rhetoric was not devoted to aspiration, for real social problems must be addressed, especially the corrupting influence of capitalism. A substantial portion of Ward's lectures included not only ethical and practical critiques of capitalism but also a powerful defense of socialism. Along the way, he addressed some of the typical criticisms of socialism, especially its Russian form, which entailed impersonal bureaucracy, violence, and economic determinism. His description of economic determinism as a valuable tool for social analysis rather than a fatalistic metaphysical claim reflects the significance of his reading in Marxist literature. Ward had come to believe that "Freedom has never been found by letting people do simply what they like. Freedom can only be discovered in relation to organization."[74]

As Harry wrote Gandhi later, there was a persistent demand among the Chinese for a speech on "Gandhi and the Future of India,"[75] a piece Ward published in the *Christian Century* shortly after his arrival back in the States.[76] This essay represented Ward's attempt to assess Gandhi's impact both on India and the larger world with respect to the Indian leader's recent withdrawal from national politics. On the whole, Ward lauds the moral discipline of Gandhi, especially "his humility of soul and complete disinterestedness." As Ward continued to struggle with the promise and peril of the machine age, he was delighted to observe that Gandhi "vindicated personality in the age of mechanism," which was a striking contrast with the impersonal emphasis on organization in Russia (727): "It is more than social reform that he is after. It is social transformation and the remaking of personality. Whatever may happen to his political program this is his permanent contribution to the freedom of India" (728).

This last phrase—"whatever may happen to his political program"— may be an indication of unrest in Ward's mind. He could not endorse pure motives except in the context of strategy. Success mattered. He had observed enough rocking-chair, theoretically sound liberals who failed to commit to the struggle. Gandhi was certainly not viewing the struggle from a comfortable vantage point, but Ward was nevertheless concerned about Gandhi's tactics and social analysis. Gandhi's call for hand-spinning and hand-weaving might be a first step toward India's economic independence, but there was no evidence of a "detailed analysis of India's economic need or constructive program to meet it." Nor was Ward enthralled with what he perceived to be a growing "dangerous separatism" in Gandhi's mission (728); India could not go it alone.

For all his opposition to war and militarism, Ward was never enam-
ored with pacifism as such. Like many with socialist inclinations, he
regarded war and militarism as tools of the status quo, and the negative
effects of the First World War on constructive social change provided
more than enough evidence of this. Still, there was something right and
compelling about Gandhi.[77] Ward puzzled over strategies for social
change, especially in light of his disappointment with progress in Russia. He had expected a better showing there, though he could still offer
the backhanded compliment that Soviet repression was "no worse than
under the czars."[78]

As Ward observed the currents of social change in China, he wondered which path—Lenin's or Gandhi's—would lead to that country's
well-being. Between engagements in China, Harry penned a short article on "Lenin and Gandhi" for the *World Tomorrow*, in which he argued that while Lenin advocated a "philosophy of power" with a "program of force," Gandhi promoted a "philosophy of love" and a "program
of non-violence." To the typical reader of the pacifist the *World Tomorrow*, such a contrast made the choice easy, but Ward refused to be limited
by theoretical postulations. Results mattered, and he gave a measure of
credit to each ideology. Lenin's philosophy of power had protected Russia from counter-revolution and thus allowed the cooperative state to
develop. Gandhi's approach had provided his people with strength and
given India "a standing before the world which no other policy could
have done." But the stories were not finished. Could "the coercive prole-
tarian state" really give Russia freedom, and would England yield to
Gandhi's method?

Over the next decade Ward paid close attention to events in other
parts of the world, and he knew that developing countries like China
and Japan were watching also.[79] Lenin and Gandhi offered disparate
options for aspiring peoples: "ideals or mechanism."[80] Ward's preference
in 1925 for Gandhi's way is clear, which is noteworthy, given Ward's persistently keen interest in the Russian Revolution. The question for Ward
was whether Gandhi's way would yield practical results. "They want to
know whether India's freedom can come by non-cooperation and non-
violence, or whether in the end can an armed struggle be avoided?"[81]

Arriving home in time for fall classes in 1925, Ward helped form the
American Committee for Justice to China and chaired the national

committee, which included Jane Addams, James Weldon Johnson, Vida Scudder, and William Allen White.[82] In that role Harry wrote President Coolidge on behalf of the organization, calling for the United States to withdraw troops and ships from the area, to alter or cancel unjust treaties with China, and to allow China autonomy over its own affairs.[83] He also undertook fund-raising lecture tours to provide aid for progressive Chinese forces.[84] In print he continued to challenge the imperialist agenda of the United States and Britain in China. Once again, he identified the profit motive as one of the key problems, calling attention to the common assumptions of commercial interests and many Christian missionaries.[85]

A December essay on "The Future of Religion" is a revealing window into the state of Harry Ward's mind just after his sabbatical. The essay opens with a grim view of the times—"the present unsettled and dubious state of the world." Upon his return to America, he had scrutinized ongoing Protestant endeavors, and he was not impressed. The modernist-fundamentalist controversy dominated religious news and sapped the energy and interest of Protestant liberals who were needed in the fray for social change. The progressive forces had turned their attention to intellectual issues identified with modernism, resulting in a "lack of passionate conviction and fighting spirit"; though they were obsessed with applying scientific methodologies to the past, they were all but indifferent to the present and future. Ward opined that these intellectual pilgrims shared no common interest with the rest of humanity. What unified religions was "an ethical emphasis," and therefore "the religion of the future will be basically and dominantly ethical. It will be primarily a humanitarian religion. The question is whether organized Christianity can transform itself into the growing, developing religion of Jesus or whether those who take his name will have to start once more upon a new road."[86] It is no wonder that with their children gone from home and with their rather jaded view of institutional Christianity, the Wards rarely attended their local Methodist congregation anymore.

In 1926 Harry and Daisy began building a new home, closer to Union Seminary yet still in New Jersey. Their new residence was built in the style of an English cottage on the bluffs overlooking the Hudson River. No other homes were close by, so there was plenty of room for a garden as well as open spaces for long walks among the trees rising above the river. All three of the Ward offspring settled nearby, with Muriel living with her parents and opening a nursery school in their home. Harry Ward's family was at the front of his mind when he, along with a number of other religious leaders and public intellectuals, was asked to write an essay on "Why I Have Found Life Worth Living" for the *Christian Century*. Harry was approaching fifty-five years of age and nearing the end of a difficult decade. Family ranked first and the job second in Harry's response to the essay's title. Of course, for him this could not be just any job, for only one that contributed to "lessening of misery and ignorance, of the search for freedom, justice, and fellowship" would bring him real happiness.[87]

"Why I Have Found Life Worth Living" is perhaps the single most revealing public piece Harry Ward ever penned, yet several articles he wrote during 1928 and 1929 tell us more about his inner self than can be accumulated from decades of his articles and books. It may be that in this period of challenge and reassessment he felt it was time to set forth his basic convictions. If nothing else, these articles represented an opportunity for him to come to terms with what was most important in his life.

Another piece from 1928, "Progress or Decadence?"—a chapter in a book[88] edited by the well-known Protestant liberal pacifist, Kirby Page—reveals Ward at his most scathing. Page had invited a number of major public intellectuals, including John Dewey, Harry Emerson Fosdick, and Norman Thomas, to participate in a symposium reflecting on the theme "Recent Gains in American Civilization." Ward objected to the title's presumptions about "progress" and "civilization," a theme, he said, that was "likely to fortify our comfortable, middle-class religionists in the false security which emanates from the idea of automatic progress that left them so unprepared and helpless when the World War hit them" (279). He proceeded to trash virtually every so-called accomplishment of the postwar years and raised all the hard questions of the hour, especially with respect to the other contributors' efforts to describe gains in such areas as government, industry, race relations, education, arts, literature, science, and religion. For example, Ward asserts that "the challenge of the Goose Step and of Teapot Dome with all its ramifications is yet to be faced by the people of this nation." He wonders aloud if "the few who have accepted the ethics of Jesus in the matter of race relationships" will really make any difference as "black people join the issue on economic and cultural equality" (280).

In this essay Ward argues that perhaps the most accurate assessment of Western "civilization" comes from those outside the West, especially "scholars of the Orient who have been trained in the cultures of both East and West and have seen the best and the worst of life in both hemispheres" (282). These are remarkable words for a Western intellectual in 1928. Ward is unrelenting in his criticism of the postwar United States, whose culture he describes as decadent. Others used this word to describe the hedonism of the "Jazz Age," but Ward had something more fundamental in mind: the unbridled power of capitalism. The problem was not only people's tolerance of "bread and circuses as a substitute for the [democratic] control of their own [economic] development" but the repression of "those who seek to change our political and economic institutions in the direction of the original American ideals of freedom and equality" (289–90). Ward is forthright in his criticism of the power linkages between government and big business. Against those who seek change "there are blacklists, injunctions, the fists, clubs and horses' hoofs of the police. If these prove insufficient, then there are frameups, long jail sentences, and in extremity, the electric chair" (290). Ward's charges are sweeping and angry; for example: "The denial of free speech is therefore now entrenched in legal precedent. The courts have torn up and thrown away the Bill of Rights and rewritten the Constitution" (291). Unless these developments are checked, the future looks grim; agents for social progress will be forced to use violence if this trend continues. The loss of democratic values at home has been translated into imperialism abroad. Nations in the southern Americas now regard the U.S. as "a great predatory power" (297). Ward's judgment is harsh: "No way of life that draws tribute from others, that waxes strong at the cost of making others weak, can henceforth be regarded as civilized, no matter what the state of its machinery, art, literature or religion" (296).

Repeatedly Ward insists that Westerners would truly understand their plight if they took seriously the perspective of non-Western folk. "A sophisticated, imperialist United States is more dangerous" to human civilization than an "ignorant and isolated" America (302). Ward's solution to these maladies is no surprise. The fundamental problem is the economic system, for a machine age civilization especially requires "social planning and social control." Ward concludes with a prophet's warning of doom. These are "dark days," which, if unchecked, will yield decadence, not progress.

A similar tone is evident in another 1928 article, "Twenty Years of the Social Creed." Writing about the events that shaped liberal Protestantism after the adoption of the Social Creed in 1908, Ward allows the emotions of that period to become part of his article. His attacks on organized Christianity are particularly harsh: "The settlement movement was getting started, and how could most preachers understand that? It asked people to live with the poor[;] . . . it let the young people dance and taught them dramatics and that was to put their feet on the road to damnation. How could Jane Addams be Christian when all she gave her neighbors was her life, while declining to offer them the choice of coming to Jesus or going to hell?"[89]

It was not just the shallowness of the church's past record. The postwar Protestant church had lost its way, focusing now on "mystic communion with the eternal or the esthetic satisfactions of beautiful services of worship." For these folk "the 'social gospel' was but a temporary and shallow emphasis; so the pulpit weathervanes tell us. And of course it was—for them."[90] Ward retained little tolerance for fair-weather liberals whose embrace of the Social Gospel was fleeting or who were forever stuck on words and could not be moved to action. They "were going to redeem the world through the evolutionary process, and a Christian social order was to come without any more Calvary."[91]

The all but jaded attitude of Ward's "Progress or Decadence?" article was not the whole of Harry F. Ward. He declared that war is always destructive and therefore "must be destroyed root and branch"; the state can no longer be "blindly accepted as the instrument of God" and therefore must be judged carefully; and "[t]he machine, which requires a world order for its fulfillment, may give us world conflict and anarchy unless religion on the world scale can show men what to do with it."[92] These positions had evolved in Ward's mind over at least a decade. What was crystal clear now was that five factors enabled him to sustain his hope through these difficult years and beyond.

First, though Harry Ward clearly relished leadership opportunities and recognition in the religious mainstream, his family's sectarian origins and his experiences as an immigrant enabled him to feel comfortable as an outsider. Though vilification at the hands of reactionary forces was personally painful, he could in the sectarian tradition embrace these experiences as a badge of honor. He also came to recognize the value of outsider status for those who wished to remain prophetic. People who are forced outside the system are able to discern more clearly the system's faults, for they have not been co-opted by the system.

Second, there was perhaps nothing quite so important for the staying power of the Social Gospel as radicalizing life experiences, which began for Ward when he encountered capitalism's victims in Chicago's back-of-the-yards. But it was not just the experience of observing oppression that radicalized Ward. Other factors included his own harassment at the hands of reactionary forces, especially during the war and the twenties: his awareness of being watched by industrial spies; the furor over the Methodist Book Concern, and the knowledge that he was increasingly regarded as a troublemaker by politically conservative Methodists, including former MFSS allies; the firestorm surrounding his controversial analysis of the Russian Revolution; and the accusations of the Lusk Committee and prominent political leaders.

Third, a structural analysis of his radical Social Gospel tradition drove home the reality of the war's destruction of Progressive Era optimism. His prewar Chicago experiences and his radical Social Gospel analysis of unjust social structures had long enabled him to recognize evil's presence, power, and persistence. Therefore the fierce challenges of the war and the 1920s could not undermine his commitment to serious social change, despite the strong forces of reaction. Furthermore, his growing appreciation for Marxist analysis led him to consider it a scientific tool to verify the radical Social Gospel's moral diagnosis of capitalism.

Fourth, Ward carried into the war years and their aftermath a sense of vocation as a Social Gospel prophet. Repeatedly others had affirmed this role for him and encouraged him in it through those dark hours. By virtue of his sectarian disposition, the radicalizing experiences of his life since Chicago, and his conclusions about capitalism arrived at through his radical Social Gospel analysis, Harry Ward became increasing committed to a holy war dualism.[93] Still, he had always understood the value of plodding on toward one's goal, of thinking strategically, even pragmatically.

This pragmatic holy war dualism is the fifth and ultimately most significant factor underlying Ward's hope for radical social change, and this factor most clearly of all began to solidify in the late twenties. His pragmatism worked at two levels of religion: (1) organized religion is only valuable insofar as it is the most useable tool in his holy war for dramatic structural change; (2) as he expressed it to his daughter Muriel, "Which view of God produces better lives and makes for a better world?"[94] Ward had finally abandoned the threadbare orthodoxy of Protestant liberalism and chosen a pragmatic, religious humanism that employed the terminology and moral framework of his dearly cherished radical Social Gospel. The liberal certainty of a universe on the side of justice sustained him through the struggles of the Chicago pastorates, through the war, and even through the painful accusations of the "Red Scare," but the relentless pounding on this basically optimistic metaphysic had taken its toll: "Faith is betting your life that there is a God. Faith is betting your life that there is a universe that is on the side of truth, justice, and fellowship. The only way that you have in which to satisfy yourself of the truth of this is to make your hypothesis and act on it. Live as if there was an ethical God. Take the risks and you will find it out one way or the other. . . . Better be defeated than never make an effort."[95]

Harry had seen enough of the church's backside during the last twenty years—both professionally and personally—to sully even the brightest optimist's perspective.

We were going to make a new world, a world fit for heroes to live in—but now we look upon one which in large measure is nothing but a hog run, where the struggle for gain tramples into the muck many of the finest possibilities of the human spirit. We were going to end war, but newer and more powerful conflicts are at this moment in the making. We were going to have done with the ancient pagan doctrine of the right of the strong to rule; but now in land after land democracy is trampled under foot and spiritual wickedness is entrenched in high places. Where now are the millions who were going to make a new social order? The vision has departed, and according to our lack of faith it is being done unto us.[96]

And, if all else failed, there was a place called Lonely Lake, where annually he could again find perspective.

For complete release from the pressure and the artificialities of modern life there is nothing like a journey into the far places of the forest or the mountains—on your own. . . . And when you come back you can look at yourself and your job from the outside. And if you cannot find a way to do that, you can neither laugh at yourself nor know your job.[97]

7

The Unraveling of Radicalism

Ward and Niebuhr during the
Great Depression

1929–1939

We had a struggle for the souls of the young men and he [Ward] got
some and I got others.

—Reinhold Niebuhr to June Bingham, 14 January 1957

THE STORY OF Harry Ward during the Great Depression is
more than an account of one person's curious journey. It is an essential
subplot of a larger story, part of a watershed period in American Protestantism. Entering this period, Ward, for all his notoriety, was a major
force among Methodists and the larger Protestant community, not to
mention his ongoing leadership in the ACLU. But by the end of the
1930s he was regarded by most mainstream Protestants, even by many
former allies and friends, as a pariah or a prophet who had lost his way.
And by that time Reinhold Niebuhr, the other half of Union's ethics
department, was the formative influence among American Protestants
and privately hostile to Ward. The feeling was mutual. Thus an account of the interweaving narratives of these Union Seminary ethics department colleagues during the thirties sharpens our understanding of
Harry Ward and his place in the developing story of American Protestant social ethics.

Niebuhr came from a Detroit parish to Union Theological Seminary in 1928 with arrangements similar to those Ward enjoyed when he, too, made the transition from pastor to professor. Just as Ward had split his time between the MFSS and the Boston University School of Theology, so Niebuhr divided his time between teaching responsibilities at Union and work for the Protestant, pacifist-socialist journal the *World Tomorrow*. Like Ward, Niebuhr came to his professorship as a pastor with a national reputation by virtue of his powerful oratory and his prolific writing in popular religious and secular journals.

Like other Protestant leaders, Ward recognized the talent of the outspoken and insightful pastor Niebuhr. Ward's lengthy review of Niebuhr's 1928 *Does Civilization Need Religion?* is very positive and includes references to Niebuhr's "penetrating insight." Always one to value people who devoted their lives to working in the trenches, Ward states, "That work of this kind can be done by a practical pastor is a sign of hope." He concludes by lauding Niebuhr's value for the larger church: "Mr. Niebuhr has a talent for this kind of work. Will our religious and economic machinery give him time and space and means to do it?" Ward's review is not without a measure of criticism, however. He expresses concern that Niebuhr pays too much attention to metaphysical issues rather than concrete problems; according to Ward, this illustrates "the common tendency of traditionally educated intellectuals to overweight the influence of abstract ideas upon life." Ward also takes a swipe at Niebuhr's negative judgments on the Soviet project: "[T]hey cannot be dismissed from the stage with telling phrases about Marxian cynics or brutal determinism. At some points we have to go to school with them." Repeatedly he chides Niebuhr for generalizing: "His positions need more documentation from concrete circumstance."[1]

Decades of observing these concrete circumstances had led Ward to write *Our Economic Morality and the Ethic of Jesus* that very year. This book was the outcome of Ward's search for hope throughout the 1920s. The postwar "Red Scare" did not deflect this warrior from his duty to demolish an unjust social order. He traveled the nation and even the world. He was encouraged by revolutionary activities in China. He conversed with Gandhi and with Lenin's widow in their homelands and pondered what sort of leader and strategy could lead humanity toward a fully democratized social order. And he continued to worry about the ongoing brutality and loss of civil liberties in Russia. During his stay in camp the summer of 1928, Harry built himself a six-foot writing table under a simple lean-to roof at the top of the bluff overlooking the lake and labored five hours a day on the manuscript. Rising early, he worked in the garden until ten o'clock and then wrote until lunchtime. His traditional after-lunch nap followed, and then it was up to the bluff for three more hours of writing.

The first chapter title—"An Irreconcilable Antagonism"—states well the problem concerning the conflict between capitalism and the ethic of Jesus. It was well past time to draw a line in the sand. If economics was meant to be ethical as John Gray had taught him as an undergraduate, then it was now time to set a new course and abandon all attempts to reform an evil economic system.[2] An economic system that allows, even encourages the inordinate accumulation of power by the economically dominant negates any real opportunity for reform: "Those who rely upon the democratic state as the instrument for the transformation of economic society neglect its use by capitalism to preserve its structure." The structure itself is corrupt and must be replaced by "a society consciously controlled for chosen ends."[3]

Niebuhr's response to *Our Economic Morality* was very positive. He hailed Ward as "one of the few religious leaders of our generation" who recognized that the real challenge to Christianity is not science but the unethical economic system. Niebuhr was obviously impeaching Protestant liberalism, which spent much of its energy in the 1920s finding ways to become more compatible with scientific advances and wrangling with fundamentalism's resistance to modernity. Ward's book, said Niebuhr, "is as clear and as challenging a statement of the real problem of modern Christianity as anything which has been written for a decade."[4] Niebuhr's high regard was shared by the Religious Book Club, which selected *Our Economic Morality* as a book-of-the-month.

Niebuhr's assessment was not entirely positive, however. Anticipating a theme that would unsettle his pacifist friends within a few years, he remarked on Ward's inattention to the role of coercion in a just society. An even more fundamental issue, argued Niebuhr, is precisely how Ward intended to achieve social transformation. Ward had criticized Niebuhr's own book for what he saw as its lack of concrete evidence in support of an analysis of civilization's problems. Now Niebuhr called on Ward to provide concrete illustrations to validate his strategy for moving civilization toward the right kind of social order.

In 1929 Niebuhr assumed the seminary's Dodge Chair in Applied Christianity; this honor was part of the plan that Henry Sloan Coffin, Union's president, used to retain this brilliant professor in the face of the enticements of Yale. Niebuhr was a hot commodity. Though Ward was probably pleased that Niebuhr's position at Union had been stabilized, he seemed unhappy that Niebuhr was given an endowed chair with the rank of full professor in only his second year there.[5] Still, most evidence points to genuine camaraderie between them during those early years, and the Wards regularly invited the bachelor for dinner and conversation.[6]

Though the two ethics professors were different in personality, theology, and background, they had in common what we might label today a "blue-collar" perspective. In contrast to the blue bloods who constituted the majority of Union's faculty, both Niebuhr and Ward grew up in rather ordinary circumstances. Niebuhr's midwestern, small-town pastor's family was solidly middle class though not yet fully part of mainstream America, for his Evangelical Reformed German subculture was uncomfortable with the American notion of melting-pot assimilation. His cultural heritage and his rather provincial education at an Evangelical Reformed college and seminary encouraged Niebuhr to regard himself as a "mongrel among thoroughbreds" when he entered Yale's master's degree program.[7] Like Ward, Niebuhr overcame the limitations of his family background and its religious subculture, excelling in his schooling and pastoral vocation. Niebuhr and Ward brought a certain rough-edged enthusiasm to their teaching at Union. Both had seen the corruptions of capitalism firsthand, though in different settings. Whereas Ward had observed the worst sort of human degradation in Chicago's stockyards, Niebuhr witnessed the more clever manipulation of workers by Henry Ford in Detroit.

Niebuhr was a far more charismatic teacher than Ward, and Union students flocked to his lectures. There is no evidence that Ward envied Niebuhr in their first years together in the ethics department; rather, he regarded Niebuhr as a fellow advocate of social transformation. To be sure, Niebuhr's own strategy for dramatic social change differed from Ward's, for by 1929 Niebuhr had found a place in Norman Thomas's

Socialist Party. Though presidential candidate Thomas accumulated only a small percentage of the 1928 popular vote—in an election that Republican Herbert Hoover won with over eighty percent of the electoral college vote—the world changed quickly in the months after the election. The stock market plummeted on 24 October 1929, and despite the Hoover administration's efforts to paint a rosy picture of current circumstances, an economic depression settled over America and the world. Ward's *Our Economic Morality* now made a lot more sense to a lot more people; capitalism was indeed a mess, and change was in the air. In 1930 Niebuhr agreed to be the Socialist candidate for the New York state senate, dismaying Union's politically conservative board of trustees.

The Socialist Party was too tame for Ward, though ever since they began serving together on the ACLU board in 1920, he had maintained a useful working relationship with Norman Thomas. A decade later the two men still shared many values, but Thomas's reformism was not radical enough for Ward. Only a fundamental change in the economic system would do, the sort one could see at work in Marxist Russia. As Ward had argued earlier, there were points at which "we have to go to school with" the Marxists. With the bleak prospects of the growing Depression, it was now high time to enroll.

Ward was not alone in this conviction. As the Depression deepened, American liberals expressed heightened interest in the progress of the Soviet Union. While America floundered, Russians gained momentum with their first Five Year Plan. Life was not easy in Russia, of course, and even open-minded liberals were dismayed by Stalin's "liquidation" of uncooperative kulaks. But what mattered most was Russia's rational economic planning, which was in stark contrast to the American and European economic chaos. Leftist Americans were curious about what they called "the Soviet experiment" as it entered its third decade, and many made the pilgrimage to see this for themselves. Though Niebuhr was not one to romanticize organizational achievements, during the summer of 1930 he became one of these visitors. Earlier that year he joined Ward, eight other Union faculty members, and sixty-seven student members of the Liberal Club in a formal protest of the harsh criticism heaped upon the Soviet Union by many church folk. They drew up a petition that stated: "While professing no allegiance to the political creed of communism, we believe that the social experiment of the Soviet Government

should receive the sympathetic and not the hostile criticism of the representatives of the Christian Church."[8] Now Niebuhr would see for
himself the results of this experiment.

He visited the Soviet Union in August with his brother Helmut,[9] and
both had mixed feelings about what they saw there. Reinhold's light-
hearted postcard to Jim Dombrowski expresses his disparate reactions:
"Dear Comrade, I send you greetings from the paradise of communism.
Only it's not quite a paradise. But it's full of life and hope."[10] Both Niebuhrs were impressed with the commitment and vitality of the common
people but worried by the brutality of the system.[11] The Socialist candidate for the New York state senate perceived no applicability of Russia's
system for the West, whatever merits the system might have for the
formerly czarist nation.[12]

The academic year of 1930–1931 would be remembered as a special
one in the impressive history of Union Theological Seminary. Among
the interesting developments was the arrival of a bright—though still
relatively unknown—twenty-five-year-old German theologian named
Dietrich Bonhoeffer, who came to study at Union that year. Niebuhr
became one of Bonhoeffer's special friends at Union, and Bonhoeffer's
recollections of his time there provide a useful perspective on the seminary, including the roles played there by Ward and Niebuhr. Describing
the various schools of thought in the seminary community, Bonhoeffer
lumped Niebuhr and Ward together as Union's point men for the "most
radical socialising of Christianity." He was impressed with the vigor and
commitment of the Union students who embraced the Ward-Niebuhr
radicalism, though he was horrified by their indifference to "all genuine
theology." He was struck by the students' willingness to provide food,
shelter, and advice over the course of that winter to thirty unemployed
persons, including three Germans.[13]

He observed Union Seminary during the period when Ward was most
influential and before Niebuhr became a dominant figure in American
Protestantism. Bonhoeffer wrote that he valued Ward's "The Ethical Interpretation of Recent Events,"[14] a course in which students read and
discussed recent periodical literature and newspaper accounts of current
social issues. The format of the class was structured by Ward's three
questions: What are the facts? What do they mean? What should be
done?[15] Class discussions paralleled Ward's articles that appeared in

print during that spring semester, addressing specific problems created by the Great Depression and pointing to the fundamental corruption of the economic system. Just as he did in his classes, Ward called on his readers to analyze the facts—misery in cities and in rural areas—and the meaning of the facts: a capitalist system has created this suffering. What should religion do to help move people "by orderly processes to take the economic kingdom away from the spirit of moneymaking and give it to the spirit of social creativity."[16] And in Niebuhr's "Ethical Viewpoints in Modern Literature" class, Bonhoeffer also encountered the pain, anger, and sharp criticism of American society expressed by several African-American writers and other socially conscious novelists and playwrights.

Bonhoeffer's other course with Ward was a seminar in social ethics. According to an unknown stenographer's notes of five major lectures given in that seminar, in many ways their content recapitulates the concerns of *Our Economic Morality* and its sequel, *Which Way Religion?* (1931). Liberal Protestantism must abandon neutrality and take a stand for social justice by fighting for a new economic order. Liberalism has become a "cult of objectivity," thriving on observation, experimentation, and discussion, which in turn has given rise to a "paralysis of both the critical spirit and the moral will."[17] Because liberal Christianity is "separated from the rising masses in thinking and feeling," it has no real passion and therefore advocates reform and gradualism. It has "no adequate perception of the revolutionary factor in history, in its own gospel and in the needs of the hour." Christians must take account of economic forces and relinquish their preoccupation with the individual. Otherwise they will fail "to reckon with the nature and power of evil."[18]

Like Ward, Niebuhr, too, was finding Protestant liberalism increasingly irrelevant to the social crisis, though not always for the same reasons as his Union colleague. In the election of November 1930, the Socialist candidate Niebuhr was crushed by his opponents. Despite the terrible effects of the Great Depression, socialism was not making any real headway. Yet Niebuhr was undeterred. That winter he and other leftist colleagues formed the Fellowship of Socialist Christians (FSC), which was not a conglomerate of socialists who happened to be Christians. They were first of all Christians who believed that Marxism provided a valuable analysis of the human situation. They were convinced that "the evolutionary optimism of current liberal Christianity" had reached a dead-end. The FSC meant to be forthrightly radical, leaving behind the half-hearted, reformist measures of liberalism. It called for recognition of the class struggle, "aggressive assertion of the rights of the exploited and the disinherited," and strenuous efforts on behalf of "the just development of the economic and political powers which these classes potentially hold." The FSC insisted that "the Christian Church should recognize the essential conflict between Christianity and ethics of capitalistic individualism." There could be "no adequate substitute for the reconstruction of the economic order."[19]

It is no wonder that Harry Ward received an invitation, probably from Niebuhr, to join the Fellowship of Socialist Christians. Though there is no record of Ward's response, it is unlikely he would have joined. Even if he had initially associated himself with the FSC, he probably would not have remained for very long. The FSC's interest in theologically driven ethics and its suspicion of the Soviet Union would have irritated him. Certainly he would have been alienated by its decision in 1935 to drop its commitment to the destruction of capitalism.

Ward himself was busy trying to form some new groups. This sort of organizing became common among liberals and radicals who became estranged from political parties in those desperate days. For example, it is clear that in 1931, shortly after the new year, Ward was trying to create at least one new group. George Coe responded affirmatively to Harry's call for an organization devoted to "working out the next step beyond liberal Protestantism."[20] In a mid-January letter to Niebuhr, Ward describes a proposed manifesto for "the group" to discuss. This group included the ACLU director Roger Baldwin and socialist economist and activist Scott Nearing, and therefore was probably different from the one to which Coe referred. Ward's contribution to the second group was an appeal for the middle class to stand against capitalism, aid the coming of a new social order, and help lessen the inevitable shock of such change. The group's deliberations led to several important conclusions, including the judgment that "revolutionary opportunities come through wars and economic breakdowns." With the tragedy of the Great Depression quickly unfolding, the time was ripe for change. However, the group concluded that the middle class was "more ready for revolutionary change than the working class." Therefore the immediate strategy was to "detach as many of the middle class as possible from the capitalist psychology." Implementing this strategy meant creating a central planning group, which would be kept small and anonymous and which would, in turn, spawn other groups. What Ward and his colleagues were proposing sounds very much like the United Front groups that came to prominence in the mid-1930s. There is no evidence that this particular group ever got off the ground, but its fundamental question would remain for Ward and like-minded radicals: "[W]hat changes in popular beliefs and ideas are necessary to prevent us drifting into a situation where change in our economic organization and social structure will be attempted by violence."[21]

Niebuhr, too, was worried about violence, but he was increasingly dissatisfied with what he regarded as weak-kneed liberal compromises that ruled out strong measures to ensure social justice. In the summer of 1931 he began writing a new book with the working title "The Ethics of Social Change"; this manuscript would ultimately become the anti-pacifist, anti-liberal, groundbreaking work *Moral Man and Immoral Society*.

Ward was busy writing as well, and in 1931 he produced *Which Way Religion?* This book spells out more carefully the religious undergirding of the social proposals laid out in *Our Economic Morality*, including the pragmatic religious humanism that Ward had hammered out in the 1920s: live as if there were an ethical God, and the world can only be better for it. Though there is really nothing new in *Which Way Religion?* Ward brings together in one very readable source his criticisms of corrupted religion as well as his insistence on religion's capacity to be a creative force in social change. The book concludes with a handy summary of Ward's vision and strategy, which reveals why he and his sort could sustain their commitment through dark days as well as bright ones. He hails that "minority in our churches who have the vision of an ethical religion, along with the desire to realize it. . . . [T]heir function is not to seize power but always to remain a minority, never content to rest on any ground won, always pressing on to new frontiers."[22] Ward was in top form, and others recognized this. In 1931 the University of Wisconsin acknowledged his stature with an honorary doctorate.

Niebuhr was about to make his own mark with the publication of *Moral Man and Immoral Society* the following year. It must have been difficult at times for him to concentrate on writing, for in the summer of 1931 the woman he had come to love, Ursula Keppel-Compton, sailed back to her native England. Like Dietrich Bonhoeffer, Ursula was a visiting foreign student at Union that year. The longtime bachelor Niebuhr finally succumbed to romance upon meeting this brilliant Oxford graduate. During the seven-month separation that preceded their December 1931 marriage, he wrote her often, and this correspondence reveals another aspect of Niebuhr's interactions with his colleague Ward during this crucial period. Two letters in June report evenings in the Ward home with conversations about the forthcoming marriage. Daisy Ward, never one to spare advice, gave Niebuhr "all kinds of lectures. 'Let me give you a motto,' she said, 'Work together so that you can play together,' and thereupon got me busy wiping the dishes."[23]

In his letters to Ursula, Reinhold Niebuhr reported his concerns about several Union students; at least three of them encountered legal trouble that summer because of their union-organizing activities in places hostile to unions. Though Niebuhr was sympathetic with their social passion, he was disturbed by their increasing affinity for communism. "Our young men have a curious lack of perspective. Once involved in the social struggle they become so excited about the class struggle that nothing but communism is good enough for them."[24] Was their lack of perspective attributable in part to his colleague Harry Ward?

Certainly one of the students, Jim Dombrowski, had depended on Ward the previous summer, when he was arrested in South Carolina for activities related to union organizing. Using his ACLU contacts, Ward helped Dombrowski gain his release.[25] Not surprisingly, Dombrowski's diary of that dangerous, purposeful, and exhilarating summer includes several quotations from Ward's 1919 book, *The Opportunity for Religion in the Present World Situation,* including the following: "Jesus lived and died by a faith in the ultimate supremacy of spiritual forces. He risked his life on the hypothesis that they would prove stronger than all the mailed might of the Roman Empire."[26]

Dombrowski visited the Wards in Canada late in the summer of 1931, when they were preparing for their forthcoming sabbatical in the Soviet Union. Like many leftist Americans of the 1930s, Harry Ward believed that rational and scientific planning was the answer to the moral and economic chaos so evident in Great Depression capitalism.

More importantly for Ward, planning promoted the moral qualities of cooperation and service in place of the capitalist vices of competition and greed. Harry and Daisy had seen potential during their earlier visit, but in 1931–1932 they observed real progress[27]—a striking contrast to the panic and despair they had witnessed just weeks earlier on the streets of New York City. Food shortages continued in Russia, and living accommodations were not very comfortable, but the Wards were most impressed by a new spirit and energy among the people. Certainly the Russians were putting the best face on the people's struggle to realize a new society.

Daisy, however, reported that Harry had "asked many searching questions" at the Communist Academy.[28] A week later she lamented that there were "too many Americans here—all getting material for books," so she and Harry tried to get off the beaten path for a closer look at this new social order.[29] In addition to the benefits of living separately from the other American pilgrims and going out regularly among the Russian people, Ward had the advantage of an interpreter, Julius Hecker, a former student of his who was living in the Soviet Union.

One has to wonder if Ward was able to acquire the complete story. Letters he and Daisy wrote to their children speak of abundant food for their meals, which was certainly not the typical situation in famine-stricken Russia in 1931–1932. Still, in his subsequent book, *In Place of Profit*, he comments on the country's difficulties and the abuses of power. But what matters most, he argues, is Russia's direction and spirit; these are unalterable, despite the flaws in the present system. And therefore the future looks bright. The book quotes freely from official statements and interviews with Russian people, but what seemed to capture Ward's imagination most significantly was the feeling of the place. Once again he gathered data from more than books, newspapers, and public pronouncements; his senses detected a different atmosphere: "[T]he psychological atmosphere is one of the things that causes the visitor to realize that he is in a new world."[30] No wonder that the a photo taken on this trip records one of Harry's heartiest smiles. Yet would that atmosphere have seemed so hopeful if his stomach was rumbling with hunger or if, like many Russians, his civil liberties were severely restricted?

Ward's ideology continued to be rooted in an unrepentant radical Social Gospel: social structures are meant to be "democratized." After many years and much work on behalf of structural transformation in countries still sympathetic to Christianity, there was still no real change. If anything, capitalism seemed more entrenched than ever, despite its evident failures. By contrast, after more than two decades, the Soviet Union remained the only example of a transformed economic order. This must be the path to follow, even if Russian communist leaders had repressed religion. Ward continued to believe in a historical dynamic that impelled humanity toward its full realization. Ward and other religious folk called this dynamic "God," but Harry also believed that one's faith in this dynamic was tested by action rather than by words. So what if communists denied God and religion? They were willing to cooperate with the dynamic that pushes humanity upward. Ward's descriptions of the new Soviet order include explicit religious overtones: "They do what they do, as they do, because for them the world is young; the former things are passing away, all things are becoming new."[31]

Meanwhile, back at Union Seminary the situation had become tense. President Coffin increasingly regarded leftist students as too demonstrative, and he was pressuring Reinhold Niebuhr to rein in the radicals. "Coffin continues to be so scared about what the boys are doing and saying that there is no living with him. I will certainly miss Ward around here this year."[32] The situation became very uncomfortable for Niebuhr, and he reported to Ursula that with Ward away he felt "isolated and alone. Meanwhile it is foolish to think of nothing but caution when dealing with our American people on social and political issues because there is too little active political intelligence."[33] It was daunting to be what felt like the lone voice of challenge in Union's conservative administrative atmosphere. Though Niebuhr was struggling with confidence, he did not back away from his commitments. He was working on a speech for a socialist rally and also revamping his religion and ethics course—more evidence that something new was afoot.[34] In Moscow, Harry Ward was writing Jim Dombrowski: "By this time you have . . . a bunch of new students lined up for the big fight."[35] Ward certainly did not wish to stifle student radicalism.

Part of what troubled Niebuhr was a new sense of alienation from some of the students. During the summer he had received a letter from Jim Dombrowski describing the wonderful time he was having at the Wards' Canadian camp, but when Dombrowski returned to Union in the fall Niebuhr detected an uncomfortable distance growing between them. In a letter to Ursula Niebuhr speculated whether Dombrowski and other students were unhappy with his political position: "He has like some of the other boys become very sympathetic to communism under the stress of American conditions and it may be that he thinks I do not go far enough in my radicalism."[36] Trying to mend fences with Dombrowski, Niebuhr dropped by his room, where he found a group of students engaged in a comparison of Union's two ethics professors, "trying to determine the difference between our positions." As he reported the incident to Ursula, he told the students that the difference "was very simple. I didn't have as much 'guts' as Harry Ward when it came to the realities of the social struggle."[37]

The Union context had become a real dilemma for Niebuhr. He was not radical enough for his favorite students, yet in the estimation of President Coffin, many faculty colleagues, and Union's vocal constituency, he was far too radical. In a late October letter to Ursula he reported that his friendship with Jim Dombrowski was on the mend, though he continued to worry "how the Russian business [the attraction of the Soviet experiment] is captivating the imagination of many of our best fellows." The next paragraph in the letter describes a dinner with the Coffins and their guests, which was preceded by Coffin's warning Niebuhr to avoid talking about political issues that evening, given the other guests' conservative views. Niebuhr himself believed that the other guests were told that "Coffin was altogether too sympathetic to radical opinion in the seminary so you may imagine what they told [the other guests] about me."[38] Two years later, when Niebuhr asked Coffin about the possibility of Union's hiring theologian Paul Tillich—who had been expelled by the Nazis from his university post because of his socialism—the president shot back: "We really have enough radical[s] here."[39] Though Tillich was indeed invited to Union, Coffin remained nervous about the appointment.

Niebuhr's own uneasiness with Coffin and with Union's constituency was just one source of his sense of isolation during Ward's sabbatical. Niebuhr was incensed that even with another New York winter coming on in the midst of the Depression, his faculty colleagues seemed so insensitive to human need. He wrote to Ursula about the quandary of teaching ethics "from the security of a professor's chair" while his colleagues were apparently indifferent to the desperate straits of many Americans. He noted that most of the students gave more generously during the recent "campaign for unemployment" than in previous years, though some of them were forced into "going on a meager diet to do it." By contrast faculty contributions were lower, despite a twenty percent increase in their salaries during the last two years. Students with re-sources of less than a thousand dollars gave twenty-five dollars to the campaign, while professors with an annual income eight times larger gave thirty-five to fifty dollars at most. Niebuhr was embarrassed and scandalized, as well as concerned that his commitment, too, would be undermined by the comforts of academe. "I don't like the lack of sensi-tivity of scholars to the world around them."[40]

Niebuhr was looking for a way to avoid this insularity. He had been offered the presidency of the Fellowship of Reconciliation, a tradition-ally pacifist organization, and he believed that such experience would help him "keep contact with the outside world and its problems, some-thing as Ward does through the Civil Liberties [Union]."[41] Further-more, Niebuhr was in a period of intellectual transition, seeking to ham-mer out a proper ideology as well as pursue activities that would inform that ideology. He believed that his colleague Ward was also changing, but not for the better. A November letter from the Soviet Union dis-turbed him. "Had a letter from Ward today. He is a complete commu-nist by now and says that nothing he reads from us, that is in our maga-zines, interests him. It all seems to belong to an old world while he is in the world which represents the future. I just wonder what he will be like when he comes back."[42]

This signaled the beginning of the end for the Ward-Niebuhr alli-ance. Though they never were intimate friends, they shared a feeling of solidarity because of the passions and goals they had in common. But now their chosen means for achieving these goals were diverging too greatly for real companionship. Niebuhr could sense it even across the many miles between the United States and the Soviet Union. Ward's inclinations of many years had finally led him onto one particular path toward human fulfillment, and Niebuhr found this path increasingly dangerous. Though he had his own blind spots, Niebuhr recognized that his Union colleague turned an uncritical eye toward the Soviet leaders' abuse of power.

Several factors in Ward's ideological framework contributed to his estrangement from Niebuhr. The principal one was Ward's belief that the Soviet Union was the only truly democratized economy. A toehold had been gained there, and it must not be abandoned. In the midst of a worldwide economic depression, the Soviet Union was the only nation pointing the way, despite all its problems and excesses. "While in other lands there spreads the consciousness of decline, the feeling of frustration, the temper of futility, the masses in the Soviet Union are becoming conscious of the renewing of life and the turning [of] a new page in history."[43] Secondly, Soviet society was embracing the best of science and reason to realize eternal ideals. Ward had great faith in these human achievements, for they signaled that the upward dynamic of history could be realized in human community. Moreover, the Soviet Union was a place where young people could grow up in an atmosphere of purpose and hope, a far cry from the desperation of the children and young people he had seen time and time again in Chicago's back-of-the-yards. Ward's own children were now all adults, well educated and with promising careers. They had been fortunate, for their parents could devote money and time to their development, yet the poor children of capitalism had no such opportunity. By contrast, young people in the Soviet Union were growing up "in a different atmosphere."[44] (A child's future had become even more precious to Harry, for the previous autumn Lynd and May's firstborn, David Weedom Ward, died soon after birth. Little David would have been Daisy and Harry's first grandchild.)

Perhaps the most significant factor leading to Ward's shift into the pro-Soviet camp was his holy crusade mentality, rooted in his family's English Methodist subculture and sustained through a lifetime. Ward had been fighting against capitalism for years, and he often regarded Marxist efforts, including those of the Soviet Union, as comparable to his. With the Great Depression the war against capitalism had reached a critical stage. The enemy was finally vulnerable, and when Ward visited his comrades behind the lines, he found what he believed was the true spirit of the Soviet people. These people and their social order carried the banner of true democracy: "[T]hey are turning the battle spirit of man into constructive channels. . . . Now begins the last and greatest migration. The toilers . . . are on the march in search of a new home for the spirit of man."[45] The language and imagery of Victorian manly warriors permeates Ward's description of this new world of the Soviet Union.

What is especially revealing is how far Ward was willing to extend this holy crusade imagery. It is remarkable that Ward, who treasured his English Nonconformist heritage and the values of civil liberties, would favorably compare communist aspirations for world domination and the medieval church or—worse yet, Communist Party loyalists and Jesuit inquisitors: "The Jesuits tortured and burned people for the good of their immortal souls, the Communists ask them to live meagerly and discipline them in 'Isolated Communities' [Siberia] for the sake of a nobler society on earth. The essential difference is that the Jesuits used the state to protect a religion and enhance the powers of a church while the Communists use it to realize a social ideal."[46] In Ward's mind this could only make sense within the context of a holy war, and under the assumption that human beings can maintain their noble ideals and not be corrupted by self-serving ends. Still, Ward was not satisfied with the excesses of party loyalists, and so the incredible remark quoted above concludes with Ward expressing confidence in "a new grouping of social forces which is not yet crystallised."[47] This seemingly naive assumption about human nature was what bothered Niebuhr.

In the summer of 1932 the Wards returned from the Soviet Union. Ward's struggle for certainty during the 1920s now had a focus. His experiences in Russia provided him with a concrete sense of direction; his commitments were now clear. All ambiguity was left behind. Forever the dualist, Ward eventually had to come down on one side or the other. The world needed an ethical economic system, and however flawed the Soviet structures might be, they at least represented an effort in the right direction—which is more than could be said for any capitalist society, no matter how much lip service it paid to democratic values.

That same summer Niebuhr was working furiously, sometimes frantically, to complete *Moral Man and Immoral Society*. It was published a few months after Ward's return from sabbatical, and many of Niebuhr's friends and allies were shocked by the sharpness of his attacks there. Actually Niebuhr's primary target was not people like Ward but reformist-minded liberals who believed that society could be changed by good will, education, and ideals. In this book Niebuhr was taking on the whole liberal establishment and challenging their unwarranted faith in human nature. The human problem, argued Niebuhr, goes far beyond mere ignorance; there is a deep-seated egoism that is even more stubborn in human collectives than in individual lives. Niebuhr took the class struggle seriously. Marxist analysis was not only compelling, it recognized that advocates of social change must take into account the brutality of human existence, and the sentimentalism of liberal reformism failed to do so.

On one level, Ward agreed with Niebuhr; he too felt that liberalism, even in its socialist forms, did not take seriously the economic struggle at the heart of human society. However, Ward would never agree with Niebuhr's conclusion about the foundation of social change: "The relations between groups must therefore always be predominantly political rather than ethical."[48] With his radical Social Gospel ideology, Ward was forever committed to a moral social order. The economic order, like all the structures that are of human society, was meant to be democratized, thereby realizing equality for every person.

Niebuhr believed that ideals are relevant, but he also believed those ideals can never be fully realized. As he would later phrase it, the most the social order can achieve is "a tolerable level of justice," giving each person his or her due by balancing competing interests within a society. To be sure, the ideal of love always called justice to a higher level of practice than the status quo, but love as a perfectionist's ideal could never be realized in the social order. Like his liberal and evangelical friends, Niebuhr took Jesus' ethic of love seriously, but he argued that such a perfectionist love ethic is not workable in human society. For example, if society embraced the pacifism that seemed to be called for in Jesus' teaching of nonresistance, social arrangements would become unstable. The powerful would take advantage of the weak, and justice would not be possible. According to Niebuhr, Jesus' ethic of love is relevant only as the conscience of justice.

Ward objected to Niebuhr's narrow—and therefore, in his judgment, irrelevant—definition of love. In correspondence with his best friend George Coe, Ward noted his efforts to set Niebuhr straight: "[H]e leaves out the mutualism in the 'love ethic' of the gospels. . . . [H]e has taken the non-resistant part out of its setting and context." For Ward the "mutualism" of Jesus' ethic of love is the fundamental relationship to which every human being and every human social order is called.[49] A month

later Ward reported an exchange with Niebuhr in which the latter argued that he was not defining love as a static absolute as Ward had
charged, but as a "principle of process." Ward was not satisfied with this
answer,[50] but neither was Coe.

In fact, Coe took on Niebuhr's whole project in a vigorous and lengthy
exchange in the most widely read liberal Protestant publication, the
Christian Century. He challenged Niebuhr to produce evidence of his
pessimistic description of human nature and worried that such readings
of human civilization would be destructive. According to Coe, Niebuhr
had overdrawn the argument about the human future and thereby undermined the possibility of progress. Like his friend Ward, Coe was not
an unbridled optimist, but Niebuhr seemed to be undercutting even the
possibility of the pragmatic use of hope: "We have, indeed, no proof that
society will or will not attain any ethical goal that now is distant; we can
only choose whether to aim high or to aim low. Yet there is in history
some sort of precedent-smashing power, an ethical creativity, that justifies keeping open 'the soul's east window of divine surprise.'"[51]

Niebuhr's book alienated many Protestant liberals, but the larger
American public did not yet appreciate the deep ideological and personal
rifts that had developed between Ward and Niebuhr. Because many
Protestants focused on the Marxist element of Niebuhr's analysis, particularly his rejection of pacifism, many of them continued to regard
Niebuhr and Ward as belonging to the same radical camp Bonhoeffer
had identified two years earlier. Indeed, the same month as the Coe-
Niebuhr exchange in the *Christian Century,* a college teacher wrote Niebuhr describing his own desire to enter a new field of work—"precisely
the sort of thing that you, Harry Ward, Jerome Davis [a pro-Soviet
ethicist at Yale], etc. are doing."[52] To some extent the letter writer was
correct. The degree of discomfort and disagreement between Ward and
Niebuhr was not yet critical. Their verbal sparring in the Union refectory was vigorous but respectful. Furthermore, both of them believed
that capitalism must be extinguished. Yet their tones and the means
they chose for dealing with this necessary change were very different.

Niebuhr continued to work actively for the Socialist Party, but in
1932, in the depths of the Great Depression, the American people gave
even less support to Norman Thomas's candidacy than they had given
earlier. Niebuhr became pessimistic about the likelihood of accomplish-

ing change through the ballot. From now on he would apply his energies elsewhere, though he remained a Socialist Party regular. Though nearly fourteen million Americans were unemployed, "the American people," he noted, "seem to be very inert in the face of the sufferings to which they are being subjected."[53]

The world was quickly becoming a nastier place. Before the newly elected Franklin D. Roosevelt could be sworn in as president in March 1933, Adolph Hitler was appointed chancellor of Germany, the Reichstag mysteriously burned, and Nazi roughnecks suppressed all other political parties. By year's end the Nazis were burning books, leading boycotts on Jewish shops, and building concentration camps for political dissidents. Hitler was granted the powers of a dictator. Nazi Germany and the Vatican signed a concordat allowing a free hand to each in its realm of influence. In Russia starvation was rampant as the famine of 1932 continued; the second Five Year Plan appeared to be a disaster. Roosevelt's New Deal was just beginning to be implemented, and so far it had little effect. Niebuhr's view of the West became all but apocalyptic: "[C]apitalism is dying and . . . it ought to die."[54] To many ears this critique was a sign of hope, for it signaled an opportunity for realizing the true human commonwealth informed by socialism. But Niebuhr would have none of it, even though he, too, preferred socialism to capitalism. "As a Marxian I have no illusions about the collective behavior of man in capitalistic civilization. . . . As a Christian I go a step beyond Marxism and have no illusions about the collective behavior of mankind in general in any age or under any social system."[55]

Ward agreed with Niebuhr's assessment about the death of capitalism, but in contrast to Niebuhr's wariness with regard to any meaningful, much less orderly, social change, Ward poured his energies and talents into preparing for the coming new order. The time was ripe for change, and so it must fall to the vanguard to prepare the way. It was time to propagandize and strategize for the new social dawn, and Ward went at it on several fronts, as if no possibility should go unexplored. Late 1933 is particularly noteworthy with respect to the onset of several new initiatives.

What so energized Ward that fall and winter? As famine continued to cloud the Soviet future, the miasma of fascism seemed to be everywhere. The Nazis were gaining an iron grip on Germany, and a fascist party under General Franco was increasing its influence in Spain. The U.S. Congress having granted President Roosevelt immense power over American currency and credit, the U.S. government had joined hands with American business interests to save capitalism—what Ward regarded as "state capitalism" and what he saw as the equivalent of "economic Fascism."[56] Here was plenty of moral evidence for an indictment against capitalism. With the Great Depression overwhelming the United States (and the world) and real American fascists holding large rallies, the facts seemed indisputable. Now was the time to go for the jugular and extinguish this unjust social order.

What would replace this criminal social order? Ward returned from the Soviet Union convinced that "what we need in this country is an American kind of Communism," but he was unwilling to identify with any political group—including the Communist Party—due to "the animus in people's minds created by battle cries." Ward was firmly committed to the Marxist philosophy, but he was still evaluating the Marxist program in light of "the American scene and its resources."[57]

His friend George Coe was bothered by Harry's increasingly rigid position, especially his tolerance for violence in this social transformation that was to occur. Ward seemed to respond straightforwardly to Coe's inquiry: "What you want to know is how we are going to seize power in this country and how we are going to behave while this is being done, as well as during the further revolutionary developments, toward those who do not agree with us." Yet his response was ultimately evasive: "This I cannot take time to answer now, nor am I ready to. By the time we meet in camp I hope to be."[58] Ward was, however, willing to respond directly about such practical matters as helping "the hungry and the old" during these difficult times, and his answer was blunt: "Provide for them, and take the means to do it away from those who have it." Even so he would not support any program that helped prop up the state politically or economically. "Reform measures I leave to those who want to save this system. I am interested in destroying it as quickly as possible, on the ground that this is the way to shorten and lessen the agony of mankind.[59]

Coe responded carefully to Ward's pro-Soviet *In Place of Profit*, praising the usefulness of its information but pressing Ward on matters in Soviet society that many sympathetic liberals and radicals found troubling. Much of the Coe-Ward debate took place in Canada, frequently in a fishing boat out in the middle of Lonely Lake, but some written exchanges remain from the period just after the book was released in 1933. Though Coe was retired and living in California, his still active mind could not wait for camp, because Ward's book raised important and troubling questions. Coe was always supportive and encouraging, but it is clear he had begun to wonder about Harry's critical perspective on some issues. He expressed evident relief upon receiving a letter in which Harry was not as doctrinaire as he sounded in the book and in previous correspondence: "Your letter has given me tremendous satisfaction . . . because you indicate the points at which your mind is not wholly made up."[60] Still, over the next several months he managed to prod his friend Harry gently on several key points.

Coe was particularly interested in challenging Marxist dogma, for it seemed to him to be as rigid as some Christian orthodoxy. He worried about the continued suppression of women in Soviet society and the use of indoctrination in children's education. He pressed Harry on the matter of civil liberties under the dictatorship of the proletariat. Was it not dangerous to allow civil liberties simply to become "instrumental" (Harry's term) for the greater social good? How was that any different than the industrialists who worked against civil liberties in the name of protecting capitalism? Perhaps only a friend could raise the more delicate questions: "You react strongly, if not bitterly, against American socialism. . . . I quite understand why *militaristic* communism should desire to 'liquidate' the Norman Thomas of today and the Harry Ward of yesterday, but I cannot think of you as a communist in this sense. . . . You are also, I feel certain, in opposition to the communist party in ways that are not disclosed but need to be."[61]

With his persistent references to Ward as a "communist," Coe touched a raw nerve. Harry would have none of it, even in private correspondence. As a public label, the tag of "communist" meant the virtual death of one's credibility, but there was more to Ward's resistance than public relations. He was seeking an authentically American expression of Marxism, and he felt the association of "communism" with a specific party label was too confining. Ward recognized that he had cut his ties to the reformist, gradualist ideology of liberalism, and he struggled for an appropriate label that would retain the open-mindedness of liberal-

ism coupled with a rejection of capitalism. Perhaps, Ward wondered, labels such as liberal socialist, liberal communist, or even "unattached
radical" would be preferable.[62] Of course, neither Ward nor Coe believed
that the basic issue was labels, but they continued to challenge each
other on the proper relationship between a Marxist and the persons and
groups associated with liberalism, socialism, and communism. Though
Coe persistently questioned Harry's antagonism toward natural allies in
the liberal and socialist camp, Harry would concede nothing. Ward,
warrior in the trenches, and Coe, the retired propagandist back home,
did not share the same perspective of the battlefield.

Perhaps the most vigorous exchange between the friends involved
Coe's strong objections to the militaristic nature of the Soviet Union and
its use of force against its own citizens. Like Ward, he had long regarded
militarism as capitalism's tool for protecting its self-interests. Therefore
how could a society committed to Marxism continue to employ militaristic tactics, especially internally? Coe was particularly disturbed by the
brutal tactics of the GPA and Ward's failure to acknowledge this sufficiently in his otherwise valuable book. Harry conceded the problems, but
argued the case pragmatically: "The ugly fact to reckon with alongside
of the ugliness of some of its [the GPA's] ways is that without it (and
the same applies to the Red Army) there would be no Soviet Union
today—not because of rebellion within but plotting directed from without." Though in this regard Soviet behavior was similar to that of other
European nations, Ward observed that, "Nevertheless, the GPA, as I
said, remains a dangerous anomaly." Likewise, Ward argued that the
harsh actions against the kulaks resulted from an "unauthorised digres-
sion of zealots from the Party line." He was not willing to concede that
anything could be *fundamentally* wrong with Soviet society. The Soviet
Union's direction was sound, but its new social order was at risk and of
necessity must be defended against powerful forces. Ward shifted the
onus to Coe, asking him to consider how else the problem could be
handled in light of persistent foreign threats: "[T]hese people [are] defending themselves against the exploiters. Is there any other way they can
do it? This is the curse that an exploiting world puts upon them, it infects
them with its own evil, and there is no quarantine."[63]

By contrast, Ward revealed no remorse with regard to the restriction
of civil liberties in the Soviet Union. He continued to hold to an "instru-

mental" view of civil liberties as a means of bringing about a truly democratic society. Forever the warrior in the fight for the classless society,
Ward was willing to modify desirable principles for the sake of
the greater cause. Coe, however, was not. As summer approached and
the time for hours of extended discussion at Lonely Lake drew near,
Coe fired off salvos in two letters written May 11. The first one challenged Harry indirectly by referring to a current bitter debate within
the American Communist Party. After reading about the debate in material sent him by Ward, Coe mused that "these writers make me wonder whether Marx's own dogmatism is not deeper than I had sup-
posed. Every orthodoxy is both intellectually erroneous and socially
injurious."[64] His second letter that day was more direct, for he had just
received the May issue of the *Social Service Bulletin* in which Ward
contrasted socialism and communism. Coe judged that Ward had misrepresented Socialist Party leader Norman Thomas in his remarks there,
but he was more disturbed by Ward's ongoing "silence" with respect to
communist militarism, especially in comparison with American socialism's rejection of militaristic means. Coe chided his friend for this incredible oversight: "I, for one, do not believe that *any* economic organization that relies for its existence upon armies and navies is sound.
Communists at this point are still following the capitalist tradition, but
socialists seem to be veering away from it."[65]

More than a month later, just before heading off to Canada, Ward
responded—or, that is to say, he at least wrote a letter. In his opening
lines he dodged Coe's challenges, rationalizing that Coe had not responded to some of the points he had raised in the previous letter. Ward
wrote about arrival times at camp, his work schedule, his flowers, the
poor sales of his book, and a new publication, "our Communist Bulletin." However, he eventually got around to Coe's questions, pleading that
while he recognized the problems of orthodoxy among communists,
these problems could not be attributed to Lenin or Marx. Rather, the
fault lay with Marxist-Leninist interpreters. (Coe circled the short paragraph and wrote in the margin: "Dogmatism.") In the final paragraph
Ward responded to his treatment of Norman Thomas but did not concede anything, though he allowed that the socialist leader "does well on
concrete, immediate issues." He continued to argue that Soviet militarism is "a question of fitness of tools to task" in order to defend its new

George Albert Coe on dock, Harry and granddaughter Nanda in boat at
Lonely Lake. (Courtesy of Nanda Ward and Robin Ward Savage)

social order "against the counter-revolutionaries."[66] Lonely Lake must
have resounded with spirited exchanges between the fishing partners
that summer.

After the summer months of gardening, fishing, reading, debating
with Coe, making camp repairs, and sharing time with his family, Harry
returned to the battle. In early October he met with the MFSS leadership and recommended that the organization's "objective be more clearly
defined." His proposal was adopted, and thereafter the masthead of the
Social Questions Bulletin read: "an organization which seeks to abolish

the profit system and to develop the classless society based upon the obligation of mutual service."[67] As Ward often described it, even in this issue, the MFSS had progressed through three stages: social service, social justice, and now social transformation.

The subsequent edition of the *Social Questions Bulletin* laid out the matter plainly for MFSS members, especially with respect to the near demise of the organization in recent months. First, if the MFSS was to continue it must become "a vital part in this struggle between an old and new world. If this is to be our last year we must put something into the record that will count in the future." Second, despite the changes associated with FDR's New Deal, this last-ditch effort to save capitalism must be regarded as "economic Fascism." If successful, the New Deal's state capitalism would follow the path of Nazi Germany, including "a campaign of hate and persecution against Jew, Negro, and Communist." What to do about this? "[K]eep as many of the middle class as possible from going Fascist."

The *Social Questions Bulletin* called for MFSS members to vote on the organization's new direction, though the tone of the issue seems assured, promising a series of publications to be known as "Crisis Leaflets," four-page tracts addressing important social questions to be used by MFSS-sponsored discussion groups. The issue also contained an announcement of a forthcoming four-week lecture tour by Harry Ward, who would be speaking on "What We Can Learn from the Soviet Union" and "The Soviets' Challenge to Religion." The issue concluded with a no-nonsense appeal that may be seen as an altar call: "We know that we can't get this merely by asking for it. Those who have eyes to see an old order passing and a new one dawning, and insight to know that creative human effort is a factor in this process will be eager to act."[68]

Meanwhile Ward was working on another front to help his more secular associates achieve the same ends: a group that would lay the groundwork for postrevolutionary America. He appealed to radicals and liberals who were convinced of capitalism's imminent death and wanted to begin working on the transition to new order so that America would not fall into the fascist pattern of Germany and Italy. The group called itself "New America," and it became one of numerous radical groups organized in the 1930s that are not well known to the larger public or even to historians. One organization did know about New

America—the FBI, which by this time was monitoring radical activities with a vengeance. Apparently the New America group began with conversations between Ward and various leftist professors at Columbia University's Teachers College.[69] Ward responded quickly to their interest, and he offered a strategy: the "winning of one national election putting in power a congress and president with a mandate from a sufficient majority of the population to immediately supplant the profit system with a planned economy, . . . abolition of the Supreme Court and the whole judicial system. The inauguration of a system of People's tribunals, prepared in advance . . . [and taking] all power away from the states that hinders planning and control."[70] This strategy would deter violence, which had become a nagging question among liberals and radicals as they anticipated the coming revolution.

The New America members were not alone in this concern. Having been drawn into endorsing the war "to make the world safe for democracy" earlier in the century, liberals were suspicious of using violence in the name of just causes. Socialists understood that militarism and violence had always been tools for capitalism, and so they shied away from wrongful means to establish just ends.

Reinhold Niebuhr and others sympathetic to socialism continued to lambast liberals for their naivete about the correlation between coercion and real social change. The debate became ugly within the traditionally pacifist Fellowship of Reconciliation (FOR) and the pages of its publication, the *World Tomorrow*. In December of 1933 the FOR board voted to oust one of its secretaries, J. B. Matthews, who held that it was unlikely a just social order could be created without some degree of violence. Niebuhr voted with the minority and resigned with sadness following the vote for Matthews's dismissal. Niebuhr was not alone. In July 1934 the *World Tomorrow* folded; in these difficult times the purity of pacifism was apparently an unaffordable luxury for most socially conscious Protestants.

The MFSS was struggling with the same issue. Ward proposed a new statement on violence to the MFSS leadership. Like the FOR, the MFSS traditionally rejected all forms of violence no matter what the cause. Now Ward offered a more nuanced though arguably rather muddy definition. Apparently borrowing from Coe's work, he distinguished between "force" and "violence," and focused his attention on the prevention of violence—the same tactic he used in his New America proposal. "We all agree on the necessity of preventing violence. We disagree on how this can best be done." Ward called for a "united front" approach to the matter, demonstrating unanimity on goals but employing various means to achieve them; agreement on violence would be reached in the midst of action. "Let those who believe in non-resistance put themselves passively between the attacked and the attackers. Let those who believe it is both right and necessary to use physical force in such a situation unite to do it."[71] Options would be evaluated in the heat of the battle.

All this talk among Protestant leaders about violence was making Union's President Coffin nervous. When some Union students ran the red flag up the seminary flagpole on May Day 1934, Coffin blew his stack, holding his ethics professors partly responsible for inciting this unseemly behavior. A student group known as the Agenda Club was at the heart of the radical activity. They met together weekly over lunch and invited different speakers to address them—including Ward, Niebuhr, Norman Thomas, Roger Baldwin, or "some other prophet or near-prophet of social change," as one former member recalls it. The Agenda Club was interested in more than talk, however; action was necessary. During the summers they would travel around the country, observing and often participating in protests, strikes, union organizing, and picket lines.[72] Their activities came closer to home during the winter and spring of 1934, when they investigated labor conditions at the seminary. The Agenda Club sharply criticized Union for the low wages it paid to custodial staff and kitchen help. President Coffin was even more unhappy when these students instigated public protests in New York City, carrying signs identifying themselves as Union Seminary students. In early April he scolded the students, insisting that he was the only legitimate public representative of the seminary and that they should get back to their real business: "to prepare themselves for Christian ministry." The red flag incident followed within three weeks. During the late May commencement ceremonies, President Coffin spoke about "extreme radicalism" among some of Union's students. In a subsequent letter to all students, he counseled careful examination of the seminary's purposes as stated in the charter. Students unwilling to comply would not be welcome for the fall semester.[73] No doubt his strong words had some impact, but this would not be the last time the fur flew at Union.

The following November some students invited Julius Hecker—the Russian-born Methodist minister who was the Wards' guide and interpreter during their 1931–1932 sabbatical in the Soviet Union—to be their Armistice Day speaker. Apparently seminary officials would not allow the meeting to take place in the seminary chapel. The students were incensed and denounced the administration's quashing of "free speech." The Armistice Day service was held in the seminary's social hall, and Hecker addressed the students.[74]

Six months after the red flag incident and three months after the *New York Times* reported "Stalin Not Dictator, Prof. Ward Declares,"[75] the American Legion vigorously objected to Ward's and Niebuhr's speaking in Cleveland because the legion considered both of them to be communists.[76] Though the two Union ethics professors continued to find opportunities for common cause in certain organizations, their paths were definitely moving farther apart in action as well as in theory. It is a revealing testimony to the American public's misunderstanding of Marxist influence in the 1930s that Niebuhr and Ward could be lumped together so easily in their detractors' eyes.

During this period Niebuhr all but withdrew from the arena of electoral politics and policy making. Though he abandoned the Socialist Party by 1936, he was unable to generate much enthusiasm for FDR. Niebuhr's activist efforts in this period were primarily connected to local projects sponsored by the Fellowship of Socialist Christians—for example, the Delta Cooperative, which helped poor southern whites and blacks establish a cooperative farm. By contrast, Ward, long regarded by historians as an idealist with little concern for strategy,[77] was scurrying about trying to set up new social structures to take the place of existing ones after the inevitable revolution against the American capitalist system. By the mid-1940s, Niebuhr found a home among the New Dealers, while Harry Ward was relegated to the political hinterlands when American capitalism regained its power and credibility by its efforts in the Second World War. But in the mid-1930s, neither Ward nor Niebuhr could have known how matters would turn out. Hence Niebuhr's prognostications of that period were generally as bleak as his almost apocalyptic *Reflections on the End of an Era:* "Our western society is obviously in the process of disintegration."[78]

Niebuhr did not view the death of capitalism as the precursor of a new social order, and certainly he did not see the Soviet Union as an exemplar. At best, society could only hope to sustain competing power structures in the effort to achieve some level of justice. Niebuhr's critique of Soviet Marxism was pointed: "It feels itself morally justified in exterminating its foes because it is under the illusion that such a course will eliminate injustice. . . . How cruel the spirit of vengeance may be [e.g., against the kulaks] when it has gained the moral prestige of the spirit of justice. Egoism . . . imagines itself free of the temptation to injustice and therefore indulges in the illusion that elimination of the foe will guarantee future justice."[79] In contrast to Ward's optimism about the revolution following the imminent catastrophe, Niebuhr's wariness of human egoism, especially in its collective forms, curbed his expectations. In a letter to a member of the students' radical Agenda Club, Niebuhr counseled: "Nothing that needs to be done in our present situation can be done except some holy fear is mixed in with other motives."[80]

There is no record of Ward's reaction to *Reflections on the End of an Era,* but George Coe expressed biting criticism of Niebuhr's new perspective in at least one private letter:

> Have you noticed that Reinhold Niebuhr's God is the capitalist variety? He is absolute love, says Reinie; which means that he is the apotheosis of the benevolent man of wealth. Take a sincerely benevolent man of wealth, raise his sympathy to the nth degree (so that he forgets where his wealth comes from), enlarge him to absoluteness, and behold, you have the precise object that Niebuhr says is the Christian's object of worship. If you don't at first see that this analysis is accurate, consider that this God accepts perennial class struggle as an inevitable outcome of human nature. "Human nature being what it is," you know! Consider, also, that Niebuhr has explicitly stated that religion is not fundamentally concerned with justice. God is love, but he is not engaged in the struggle for justice. Niebuhr's theories may move him out of the game onto the sidelines—just where his God is.[81]

Meanwhile, Niebuhr expressed concern about New America to Jim Dombrowski: "I am very much worried that it will begin without the labor support and become merely a middle class organization. I am afraid that would be fatal."[82]

There was nothing impractical about Ward's commitments to economic egalitarianism for his own family. As the Depression threatened the livelihood of his artist son and author daughter-in-law, Harry reassured Lynd and May that the larger Ward family would practice mutuality during this time of the "bust-up of capitalism."[83] May and Lynd's financial vulnerability was particularly important with the imminent birth of another child. Having lost their firstborn in 1930, this time every precaution was taken, and a healthy daughter, Nanda, was born in August 1932. Five years later another daughter, Robin, was born to proud parents Lynd and May. Grandfather Harry was proud, too. Even through the serious economic and political struggles of the Great Depression, these two little girls brought a smile to his face.

In 1934 Ward agreed to chair another venture for bringing in the new order, a united front group known as the American League Against War and Fascism. The economic and social crisis brought on by the Depression, including the real threat of American fascism, had encouraged advocates for serious economic change to set aside their ideological and strategic differences to make common cause in united front groups. Though they were not in the majority, communists were prominent in the league—a situation that even many liberals found disconcerting. Ward tried to break down such fears. His 1935 article, "Christians and Communists," in the *Christian Century* argued forcefully that it was past time for Christians to ally themselves with forces that sought the same moral ends. Christians did not forfeit their right to criticize communists by working with them in united front groups, but Christians had to recognize the urgency of the hour. "It is the progressives, who now have the balance of power. They can use it effectively against fascism only with the help of the socialists and communists."[84]

Meanwhile, the fledgling organization known as New America was beginning to find its wings. Its National Policy Council (NPC) called for an important meeting in September 1935. Some thirty members were present, with representatives from several parts of the country. Creating a keen sense of comradeship for the new order, they slept, ate, and met in a member's Indiana home, with everyone sharing the common tasks of kitchen cleanup. Harry Ward, the national chairman, provided much of the fodder for their discussion. He warned his fellow members that words and arguments must be connected with real historical experiences. Part of his concern was obviously the naive assumptions about progressive history; as Ward summed it up: "We cannot force the pace of history, we can only hasten it."[85]

What should New America do? Ward called on members to engage in an "educational and agitational" strategy with the goal of creating an adequate alliance to gain control of the state through the ballot. Once state power was in their grasp, they must wrest the economic sector from the hands of capitalism and protect it against the predictable onslaughts from the forces of economic fascism. In preparation for this and as a practical means of building support, New America must enter into alliances with a variety of groups, including united front groups—"the only effective revolutionary activities at the present time"—even those which were inspired and influenced by the Communist Party. Ward insisted that a correct analysis of the revolutionary situation in America must be concluded as soon as possible, but there was a certainty these new revolutionaries had to comprehend: power must not only be won; it must be retained.[86]

The 1934 elections encouraged the New America folk, for the Farmer-Labor Party in Minnesota and the Progressive Party in Wisconsin demonstrated significant strength.[87] In 1935 the NPC stated that New America would not seek to control any third-party movements but would be "constantly pushing them to the left."[88] Even the reelection of FDR in 1936 gave hope to New America leaders, for this was evidence that the electorate was at least capable of discerning the more progressive of the two national political parties. Of course, FDR's New Deal and his "brain trust" were at a dead-end. America needed a "People's Front,"[89] but since New America was an organization almost exclusively comprised of intellectuals, it had a long way to go before achieving this status.

Though he was not an adherent of New America, Reinhold Niebuhr continued to seek a similar alliance. Having virtually dropped out of the socialist political effort, he now had little in common with the pacifist camp. Increasingly his patience wore thin with those he regarded as sentimentalists and idealists. His efforts to realize an alliance with working folk took more local forms, for example, his tireless efforts on behalf of the Delta Farm Cooperative and the Highlander School in rural Tennessee led by two former students, Myles Horton and Jim Dombrowski.

Ward was thinking on a much grander scale at every opportunity. In 1935 his Christian Ethics 42 course at Union focused on the "Tactics of Social Change" by studying revolutions down through history, and in 1936 the same course offered an opportunity to scrutinize the breakdown of economic order, with heavy reading assignments in Marxist documents. In 1935 Ward also taught New America's training school, and his presentation on the "Basic Points in Winning Power" reveals how strategically oriented Ward's focus had become.

His lecture began by addressing the persistently problematic issue of violence. Right out of the gate Ward acknowledged that "we have many members who are pacifist idealists," but, he insisted, they must acknowledge and come to terms with the ongoing use of violence against American workers through "repressive legislation." Ward contrasted the position of New America with both socialism and communism. Socialists assume that all will be well if they can just win power through the ballot; communists, on the other hand, range all the way from romantic advocates of armed insurrection to those who opt for violence as a regrettable but necessary tool for change. By contrast, argued Ward, New America must begin with the larger picture: "the necessity of preserving society for the future." New America must focus on the transition to the new order as well as the preservation of that order. In both instances the issue would be how to *limit* violence, given the inevitable resistance of capitalist forces both during and after the power shift. Ward's judgment was that the more violence could be lessened in the present context, the better chance of lessening it during the revolutionary times ahead. By what strategy could this be accomplished? Drawing on his experiences in the ACLU, Ward observed that middle-class protest and intervention often prevented class war from breaking out between workers and employers, and therefore middle-class folk must actively protest the ongoing, increasingly repressive actions against workers. But Ward was even more specific with respect to the long haul: revolutionary forces must "win the armed forces," "put the instruments of war out of commission," and "restrain those who start the war." Without such actions civil war will be inevitable. New America was working for a more democratic state—with all sectors, including the economy operating democratically—but New America's first order of business must be to defeat "the Fascist State." "It is a question of which side gets its forces united and organized first. Hence the united front strategy is important now."[90]

At every turn Ward was channeling his various organizational connections to the United Front and in particular to the group he had chaired since 1934, the American League Against War and Fascism. By the summer of 1935 the Communist Party had set aside its differences with various progressive groups and offered to make common cause with them in united front groups. General Franco's fascist war against the popular front government of Spain, which began in the summer of 1936, made the notion of a united front among leftist groups seem more urgent than ever. To his New America colleagues, Ward reiterated his concern about the army in the coming American revolution. General Franco's ability to use the military should illustrate how the army could be used by American fascists.

Under Ward's leadership not only New America but, more importantly, the Methodist Federation joined the American League Against War and Fascism. Throughout the 1930s a number of well-known Americans became members of the league—including Norman Thomas, Lincoln Steffens, John Dos Passos, Langston Hughes, Theodore Dreiser, Roger Baldwin, Adam Clayton Powell, and Reinhold Niebuhr—but there were also members like the communist leader Earl Browder. This communist influence was bothersome even to left-leaning members, who resented the clever power plays of communists in many united front groups. New America members persistently debated the legitimacy of working with the communists.

Many Methodists were none too pleased with MFSS membership in the league, for the MFSS was the only explicitly religious group affiliated with it. Of course, conservative Methodists' unhappiness with Harry Ward and the influence of the MFSS existed long before 1936, but now that the MFSS was associated with the league and had also declared war against capitalism, the conservatives were convinced that they must now regain control of their denomination. At the General Conference of 1936 they were successful in two of their three objectives: (1) gaining control of the Educational Board, through which much

MFSS material was distributed; (2) denying the MFSS official status among Methodists; and (3) investigating the MFSS. The last of these three efforts was thwarted by MFSS supporters, but success with the other two meant a dramatic loss of influence by the MFSS among Methodists. Never one to concede defeat, Ward took the loss of official status as a badge of honor for the MFSS—evidence that the prophetic voice was always unwelcome in the temple. Hereafter MFSS publications proudly and voluntarily printed "Methodist Federation for Social Service (unofficial)."

Conservative Methodists were not the only ones who found it increasingly difficult to deal with Ward. His relationships with his Union colleagues had soured badly. George Coe was concerned, for he was hearing about this even in California. Knowing his friend Harry's temperament, he broached the subject gently but nonetheless straightforwardly, noting that "friends and admirers" perceived an unhealthy public antagonism on Ward's part toward President Coffin. Acknowledging the limitations of Coffin's liberalism, Coe admonished Harry to recognize the practical value of liberal alliances for the greater cause. Ward was not persuaded, however, and he responded defensively. Denying that he held any antagonism toward Coffin, Ward proceeded to tee off on so-called liberal allies. Once again the warrior showed no sympathy for those who gave aid and comfort to the enemy: "I recognize the value of Coffin's liberalism and tell him so, but I have seen too clearly where it stops to put my trust in it in the time of crisis. . . . As long as they are only liberals they cannot help serving to deliver us into the hands of the Fascists."[91]

Coffin was on the rampage again that spring of 1936 because of some seminarians' ongoing radical behavior. In April he and Niebuhr went head-to-head, with the seminary president accusing Niebuhr and his radical colleagues of irresponsibility: "You fellows make me tired. I am sick of this place and wish I had accepted a church. I am going to carry this matter to the board." Niebuhr was fed up and responded in kind: "You make me tired too. I feel just as much like quitting and taking a church as you do," and concluded by admonishing Coffin to stop treating the faculty like children.[92] Coffin and Niebuhr kissed and made up, but the differences between Ward and Niebuhr were creating more problems.

Given Ward and Niebuhr's physical proximity and the intensity of their discord, it is no wonder that their disagreements became what Niebuhr would later describe as a "struggle for the souls of the young men."[93] The rivalry was evident to the students who fiercely debated the relative positions of their mentors in class, during meals in the refectory, or into the wee hours in their dorm rooms. It was an exhilarating time for these young people, and they turned out in droves when their mentors held court. On designated Thursdays the Niebuhrs hosted students in their apartment for snacks and conversation. Those stimulating evenings were memorialized in a student ditty sung to the tune of the gospel hymn "When the Roll Is Called Up Yonder."

When it's eight o'clock on Thursday night and books become
    a bore.
Then we'll leave our desks and climb the golden stair.
We will gather at the master's feet a-sitting on the floor.
When the beer is served at Reinie's, we'll be there.[94]

By contrast, Daisy Ward came into the city once a week from New Jersey to pour tea and pass cookies to the students who jammed Harry Ward's office to hear him expound on current events.[95]

The contrast between tea and cookies and beer and doughnuts may serve as a useful metaphorical representation of the differences between the two men. For all his radicalism, there was something very "old world" about Ward—not in the aristocratic sense, certainly, but in his deliberative and logical way of interpreting historical development and social change. He was able to place the unfolding events of the 1930s into clear categories, even moral categories, in good Victorian style. Orderly, purposeful effort would bring proper completion to these historical developments. By contrast, Niebuhr's creative, sometimes startling insights were at least as intoxicating as the beer he served the students. One minute he seemed to stand outside history, observing the ebb and flow of civilizations, then the next minute he would penetrate the depths of the human heart. Whereas Ward remained seated as he slowly and carefully developed a logical argument for the students, Niebuhr paced about the room, rapidly firing off his discernments at the students gathered there.

Of course, their differences extended beyond style to ideologies and

social strategies. However, the growing division between Ward and Niebuhr was never publicly cited by either of them, for seminary decorum
discouraged personal attacks on colleagues. Students would remember
these debates as "friendly arguments,"[96] but the private correspondence
of each man reveals a festering antagonism. Niebuhr continued to find
himself at odds with Union's administration and much of its faculty's
"liberal moralism that sees only the surface of life," but he lamented in
a 1936 letter to his wife that he found "Ward's sneering almost as difficult to bear."[97]

It is difficult to identify the moment when this sneering began, though
Ward's impatience with anything less than an American form of the
Soviet experiment can be dated as early as his November 1931 letter to
Niebuhr. Two years afterward, Ward reported to Coe that he was still
trying to set Niebuhr straight, especially with regard to his strategy of
"realism" and his interpretation of Jesus' love ethic. With respect to the
latter, their disagreement was fundamental. Niebuhr read Jesus' ethic as
a perfectionist system of self-denial applicable only to the individual.
Ward argued that Jesus' love ethic emphasized "mutualism" and therefore it need not be regarded as an ethic of nonresistance to evil. Ward's
complaint against Niebuhr's "alleged realism" became more passionate,
for he regarded it as "only romanticism in reverse gear from that of the
evolutionary optimists whom he properly skins."[98] In his judgment, this
"reverse gear" stemmed from Niebuhr's growing fascination with more
conservative theology. Indeed, Niebuhr was deliberately wedding orthodox theology and radical politics, though he understood early on that
his colleagues would undoubtedly reject such a union. "It will satisfy
neither the liberals in politics and religion, nor the political radicals nor
the devotees of traditional Christianity."[99] Certainly Ward, one of the
political radicals, was not satisfied. As he told his student assistant,
melding conservative theology and leftist politics was like "having two
horses pulling a wagon—one horse moving east and the other horse
moving west." Ward believed that the horse of conservative theology
would ultimately stumble and bring down with it the horse of leftist
politics.[100] No doubt Ward agreed with George Coe's assessment of
Niebuhr's capitalist God.

An undated letter from the 1930s relates a painful occasion on which
Ward and Niebuhr spoke at the same banquet. Perhaps it was a meeting

of the United Christian Council for Democracy (UCCD), a united front of nine religious organizations created in 1936. Both Niebuhr's Fellowship of Socialist Christians and Ward's Methodist Federation belonged to the UCCD. At any rate, on this evening Niebuhr was all but sick with Ward's presentation and its reception by the audience: "He [Ward] gave a pathetic defense of Russia. I thought he had learned a little more. The conference is *terrible*. American liberalism tinctured with radicalism . . . [in its] most *superficial* and most vapid form. I never thought Christianity could sink to such a farrago of nonsense. . . . This is the straw to break the camel's back for me."[101]

From the perspective of most Soviet sympathizers, the camel's back was broken by the Nazi-Soviet Nonaggression Pact in August of 1939. At this time, Niebuhr was in Britain delivering the prestigious Gifford Lectures, later published as his magnum opus, *The Nature and Destiny of Man*. Niebuhr's years of toil in the theological vineyard had yielded a compelling analysis of human nature that precluded romantic assumptions about history and human progress. In light of the world-shocking events of 1939, Niebuhr's conclusions appeared to be beyond dispute. The Hitlers could not be pacified by words and treaties, and the Stalins were no more committed to justice and equality than their new Nazi allies. Niebuhr found a certain amount of satisfaction in the painful discomfort of liberals and radicals. The true colors of Stalinist Marxism had been revealed for all the world to see. Most liberals—including members of united front groups like the American League for Peace and Democracy (formerly the American League Against War and Fascism) —abandoned all association with communism. But Ward did not join the exodus, and the consequent strain for Niebuhr became almost unbearable. In a letter dated two months after the signing of the scandalous treaty, he wrote Ursula:

I find travelling with him difficult. He sent me a circular yesterday explaining why the American League [for Peace and Democracy] has not condemned Russia and why they have suddenly discovered that this is a war between rival imperialisms. In their words merely following the communist line. . . . Of course this is a war between rival imperial powers just as any struggle between two men is not just a struggle for principles but a struggle between two selfish men. . . . Incidentally I sent the Nation an article on this. I haven't the slightest idea whether they used it.[102]

The *Nation* used the article all right. That essay, "Ideology and Pretense," represents Niebuhr's most damning critique of Marxism, and its principal argument is one he would employ often in the years to come, especially during the cold war. Marxism is particularly dangerous, maintained Niebuhr, because it poses as a purely moral ideology, claiming to rise above the limitations of coercion. But in reality Marxism uses this cloak of moral innocence to hide its totalitarian agenda. Niebuhr's break with Ward was now complete.

Earlier that year, in an article describing his journey away from liberalism—"Ten Years That Shook My World"—Niebuhr came close to equating communist and fascist tyrannies, though he conceded that "it is impossible to destroy all the universal hopes in communism." He also expressed sorrow for the situation of people like Ward (though he did not name him or anyone else): "I feel genuinely sorry for my friends who seem to be under a spiritual necessity to deny obvious facts about Russian tyranny."[103] For those who still stood by Russia after the Nazi-Soviet pact and the Soviet Union's invasion of Finland and eastern Poland, Niebuhr had no tolerance left. "Thus the same comrades who tore their hair over Chamberlain's disloyalty to democracy through his policy of appeasement are quite complacent toward Stalin's pact with Hitler, though the latter obviously freed Germany to make its attack on Poland and to plunge Europe into war."[104] Niebuhr argued that it was now time to do more than critique the Stalinist version of Marxism; Marxism itself needed more careful scrutiny because it had "become a source of moral and political confusion."[105] Recent events had shocked many leftists, even those like Niebuhr who early on had recognized the brutality of Stalin's regime. On first hearing the news of the Nazi-Soviet agreement, Niebuhr wrote to Ursula: "The damned Russians are even worse than we thought."[106] As Russia stood ready to conquer Finland, he was indignant: "But if this isn't pure imperialism, I would like to know what is."[107] No wonder that this period became for Niebuhr the litmus test[108] for judging his colleagues' critical acumen. His sympathy for previous allies, like Ward, had evaporated.

Niebuhr was not alone in his disgust. The American League for Peace and Democracy (ALPD) listed in the choppy seas of accusations and recriminations, and the MFSS lost most of its influence among Methodists. Ward had walked away from New America in the late thirties, when the group's leadership seemed determined to remain theoretical rather than become action-oriented. He insistently claimed that New America publications had become "liberalism tinged with Socialism and an occasional slight odor of Trotskyism."[109] However, the breaking point actually came with the conflict over attitudes toward communists,[110] including their role in other united front groups like the ALPD.[111] Ward's pragmatic strategy of working with the communists is evident in this debate. "It comes down to this—can we learn to get along with the CP (and they with us)? If not, of course, we can play no active role in the development of the peoples' front, but will carry out the correcting function of a theoretically sectarian movement."[112]

8

More Wars

1939–1945

The significant fact is that the center of spiritual gravity is now outside the churches.
—Harry F. Ward, "Pulpits at War"

DESPITE HARRY WARD'S experience in dealing with adversity, it is difficult to imagine the challenge of keeping his sea legs in the furious storms that came crashing across the bow of his life in 1939. The major storms were the furors over the nonaggression treaty signed between the U.S.S.R. and the subsequent Soviet occupation of eastern Poland. Many pro-Soviet American liberals abandoned democratic front ships, including the American League for Peace and Democracy.[1] Roger Baldwin's letter of resignation from the league is instructive, for he recognized that some would misunderstand his allegiances: "My reluctance is increased by my dislike of appearing to play into the enemies of the League or to encourage 'red-baiting.'" American communists seemed to walk in lockstep with the Soviet party line. Baldwin's letter continues:

[I]t has become painfully evident since the mutual assistance pact between the Soviet Union and Germany that Communist international policy is now dictated by the national interest of the Soviet Union wherever it may lead. Up to that sharp turn, we could count in the League on a fairly stable Communist policy in the international terms of democratic forces in all lands, without undue reference to the Soviet Union. . . . I shall of course continue to work with Communists, as with all others, on specific issues of civil rights in the United States in which they are engaged. The notion that Communists are outside the pale of cooperation on any matter because of their adherence to Soviet foreign policy is so irrational as to be almost hysterical.[2]

Baldwin also referred to the league's initial neutral response to the Nazi-Soviet pact; the ALPD board had stated that "at this time, we neither condemn or approve the actions of the Soviet Union. Our members will have their own opinions on these matters and will express and implement them in their political organizations outside the league."[3] ACLU board member Norman Thomas was not as diplomatic as Baldwin about the league's behavior. Thomas's tolerance of communists had long since vanished, due in large part to their persistent obstruction of his socialist political ambitions. His letter to Ward arrived a week before Baldwin's. The issue here, he argues, is not just the Nazi-Soviet pact; Thomas specifically complains about Ward's ongoing failure to condemn Soviet transgressions.

> Ever since I heard that you were unwilling to sign any sort of protest against any of the crimes against civil liberty committed in Russia, I have felt that you were not the man to be Chairman of the [American Civil Liberties] Union. You will remember that I was one of those who persuaded you to undertake that task and I rejoiced in the work you did. But I do not think that one can be for civil liberty, as the C.L.U. ought to be for it, and condone the manifold and brutal denials of liberty and justice under Stalin's regime.[4]

These were not just idle words. Thomas and other anticommunist board members were determined to remove Ward and his ilk from ACLU leadership positions. The situation had become more difficult for the ACLU because it was being scrutinized by Congressman Martin Dies's House Special Committee to Investigate Un-American Activities (HUAC), which was established in 1938. Given the ACLU's record of defending free speech for all, including communists, passionate anti-communists regarded the ACLU as just another communist-front group eroding American values. However, it was not Ward's connection with the ACLU that brought him before the Dies Committee but his leadership of the American League for Peace and Democracy, whose board he had chaired since 1934. To the anticommunists on the ACLU board, Harry's appearance before a congressional investigative committee would mean more bad press for the ACLU, since Ward still chaired its board— even though Norman Thomas and other anticommunist board members pressured him to resign.

Harry Ward's seven-hour testimony before HUAC on 23 October 1939 is a useful window into various agendas that swirled around the proceedings. The questions put to Ward probed communist influence on the league. The charge was led by HUAC's director of research, J. B. Matthews, Ward's predecessor at the ALPD and now a rabid anti-communist. In testimony fourteen months earlier, Matthews identified the Ward-led Methodist Federation as "entirely in accord with the Communist Party."[5] Harry savored this opportunity to jab at Matthews,[6] and his sarcasm sometimes gave way to outright hostility. He repeatedly interrupted Matthews's questions to correct him or challenge his knowledge or his motives: "You have got the history wrong, Mr. Matthews. You do not know the inside situation [with the ALPD] or you would understand the situation."[7] Even Chairman Dies found Ward's best shot at Matthews humorous.

Mr. Ward: Mr. Matthews, you ought to realize that Communists, Republicans, and even Methodists, can change. I am a Methodist and believe in repentance, and also in the possibility of backsliding, Mr. Matthews.
The Chairman: All of which was meant for Mr. Matthews' benefit?
Mr. Ward: For his personal benefit; just a little instruction for him.[8]

With other questioners, Ward was more polite but no less evasive. He bobbed and weaved as interrogators tried to pin him against the ropes with questions about the amount of money contributed by communists to the ALPD, the influence of communists and communist sympathizers in key leadership positions, and the ALPD's apparently consistent support of the Soviet Union's agenda. Harry Ward remained unbowed.

Mr. Ward: Mr. Dies, you certainly know, sir, that there are lots of people in this country who are against capitalism who are also very strongly anti-Communists.

The Chairman: You are speaking about socialists.

Mr. Ward: Yes; and there are lots of other people too. There are lots of economists on technical and practical grounds. You can be against capitalism on moral grounds as I am and practical grounds, as I am. That does not make you a Communist by a long shot.[9]

In a rare moment of public revelation, Ward connected his own aspirations as an immigrant with the convictions he now espoused:

I am talking about American democracy, sir. I am talking about that, because I came to this country when I became old enough to choose for myself. . . . I believe that [American democracy] is the only way mankind is ever going to be saved from the perils that confront him, [which] is by the perpetuation and extension of those principles into every area of human life.[10]

Ward's answers to questions about the ALPD's response to the Nazi-Soviet pact were vague. He insisted that there were differences of opinion within the ALPD and asserted that the Soviet action "in regard to Hitler has given him more of [a] check than it has helped him."[11]

The committee quizzed Ward about the information supporting his more positive assessments of Soviet society. Despite Dies's own ideological blinders, his persistent pressing of the question revealed the limits of Ward's knowledge of Soviet life.

The Chairman: How long has it been since you were there?

Mr. Ward: I think that I was there in 1933. [Actually it was 1932].

The Chairman: And you have not been back since?

Mr. Ward: No.

The Chairman: Then you do not know what has happened, do you?
Mr. Ward: I know it as a part of my studies.
The Chairman: How do you know what has happened since 1933?
Mr. Ward: I have studied conditions.
The Chairman: But how do you know since 1933?
Mr. Ward: Through publications.
The Chairman: That is, through papers; that is based on newspaper reports?
Mr. Ward: Yes; and by keeping in touch with documents sent over to this country. [This was followed by some probing about the nature of these documents.] . . . [P]lus the conversations with acquaintances of mine who have come back from Russia, who have, from year to year, made their studies and come back with reports.
The Chairman: Quite a good many of them?
Mr. Ward: No; two, perhaps, travelers.[12]

After further testimony, Dies, somewhat abruptly, asked Ward to stand down while two witnesses addressed some points of contention. Following their brief testimony, Dies then called the committee into executive session.[13] Two days later the committee declared its work on this matter done and asserted that the year's worth of testimony had "established conclusively that the American League for Peace and Democracy was organized and is controlled by the Communist Party."[14] An appendix to the report provided names of government employees who were associated with the ALPD.

The abrupt conclusion of the proceedings must have seemed suspicious to Ward and others. Unbeknownst to him, the day before his HUAC testimony informal meetings took place between some of the ACLU's anticommunist leaders and Dies's committee. This may explain Dies's quick interjection, when a committee member inquired into Ward's relationship to the ACLU, that "this committee found last year, in its reports, there was not any evidence that the American Civil Liberties Union was a Communist organization."[15]

Meanwhile the Soviets soiled their reputation even further when they invaded Finland on November 30. Many old friends abandoned their Soviet sympathies in droves, but Ward continued the fight. A year later, for example, he tried to gather signatures on a petition to the president and the Congress protesting any attempt to outlaw the Communist Party, but his efforts were repeatedly rejected by correspondents who cited the "outrageous attack of Communist Russia on Democratic Finland."[16] Soviet behavior in 1939 had crossed a line that even some of the most tolerant could no longer traverse. For example, Halford Luccock refused to sign Ward's petition, though "not because I am at all squeamish about Communism. . . . I was glad to sign a statement a year ago just before the Russian-German agreement asking for a fairer understanding of Russia. I have nothing whatever to retract from what I signed."[17]

Throughout 1939, factions on the ACLU board warred bitterly over the question of communist membership on the board and over Ward's leadership. John Haynes Holmes charged that the ACLU was "under the strange control of a minority, headed by the Chairman [Ward], which is primarily concerned not with civil liberties at all but with the interests of a radical minority group which follows the party line as laid down by Moscow."[18] At the annual meeting in February 1940, the matter was resolved, though hardly to Ward and company's satisfaction:

> While the American Civil Liberties Union does not make any test of opinion on political or economic questions a condition of membership . . . the personnel of its governing committees and staff is properly subject to the test of consistency in the defense of civil liberties in all aspects and all places. . . . It is inappropriate for any person to serve on the governing committees of the Union or on its staff, who is a member of any political organization which supports totalitarian dictatorship in any country, or who by his public declarations indicates his support of such a principle.
>
> Within this category we include organizations in the United States supporting the totalitarian governments of the Soviet Union and of the Fascist and Nazi countries (such as the Communist Party, the German-American Bund and others).[19]

This resolution represented more than political posturing. It meant that longtime board member Elizabeth Gurley Flynn, an avowed member of the Communist Party, would be purged from the ACLU board. This new policy was intolerable to Harry Ward. Shaking the dust from

his sandals after two decades of chairing the ACLU board, he resigned "in protest against their resolution setting up doctrinal tests for
membership."[20] "The essence of civil liberties is opposition to all attempts to enforce political orthodoxy. . . . Throughout its existence . . .
the [American Civil Liberties] Union has had only one test in selecting
the members of its Board and National Committee . . . the Bill of
Rights. . . . The Civil Liberties Union which did this [resolution] is
not the same Civil Liberties Union with which I have been glad to
work for twenty years."[21] Sadly, as one historian of the organization has
rightly observed, Harry F. Ward "vanished from the ACLU's institutional memory."[22]

There was pressure on another board to force Ward out of the other
primary institution in his life—Union Theological Seminary. But despite President Coffin's ideological disagreements with his senior ethics
professor, he supported academic freedom for his faculty, including the
increasingly controversial Harry Ward.[23] Though Ward had reached retirement age, Coffin allowed him to continue to teach at Union for another two years. Ward's course offerings from the mid-1930s onward
had reflected his agenda. As early as 1934–1935 he was offering a year-
long course on the "Ethics of Social Change," with the first semester
devoted to readings in anarchism, utopian socialism, syndicalism, liberal
evolutionism, Marxism, revisionism, and Leninism. In the second semester Ward focused on various European revolutions, and he titled the
final unit "Strategy for the American Revolution." He offered this
course, now known as "Tactics of Social Change," during his final year
at Union. According to the syllabus, only the first two weeks of the
thirteen-week fall semester course were devoted to non-Marxist theories of social change; the rest centered on various forms of Marxism. In
Ward's final semester, spring 1941, he taught the second half of the
course, with its emphasis on historical revolutions. Lecture notes from
the last two weeks, which were titled "The American Scene," reveal
Ward predicting that capitalists would seize power and establish a fascist United States government "either when war is declared or when a
national emergency is declared as a result of increasing strikes."[24]

Ward was grateful for the seminary's support, for he faced strong opposition on multiple fronts. The old warrior was willing to wage his fight
even against great odds, through public speeches, correspondence, testi-

Harry F. Ward, 1960s.
(Courtesy of Nanda Ward
and Robin Ward Savage)

mony before governmental bodies, and in print. Though family and
friends later recalled that Ward was "shaken" by the Nazi-Soviet pact,[25]
one would never know it by his public comments. He thundered against
the Dies Committee for "creating the Communist myth" concerning
the ALPD, which folded 1 February 1940. "Before the Dies myth . . . it
was charged that we were being used by the Communist party. Our
answer was: 'What of it? We are using the Communist party, too.'"[26]

His *Democracy and Social Change* (1940) also revealed a warrior un-
daunted. Though not very well known by comparison with his earlier books, *Democracy and Social Change* sets forth Ward's longstanding
agenda, dating back at least to his efforts through New America in the
1930s. Ward believed that the world's future lay in economic democracy,
and that the future depended in large part on the world's greatest democracy "transplant[ing] our democratic principles into new soil" (7).
Though his enthusiasm for the world's first socialist state remained un-

abated, he was most interested in promoting a genuinely American form of economic democracy, and he cited the American traditions of Jefferson and Lincoln to make his case. This was not just rhetoric, for Harry truly valued America's democratic traditions. As an immigrant he knew all too well the democratic limits of other nations. So it was fitting that in 1941 he took his family, including his two granddaughters, to the Statue of Liberty fifty years after he immigrated to the United States.

Ward's view of democracy, both historically and sociologically, is essential for understanding not only this book but Ward himself. According to Ward, democracy is an evolving embodiment of self-government that reaches its climax in "economic democracy," where the economic system is owned and controlled "by the people." This is the final step in a long historical process that has seen human beings progress from feudalism to capitalism, and now to the era of socialism, which began with the Soviet project. America's problem was that its emphasis on a "democracy of individual rights" was being maintained at the expense of a "democracy of interdependent community" that focuses on social equality—democracy's highest expression. Worse yet, the forces of American capitalism were, in the name of individual rights, actually asserting class power, which is in reality autocratic, not democratic.

Ward's sociological interpretation of democratic institutions, especially his analysis of power, sets this book apart from most of his previous work. His experiences with New America, the ALPD, and the ACLU, his continuing engagement with Marxist texts, decades observing domestic and international politics, and perhaps even the challenges of Niebuhr's analysis of power had pushed Ward to articulate more carefully the function of social power. All nation-states, including democratic ones, employ coercion, he stated. The issue for democracies is how to put this power in the hands of all people. The alert reader senses a dig at Ward's junior colleague's association with the increasingly popular "political realism": "The essence of political realism is to understand that the state cannot represent the community as long as there are economic classes struggling for power" (114). Social equality cannot be realized so long as the economic sector is not controlled by the people; social equality entails a planned economy, not one subject to "the blind struggle of monopolistic capital" (98). Therefore in order for democracy to achieve its ultimate goal of social equality—putting power (including economic power) in the hands of all people—democracy may have to repress certain groups, especially those who resist change in the name of capitalism, in order to save democracy's life. Otherwise the present situation would continue. Even with all its welfare state trappings, the New Deal government was using its power to maintain capitalism and thereby class power. This power play of what Ward labeled "state capitalism" is nothing short of fascism, he believed. Americans are wary of fascist threats elsewhere, he noted, but they fail to see its growing presence at home. One has only to look at capitalism's funding of various fascist governments in recent years and at the domestic repression of civil liberties as well to recognize the threat.

Democracy and Social Change offers more than a theoretical discussion. It also includes the outline of an action plan for changing the United States to an economic democracy.[27] Intellectuals in particular bear a heavy responsibility for enabling change in the American economic system, for educated folk can discern the movements and necessities of history and therefore ought to be able to point the way for humanity. Human beings need leaders for the great movements of history. Religion, too—especially that "saving remnant" which promotes prophetic religion against institutional religion—bears a special responsibility, for religion has always played a significant part in civilization's great transitions.[28]

What else must be done? Civil liberties must be protected, and supporters of true democratic development, including communists, must be free to help move American society in the right direction. A democratic front is essential to success, for such an alliance is needed to counteract the inevitable "coalition of class interests and political forces which naturally forms to oppose this change" (243). There must also be a strategy that addresses seriously three key areas of American society: the political, the economic, and the cultural. (By "cultural" Ward meant primarily the "war of ideas" that must be won in America.) The psychological appeal of the profit motive, and the American myth of rugged individualism that supports it, must be exterminated.

Ward is fuzzy with regard to the political and economic realms. He repeatedly refers to making the right decisions at the right time in the "main offensive against capitalism," yet one has to wonder if he has in mind a general strike that might significantly affect a key policy decision or even a national election. Is he counseling a coup d'état? Probably not, but like his proposals for New America in the thirties, the specifics of seizing power are nebulous.

Can it [the Democratic Front] develop a leadership able to select the right moment and the right point of attack for the democratic taking of economic power? Will enough of the Center go with the Left to make the bid for power successful? . . . If it [reactionary forces] can be stopped before serious losses occur, if sufficient education concerning the economic causes of present needs and the failure of present remedies can be carried on in the Democratic Front, then the forces it is training to act together will not disintegrate, but will consolidate for effective social change when the possible moment arrives. (254)

(Perhaps this is an indication of why, in 1940, Ward finally registered to vote—though twenty years later he insisted to his granddaughter Robin that he never cast a ballot in his life.[29])

Part of this strategy must include resistance to joining the growing war effort, for the earlier world war had all but quashed serious reform and the exercise of democratic rights. Ward argues that the American people need to feel a comradeship less with Europe and more with China, India, Mexico, Chile, Cuba, and Russia, where democratic forces are clearly at work (288). This is a turning point in history, he insists. Three key events of the twentieth century signify that we have reached the end of an era: the organization of the first socialist state (the Soviet Union), the breakdown of the capitalist economy (the Great Depression), and the rise of fascist powers. "The energy of the universe is waiting to be used," and humanity has "forces within it that cannot be defeated" (39).

Ward's critique here of America's unrealized democratic potential is crystal clear, but his defense of recent Soviet behavior is thin at best. On the matter of tyrannical bureaucracy—where the issue is more than arbitrariness, for it involves serious bloodletting—Ward appeals to what seems to be a kind of historical determinism ("[t]he machine age decrees collectivism") and the dependability of human reason ("recognition of the danger is half the battle"). Despite his keen understanding of the machinations of power in the economic sphere, his description of political power all but begs the question: "Those who defeat plutocratic autocracy should be able to vanquish socialist bureaucracy" (95). And there is more than a wisp of utopianism and naive faith in the goodness of human nature: "[T]he future belongs to the forces which seek to push life forward. The forces of death may win some battles, but they are doomed to defeat in the end. . . . Time after time the people plunge themselves into darkness and disaster by their ignorance and folly. Then once more they move toward the light, and each time new light breaks upon their path" (292–93).

And what about the Nazi-Soviet pact and the Soviet invasion of Finland? He offers a defense by way of larger Soviet history, reminding his readers "that temporary diplomatic and even military arrangements between states founded on different basic ideas are a commonplace of history." He notes that the United States and Britain also formed alliances with dictatorships, to foster trade and improve diplomatic relations (an odd example, given Ward's denunciation of American capitalists' support of fascist powers earlier in the book). Ward mainly addresses the Soviets' behavior in terms of the recent purges in various American organizations, including the ACLU, and what he labels "emotional reaction" to these Soviet actions (138). He quickly moves on to what he had continually argued was the distinction between fascism and communism, a distinction that prohibited their being lumped together as two forms of totalitarianism: "It is a matter of common knowledge that the fascists propose to destroy democracy root and branch, while the communists propose to develop it in a new direction" (138–39). Regarding the suspension of civil liberties in the Soviet Union, Ward argues that these strong actions were only used against counterrevolutionaries; moreover, they were only temporary and undertaken when necessary. Obviously the loyalty inspired by his holy war dualism and the propaganda war were undermining the warrior's sharp vision.

Despite growing reports of anti-Jewish atrocities in Germany and Poland, which he had so passionately denounced just two years earlier, Ward opposed American intervention in Europe. In the fall of 1941 he encouraged the MFSS not to take a stand on the war.[30] Elliot Field, a Presbyterian minister, stated the problem well after reading Ward's article, "Keep America Out of War." Field expressed his own desire, which he shared with Harry Ward, that the United States should put its economic house in order, but he protested Ward's "assumption that all this must be done *before* we have a right to take any hand in meeting the peril of the dictators." He acknowledged Britain's imperialism but argued that there were more urgent questions to be addressed, especially given Nazi and Soviet behavior, which Ward conveniently ignored. Field's analysis is pointed and scathing.

> In one breath you say that we should appeal to the peoples of the conquered lands, and of Germany, in a negotiated peace, without recognizing adequately the fact that they [the conquered European nations] are helpless and voiceless; and at the same time you opposed the use of force against those powers which have made slaves of those peoples. How can we collaborate with "the genuine democratic forces of the rest of the world" when they, as you say, "are suppressed and driven underground"? The only collaboration at this moment is with those forces which are free to oppose Hitler, and Britain is the foremost of these.

> You sneer at Britain's democracy, chide her for not giving independence to India—but there is not one word in your article of blame for the Soviet Union whose war against democratic Finland gives the lie to all claims that she is a "democratic" nation. You even speak of the people of the Soviet Union as having natural affinity for peace and for democracy—when we know that the *people* of the Soviet Union are voiceless and helpless in Stalin's hands. Your equating of the Soviet Union with the democracies simply staggers belief. . . . It is just this type of argumentation which gives the opportunity to the reactionary elements in our country to claim that all radical—and labor—movements are communistic. Why this admiration of the Soviet Union? Do I understand you to claim that the Soviet Union is a democratic government? I'm not speaking of Marxian or proletariat *theory.* I'm speaking of the government of Russia, which is the cold, hard fact facing us.

> We do need prophets whose zeal flames with indignation, but in your article there is the merest reference to Germany's acts. . . .

Six pages of inveighing against capitalism—hardly a sentence to the brutal, unspeakable warfare which Nazism is carrying on. Is there to be no moral indignation against this greatest scourge which the world has ever known?[31]

Without taking anything away from Field's penetrating analysis, it very well may be that the most damning effect of Ward's pro-Soviet blinders is not his response to the Nazi-Soviet treaty but his refusal to see the naked brutality of the Stalinist purges of the 1930s. Strategically one might concur with Ward that the Soviets had few options in the late thirties, for the antagonism of the United States and its allies was evident. Stalin also understood that Hitler was certainly no friend of communist aspirations, even modest ones, and that Nazis despised Slavic peoples. The German assault against the Soviets would inevitably come. Ward argued that Stalin and his advisors knew they needed to buy time, so the nonaggression pact with Germany seemed the most prudent strategy. Of course, this realpolitik could only be justified if one shared Ward's assumption that "the self-interest of the Soviet Union is more in the interest of world-wide democracy than the self-interest of the British and American financial imperialists, just as it was in the pre-war efforts for disarmament and collective security."[32] This is not to justify Ward's conclusions, but rather to nuance them as carefully as possible. However, no nuancing is possible with regard to what took place in Stalin's Soviet Union of the thirties, especially when it becomes clear that for Harry Ward this was not just a theoretical issue; he was personally acquainted with someone who had "disappeared" in Stalin's purges.

The face that should have haunted Ward from the late thirties onward was that of his former student Julius Hecker. A native of Leningrad, Hecker immigrated to the United States as a young man and gained American citizenship. After graduating from Union Theological Seminary, he served as a Methodist pastor in New York City and earned a Ph.D. at Columbia University. Inspired by the revolutionary developments in the Soviet Union, he returned there in the 1920s, giving up his U.S. citizenship. Julius Hecker hosted Harry and Daisy during their month-long visit in 1924 as well as their 1931–1932 sabbatical, helping his former teacher gain access to places and agencies that Harry Ward described so favorably in his book *In Place of Profit*. Hecker believed in the Soviet Union; he regarded this communist project as the wave of the future. Perhaps no existing photograph shows Harry Ward with a broader smile than the one taken in Moscow in 1932 as he sat in a car with Julius Hecker. Given what happened to Hecker, this is a very disturbing photograph: Ward, the grinning Social Gospel warrior committed to social justice, in the company of a young man who unbeknownst to them faced a grim future. In 1938 Hecker was arrested, and later he was shot—just one of Stalin's victims among millions. How is it possible that the ghost of Julius Hecker did not dissuade Harry Ward from rationalizing his support of Stalin's Soviet Union?[33]

Perhaps, in fact, that torn (how?) photograph did haunt Ward, for it was found among his personal papers, not with other snapshots and family pictures. Perhaps in private moments over the years Harry did ponder that picture, remembering his kind, idealistic student and wondering how things could go so wrong. Whatever questions and guilt that photograph may have elicited, there is no evidence that it affected Ward's publicly expressed belief system, his attitudes, or his actions. His holy war dualism betrayed him as well as his friendships with others. By investing his entire moral universe in the survival of a particular social system, Harry Ward and others of his persuasion were left without a reference point that, according to his onetime colleague Reinhold Niebuhr, "would have enabled them to detect or to anticipate *the possibility of new forms of evil arising in a new society.*"[34]

As Ward approached the day of his retirement from Union Theological Seminary in 1941, he continued to challenge the dominant forces of power in American society. At least one of those forces of power was not happy about his persistent attacks: in 1941 the FBI file on Harry Ward began to swell in size. The bureau's renewed interest in Ward seems to have been stimulated by a speech in which he not only decried the "war hysteria" of the country but specifically likened the abuses of the FBI to those of the Gestapo.[35] He was particularly incensed in May when FBI agents took numerous pictures of participants at a Mother's Day Peace Meeting in Cleveland, and he protested the action in a letter to the U.S. attorney general.[36] In a speech to a Maryland audience later that month, Ward denounced Hoover in particular for such domestic spying; he charged that the FBI director had "boasted" he was going to "make lists of everybody they are going to get."[37]

Harry F. Ward in
his study, 1960s.
(Courtesy of Nanda
Ward and Robin
Ward Savage)

Apparently Ward's attack got the FBI's attention, for an important person[38] called at the FBI central office before ten o'clock the morning after that speech. The unnamed person stated that

> [H]e knows the background of Ward, and . . . he has a nasty tongue and pen. He stated he wouldn't suggest getting into any controversy with Ward. . . . ▮▮▮▮▮▮▮▮▮ states he merely wanted Mr. Hoover to know about this and it is just in the nature of a friendly tip. I told him how much Mr. Hoover would appreciate his calling.[39]

Obviously Mr. Hoover and company did appreciate the tip and act on it, for close surveillance of Harry Ward began immediately and continued for the rest of his life.

Harry F. Ward speaking at a labor rally in Paterson, New Jersey. (Courtesy of Nanda Ward and Robin Ward Savage)

When Harry F. Ward retired from Union Theological Seminary in 1941 at age sixty-eight, few persons, including Harry himself, could have guessed that he would live for another two and a half decades. Still, it is clear from his closing address, "Christianity, an Ethical Religion," that this old warrior did not intend to relinquish the cause. He reviewed his years at Union with a focus on the future: "Looking back through twenty-eight years of teaching the Christian Ethic, certain points stand out like rocky promontories in a long coast line against which the waves are always breaking. Looking ahead at the uncharted and dangerous course which lies before humanity in its long pilgrimage, these points are like mountain peaks rising above the mists that obscure the way."[40]

Three "mountain peaks" were familiar landmarks to anyone who knew Ward during those years: (1) the necessary relationship between the individual and society—meaning, of course, that religion is necessarily social and individual; (2) the religion of Jesus "requires a more effective relationship between religion and science,"[41] especially with respect to the economic foundation of society; and (3) "ethical religion is continuously revolutionary . . . [for] it continually criticizes and denounces all tendencies to injustice and to power . . . and demands the kind of [social] organization that makes it difficult for them to grow."[42]

It is telling that Ward concluded his address with a paraphrase of what he called "an historic phrase"—actually the famous epigram from the young Karl Marx's "Theses on Feuerbach."[43] No doubt Ward intended this as his legacy to the seminary: "If Christianity is an ethical religion, then the whole Seminary exists to promulgate it, and effectiveness in that task becomes the test of every department. To paraphrase an historic phrase, *the Seminary exists not to explain religion but to change life.*"[44]

In an essay titled "Some Things I Have Learned While Teaching," which was published in the seminary's alumni magazine, Ward reflected on his years of teaching. For those who might have wondered about this professor who never went to church except to preach and who was hardly at ease among typical American church folk, the answer was simple and pragmatic to the core: "When I left college [probably a reference to Harvard] some of my friends who helped to make American socialism said, 'Why waste your time with the Church?' I replied, 'Here is the machinery and power dedicated to the achievement of the highest life for man, I will try to use it for that purpose.'"[45]

Those who had him under surveillance put a different spin on those decades of increasing radicalism:

> *Ward is a man of some education and has been interested in social service work for years. His experience in this work has warped his perspective and since 1917 he has been led astray by various forms of propaganda with which he has come in contact. Being an author and speaker of no mean ability, he is a valuable propaganda agent for any movement of radical or semi-radical nature which might choose to use him.*[46]

Clearly the watchers understood their subject's strong points.

Harry Ward's students understood him too. Normally students raised about $200 for a retirement gift, but Ward's students respected his values. They purchased a ten-dollar vase in which he could place his cherished homegrown roses and designated the rest of the money they had raised for a cause of Ward's choosing. Their notes of gratitude reveal the powerful influence he had on their lives. Jim Dombrowski spoke for many in his appreciation of Ward's "unflagging zeal to keep theory and practice together."[47] Another former student, Sam H. Franklin, expressed gratitude "for showing us how important moral indignation can become implemented with techniques of effective social strategy."[48] With what was perhaps a none-too-subtle dig at the now more popular Niebuhr, Frank W. Herriott applauded Ward's "uncompromising devotion with complete understanding of the forces with which you were dealing, and hence with no easy optimism."[49] Students from his early days of teaching at the Boston University School of Theology commemorated their old professor's retirement by renaming their eating club the "Harry Ward Cooperative." Begrudging Union colleagues recognized Ward's contributions to the seminary even as they privately breathed sighs of relief. Ward's body needed some relief, too, and he spent the next six months in the warm climate of Mexico.

However, events would not let his mind rest. Within weeks of his retirement Germany violated its nonaggression treaty, declaring war on the Soviet Union on 22 June 1941. Immediately Britain and the United States promised aid to the Soviets. After their initial successes the German troops stalled, and by winter the Soviets had begun a counteroffensive. Ward, too, began a counteroffensive: against the continuing detractors of the Soviets. Whatever personal reservations he may have had about the Soviet actions of 1939, the old debater did not blink at the task; in fact, he marshaled his best evidence and arguments. He insisted that the Nazi-Soviet pact and the Soviet invasion of Finland were acts of Soviet self-preservation rooted in the 1938 compromises at Munich. In the minds of antagonists and even some friends, Ward's logic demonstrated that he maintained no critical distance with respect to the Soviet project. Yet in Ward's mind the logic was crystal clear: "*[T]he self-interest of the Soviet Union is more in the interest of world-wide democracy* than the self-interest of the British and American financial-imperialists."[50] A telling statement indeed.

As 1942 began, the Germans continued their advance against Russia, and they laid siege to Stalingrad in September. On January 9, Ward spoke at a Reading, Pennsylvania, church on "Soviet Democracy and American Ideals." "An anonymous source" sent an advertisement for the meeting to the FBI and penciled in, after Ward's name, the label, "Sabotager." An accompanying handwritten, anonymous note all but screamed:

> *Sabotage. Sabotage. Just got my hands on this card. Russian Jews are working against U.S. . . . The strikes are the beginning of Revolutionary War they predict. . . . I am American born.*[51]

During the war years, Ward's association with Jews were of special interest to federal authorities.

> *On April 20, 1945 Confidential Informant T-2 observed the subject entering the Temple Emanu-El located at 119 Tenafly Road, Englewood, New Jersey. A sign outside the temple indicated that the subject was to be a guest speaker and his topic was to be Soviet Democracy and American Ideals.*

> *Confidential Informant T-1 also reported that this meeting was attended by* RUTH DOBRER, *Bergen County, CPA President.*[52]

Anti-Semitism was thriving in the United States as well as in Germany.

Meanwhile, in the face of overwhelming German firepower, the Soviet resolve at Stalingrad was remarkable; the Germans were forced to fight both the Soviet army and the brutal Russian winter. In November a Soviet offensive broke the siege of Stalingrad, and by late January/early February 1943, German troops stationed around the city surrendered. For Ward this was confirmation of the payoff that comes when a society promotes solidarity and planning rather than greed and the chaos of market forces. His 1944 book, *The Soviet Spirit*, rehashed material dating back to his visit to the Soviet Union in the early thirties, but in Ward's mind the recent Soviet military triumph provided further verification of what he had observed in 1931–1932. The strength of Soviet resistance against the Nazi war machine was compelling evidence of socialism's success. Citing a Russian religious leader, Ward offered his readers his most evangelistic interpretation of the Soviet project: "Today, twenty-five years later, we see the face of the generation which has grown up in those years. It is the face of a true human. I repeat the universally known truth of the gospel: 'A good tree cannot bring forth evil fruit, neither can a corrupt tree bring forth good fruit. . . . Where-

fore by their fruits ye shall know them!'" (144). Borrowing another favorite quotation, Ward recalled Lincoln Steffens's exclamation during
one of the thirties pilgrimages to the Soviet Union: "I have seen the
future and it works" (10).

In 1942 Ward became a member of the board of contributing editors
for *New Masses,* a leftist journal often associated with communism. (For
the rest of his life most of his published writing would appear in leftist
and pro-Soviet journals that were generally out of the mainstream.) An
informant told the FBI that Ward was "*a suspicious character and deserved
watching,*" and the local police reported that "it was common gossip in
the vicinity that Dr. WARD was active in any and all Communist groups.
Further, that the subject had from time to time had meetings of women
at his home at which he lectured." Digging for scandal, FBI agents
interviewed the Wards' neighbors. One neighbor reported that

> *[T]here were many rumors about three or four years ago that Dr. WARD
> and his family were very Communistic and that it was known that Dr.
> WARD had made numerous trips to Russia. . . . [The person inter-
> viewed said] [T]he doctor and family had very strong Communist
> leanings, but that they were in no way disloyal to the United States. He
> advised that both WARD and his wife were buying a great number of
> war bonds and stamps, and he believed the son was a lieutenant in the
> U.S. Army.*[53]

Indeed, Lynd Ward was fulfilling his draft obligation by working on
gyroscopes in a nearby New Jersey bomb factory, and Harry was not
only buying war bonds, he was also serving as a community air-raid
warden.[54]

Despite the confidence expressed even by wary neighbors, the FBI
regarded Ward as a serious security risk. His passport was withdrawn in
1943. Federal agents inquired about his status at Union Seminary "under
a suitable pretext," reported the investigator. The bureau ran a credit
check. And eyebrows shot up when Ward's name was found in the address book of the well-known pro-Soviet activist Anna Louise Strong.
Moreover,

> *T-16 advised on May 5, 1944 that the subject was loyal to EARL
> BROWDER.*[55]

In view of Ward's influence by reason of his position at the Union Theological Seminary and also his cooperation with the Communist movement in this country, it is desired that his name be carried on the New York "key figure" list.[56]

He is considered a spokesman for the Communist Party and has made many speeches following the Party line.[57]

A memorandum from J. Edgar Hoover to the New York City FBI office indicated that a "security index card" on Harry Ward had been prepared at the bureau and the label "Communist" affixed to the subject's name.[58] An informant who was listed as working at a local post office provided reports on Ward's magazine subscriptions; these included the *Daily Worker*, a publication of the Communist Party. At some point in the forties,[59] an informant—apparently the wife of a close acquaintance— reported a private conversation in an automobile during which Harry turned to the folks sitting in the backseat and proclaimed, "I have become a Communist."[60]

Even observers who were less suspicious than the FBI would have wondered about Ward's communist ties, for in the 1940s he regularly gave speeches in support of Soviet causes and an American-Soviet partnership. He also delivered addresses on major public occasions for American communists and their allies. At the beginning of 1945 he spoke to a Madison Square Garden audience gathered to celebrate the contributions of Lenin. Ward spoke with great admiration of this Soviet leader, "the most creative statesman of our time, the one whose work will most affect the course of history." Harry fondly recalled meeting Lenin's widow many years earlier and her description of Lenin's "love for the people," and he compared Lenin's leadership to Abraham Lincoln's. He concluded his speech with evangelistic zeal: "His [Lenin's] spirit . . . now moves across all the seas, into every land. It stands beside, inspires, fights and works with all those men and women everywhere who seek more freedom, more comradeship and a nobler way of living for all mankind."[61]

From Ward's perspective the war years—which witnessed such developments as the American-Soviet alliance and a more closely managed U.S. economy—provided a teachable moment about the profit motive and the future of economic democracy in the United States. Ward had seen too much change in the world not to anticipate the drastic alterations of the postwar era: "The farm, the village, the town, the city, may look the same to the boys when they come back, but the people are not the same. . . . The women who have been taking on men's jobs and sharing men's dangers will not go back to a narrower world. After what the black people, the brown and yellow peoples have seen and done in this war, white supremacy cannot be maintained, neither here nor elsewhere in the world. . . . America will change after the war because America is changing in the war."[62]

The particular change that Ward understood to be inevitable and valuable was some form of socialism. His postwar article, "The Coming Struggle within the Victorious Nations," characterizes the war as the first stage of the battle between democratic and fascist forces. Of course democracy had prevailed on this occasion. Now it was time for the second contest between democracy and fascism, and this would take place within capitalist nations. Ward insists that at the practical level the question must be "What part will organized religion play in this great change?" For which side in the struggle will "preachers serve as chaplains"?[63] In his appeal to more secular audiences, he pointed out the convergence of the American dream of equality and Marxist analysis in the search for a classless society.[64]

As Ward passed seventy years of age, he took the last step in removing himself from major organizational leadership, retiring as MFSS secretary in 1944, a post he had held since before the First World War. He encouraged members to continue to make common cause with "like-minded" Christian folk to achieve "the needed combination of analysis and action."[65] And he continued to write a column, "Behind the Headlines," in the MFSS's *Social Questions Bulletin*. His zeal for social change had not diminished one whit.

These were crucial times, and Ward sometimes employed apocalyptic language to communicate the present dangers and opportunities. The previous year he had described the futility of the capitalist society, alluding to Jesus' parable of a house built upon sand: "[I]t was not built upon the rock. So in due time the day of disaster came, the day of idle capital, mass unemployment. Against these evils no remedies availed until there came the day of total war."[66] In 1945 he wrote "Judgment Day for Churches," in which he lamented the "[f]ailure by sincere and well-meaning religious leaders to carry conviction in their teachings[,] . . . leaving the people without a vital faith to carry them through the greatest crisis in history."[67] Sometimes Ward was even more pessimistic about the future of the church. During the war he had written: "The significant fact is that the center of spiritual gravity is now outside the churches. Social forces are at work pushing mankind up to a new level of life, draining the swamps, raising the valleys. They will go on working despite the ecclesiasts with or without the support of the preachers."[68] Similarly, Ward wrote about "Fascist Trends in American Churches."[69] Since the onset of the Vatican's cozy relationships with European fascist governments,[70] he had all but given up on Catholicism, and to him Protestantism seemed almost as culpable.

Still, his pragmatic streak would not allow him to abandon the Protestant ship. Not even the posturing of the burgeoning cold war could deflect Harry Ward from his efforts to create alliances with those he thought were currently out of touch. He continued to believe in the power of words. His voice and typewriter would not be silent, despite the increasingly dominant influence of Niebuhr's theology. Without naming his colleague, Ward went on the offensive against "these ideas [that] lead to an imperialist God and an anti-democratic church."[71] Just weeks after V-E Day, Ward lamented to his MFSS successor Jack McMichael what he saw as the prevailing winds of Protestant ethics: "Then as usual the whole business is settled by a phrase about God which is entirely congenial to fascist ideology. Whereas the vital issue is what kind of God and what relationship with Him will give unending power to the democratic struggle."[72]

9

In the Trenches with Jesus and Marx
1946–1966

The demand for an anti-communist statement is both a snare and an unethical position. What followers of Jesus have to do is to find out what common ground there is on which we can live in the same world with communism[,] not how to damn it. That only helps the enemies of all that Jesus stood for.
—Harry F. Ward to Jack McMichael, 20 June 1951

Marx [is] a fellow traveler with Jesus.
—Harry F. Ward, "Jesus and Marx"

ONCE THE WAR WAS OVER, labor set out to regain lost ground. Major strikes proliferated, especially over wages. Less than ten weeks after the Japanese formally surrendered, the United Auto Workers struck in Detroit. By January of 1946 workers in forty-four states were on strike against Western Electric, and strikes had shut down U.S. steel plants. Over 400,000 United Mine Workers walked off the job in April, and in May the nation's trains came to a standstill due to strikes.

Though armed conflicts in Europe and the Pacific were at an end, international unrest continued. Mao Tse-tung's communist forces persisted in their fight against Chiang Kai'shek's army. The Soviets and the Western allies postured in Europe, laying the groundwork for what would come to be known as the "cold war." In early March of 1946 Winston Churchill proclaimed that an "iron curtain" was descending on Europe. President Truman's secretary of commerce, Henry Wallace, criticized the president's dangerously antagonistic stance toward the Soviets, calling instead for "friendly, peaceful competition." Wallace was forced to resign. Korea was also in the news with American forces stationed in the south and Soviet forces in the north. Secretary of State Dean Acheson proclaimed that the United States intended to stay in Korea until the country was united by a free government.

Still on wartime alert, the FBI continued its regular surveillance of troublemakers. Three FBI agents attended a meeting in Boston, 10 June 1946, at which Harry Ward was the principal speaker.

The meeting was to protest the labor policies of the Truman Administration and to enlist support for the National Maritime Union in its negotiations with ship owners. . . . The subject's speech was very forcefully delivered, and he elicited prolonged and vociferous applause from the audience.[1]

Ward's speaking schedule was interrupted, as always, by summers in Canada, which continued to be cherished times in his life. He could spend time with his family, including granddaughters Nanda and Robin, and provide them with running commentary on world events. He also frequently offered advice on how to perform the most mundane chores. At camp, Harry was beyond the range of direct surveillance, but the FBI kept track of him:

General inquiry in the neighborhood . . . indicated that the WARDs still reside at this address but during the summer months are vacationing at a cabin owned by them in Canada.[2]

Camp always included time with George Coe, a best friend who continued to be Harry's sounding board. At the beginning of the year Harry wrote Coe and very uncharacteristically expressed his personal affection for Coe's "long true and tried friendship." He also included a report about his ongoing work and an assessment of the challenge ahead. Perhaps no statement expresses better the mind-set of this holy warrior: "Our labor and economic policy at home is weak and dangerous, our foreign policy a compound of ignorance, silliness and wickedness. So we are in a beautiful mess and the fighting is going to be good all along the line."[3] The cold war had begun in earnest, and Harry Ward was ready for the battles, as noted by the FBI:

████████████ *advised that the subject made his speech on May 5, 1947 before the Karl Marx Society, NYC, on the "Ethics of Marxism."*[4]

Unknown to most except his family and closest friends, Ward had begun working on a manuscript he hoped would be his ultimate published legacy. Titled "Jesus and Marx," the manuscript is a spirited and heavily documented defense of the necessary compatibility of Marxists and the followers of the religion of Jesus. An important reference point in this work is Reinhold Niebuhr, the person who had come to dominate conversations about Protestant ethics in America and even Western Europe. The notes and clippings gathered for the "Jesus and Marx" project reveal that part of Ward's agenda was to make his best case against the increasingly popular Niebuhrian outlook—though traditional Union protocol and probably Ward's own grudging respect for his former colleague prevented a direct assault.

Ward and Niebuhr had only crossed swords in print once, in 1947, and that exchange was polite enough. In his copy of an article Niebuhr had written—"Our Relations to Russia"—Ward underlined Niebuhr's use of the terms "power" and "order," for this is where they parted company theoretically and strategically. (Interestingly enough, this essay was one in which Niebuhr encouraged positive working relationships between the U.S. and the U.S.S.R. He also insisted that both nations were equally self-righteous and self-deceiving.[5]) Harry penned an article with the same title as Niebuhr's, and it was published in the *Witness*.

In this essay Ward expressed his disappointment with Niebuhr's description of the competing economic systems: "free enterprise," he felt, was hardly an appropriate label for monopolistic capitalism. Niebuhr needed to recognize that this form of capitalism had no interest in peace with a competing system that threatened its well-being. Nor was Niebuhr helpful when he suggested that the West was "slightly less self-righteous" than the Soviet Union; to Ward, it seemed that Niebuhr had not taken into account the U.S. track record in developing atomic weapons. And how could the West protest Eastern European elections "after our record in the deep South, our behaviour in Korea, our complicity in Greece?" The common struggle for the U.S. and the Soviet Union, therefore, must be "the overcoming of anti-democratic tendencies on both sides."[6]

Harry continued to justify Soviet repression as emergency measures and ultimately not significant, since these measures—even the excesses—neither squelched the "overall movement toward more democracy" nor impeded the final withering away of the state. Furthermore, he continued to place great faith in the Communist Party's self-purging, despite the incredible violence that accompanied it. Paradoxically, Ward saw this self-purgation as the key to preventing abuse in a one-party society, and he persevered in his reliance on the democratic rhetoric of the Soviet constitution. For a person who talked so much about how "facts" proved theory, Ward demonstrated—even in "Our Relations to Russia"—that he would not be swayed from his assumptions about the fundamental integrity of the "Soviet view of the state" and the nature of the Soviet Communist Party. In his judgment, by their very nature neither institution could be totalitarian (whatever the facts!).

Early drafts of "Jesus and Marx" contain several explicit references to Niebuhr, though he is never named. For example, Ward refers to "preachers [who] proclaim that communism is more dangerous than fascism because it is a 'Christian heresy' whereas fascism and Nazism are 'anti-Christian paganism.'"[7] Ward takes on the Niebuhrian charge that Marxism is utopian, answering with material from Marx, Engels, and Lenin. Then Ward cites Niebuhr's statement (unattributed): "Communism justifies its cynical policies by the utopian hope that the revolutionary use of force will create a society in which no force will be necessary." Ward's rejoinder is biting, even acerbic: "Here we meet the same mental process that characterizes our anticommunist investigating committees." On scraps of paper that include Niebuhr's name and Niebuhr's description of Marxism as "Christian heresy," Ward scribbled things like "Not Jesus' way with publicans and sinners" and "That could only be written by one who had not examined the sources." In newspaper clippings Niebuhr's statements about communism are usually circled.

In later drafts there is little evidence of this acrimony. However, in the final draft there are veiled references to Niebuhr's views—for example, "A misinterpretation of the Marxist position on the class struggle widely current in religious circles is that it merely seeks to bring another class to power" (45). Ward resented Niebuhr's assessment "that when all 'socially controllable inequalities have been removed, there will always remain sources of conflict that root in the sinfulness and greed of the human heart.'" One can almost see Harry's eyes roll as he types his response: "Of course. Those who know this should also know that life, like realistic religion, is a constant 'going on to perfection,' not an arrival at a perfect state . . . Certainly history will find no excuse for them if they use their knowledge of the permanency of the struggle against evil in human life to provide an excuse for keeping out of the struggle against the root of evil in our present economic system" (68).

By the spring of 1947 President Harry Truman had asked Congress for four hundred million dollars to stop the spread of communism in Greece and Turkey, and by summer George Kennan's policy of "containment" was being touted as the most promising anticommunist strategy. Fears of communism extended to the home front, and in late March 1947 President Truman called for a loyalty program among government employees that was intended to root out any civil service worker whose loyalty was in "reasonable doubt." A few months later the House Un-American Activities Committee was in high gear, investigating the Hollywood film industry. By mid-1948 the Russians and the Americans were at a standoff in Berlin as well as Korea. And in early August Alger Hiss, a high-ranking official in the U.S. State Department, was accused of being a spy and Communist Party member. The cold war was heating up both at home and abroad.

Yet Harry Ward remained undeterred in his spirited defense of the Soviet Union. In response to the charge that the Soviets were imperialists, he admitted that "the Soviet government has its inescapable share of the original sin of nature. But that does not consist of the lust for empire, nor the desire to dominate other peoples."[8] As to the characterization of communist countries as police states, Ward conceded that the Soviet Union was a temporary police state in earlier years, but he asserted that this was out of necessity, given the forces of counterrevolution. Though some remnants of this police-state structure still existed, Ward insisted that great progress was being made toward their abolition. Then he turned the tables on the Soviet detractors, calling attention to police-state conditions in the United States: people who were labeled "subversive" were in danger of losing their jobs; the FBI was engaged in large-scale spying on American citizens; and violence against dissidents was permitted—even encouraged.[9] Ward stayed on the offensive, arguing that "the socialist era of history has begun." Opponents to this change are "trying to stop more than the Soviet Union"; they are "endeavoring to stop the course of history . . . something which cannot be done for long."[10]

Ward turned up the heat, especially on "liberals" who had formerly been allies in progressive causes; the cold war had infected everything, including liberal Protestantism. He drew a line in the sand, distinguishing between "liberals and radicals," especially with respect to their responses to the prevailing economic system. "Liberals would remove its evils by education and reform," whereas radicals call for changing "its nature by replacing the struggle for profit with democratic planning for social ends." Moreover, the radicals "believe in regeneration as well as education and reform." These two camps must come together now, as "united reaction rallies its forces for Armageddon." Ward was fed up with liberals who made outrageous accusations (à la Niebuhr) about radicals' naivete concerning Soviet behavior or their willingness to turn a blind eye to evil. Soviet sympathizers recognized that there were problems, said Ward, but they also understood that "the establishment of the first socialist state is an epochal event in the development of democracy." Energy should be focused on encouraging "the Soviet people to succeed in overcoming the evil that is present in every form of the state. . . . The point is does it [evil] recur less frequently and in lesser degree?"[11] Ward reminded his religious audience that the Soviet Union was not the only sinner on the international scene. "No voice from the headquarters of our religion reminds them [the West] of the mote and the beam, the first stone."[12] It was time for the church "to decide, as Jesus had to in the wilderness, on which side it is going to stand—with the needy people or those in high places."[13]

While Europe was dividing into two camps, it seemed that all of America was committed to the Truman Doctrine designed to contain communism. Yet Ward continued to hail the developing democracy of the Soviet Union in language dear to Methodism, insisting that Soviets recognized the dangerous concentration of power in their government bureaucracy: "Like all Marxists they [the Soviets] regard democracy as a developing process, in religious terms a 'going on to perfection.'"[14] His publicly stated positions continued to be reported to the FBI.

> *Confidential Informant T-6 advised that National Conference on American Policy in Greece was held on June 6 and 7, 1948 at the Capital Hotel, New York City. Doctor* HARRY F. WARD, *one of the speakers, attacked the Truman Doctrine and stated that "our Government is starting a Fascist Government in Greece against the Partisans who fought the German invaders. We demand the American Government withdraw its forces from Greece."*[15]

The chickens came home to roost when Gordon Ward found that his father's controversial politics threatened his own career. In a July 1948 letter to his father he noted with relief that Harry had postponed a trip to Poland and Russia: "We believe very strongly that it would have disastrous consequences for the whole family if you were to go to Moscow as long as the present anti-communist hysteria prevails. It is staggering how many normally reasonable people these days accept the idea of guilt by association."[16] Gordon wrote his brother and sister about the dilemma: "It is difficult to know how to convince Dad of the wisdom of being discreet in accepting speaking engagements. They are what get the publicity that stirs things up. . . . There is no need for you folks to worry about us down here. We will get along ok until Dad gets in the papers and magazines again."[17] "Here" was Blacksburg, Virginia, where Gordon was teaching at Virginia Tech.

In late December 1949 Harry spoke to a New York City symposium sponsored by the National Council of American-Soviet Friendship that served as a celebration of Stalin's seventieth birthday. His speech was titled "Stalin, the Man and His Work." Appearances such as this were duly noted by the FBI.

> *I have observed* DR. WARD *at the ninth floor of the Communist Party Headquarters, reporting to the Politburo as a member of the Communist Party. This took place during the early 1940's, and on several other succeeding occasions I have met* DR. WARD *in conference with*

EARL BROWDER and with sub-committees of the Politburo, always as
a Communist. Up to the time that I left the Party in 1945, DR. WARD
was known to me as a Communist, both through my personal conver-
sation with him and from official advice received from ███████████.[18]

Harry Ward's adversaries probably were not aware that he had finished his "Jesus and Marx" manuscript and submitted it for publication,
though he continued to revise the text in light of new developments.[19]
Harper and Row was the first of several publishers to reject it. In the
McCarthy-Hoover days of the late forties and early fifties, publishers
judged that this was hardly a book for the hour. Not only did Ward seek
to demonstrate the compatibility of Karl Marx's ideas with the teachings of Jesus, he held up the Soviet Union, including Josef Stalin, as a
paradigm of the world's future.

The year 1949 marked Harry and Daisy's fiftieth wedding anniversary. Daisy remained steadfast in her support of her husband's out-
spokenness and his convictions. Following some disappointing audiences
at Harry's public lectures, she wrote to a friend,

> One feels heavy with responsibility these days, when there are
> few voices and few opportunities to be heard. I marvel at Harry's
> unswerving devotion to what his informed judgment sees [as] the
> path ahead. I wouldn't have him deviate one inch from it.
>
> It is a comfort that our children understand and appreciate what
> he does.[20]

Actually Gordon Ward was not so understanding as his mother
imagined, especially when he did not receive tenure at Virginia Tech—
largely because of his father's reputation. He left his post there and took
a government job in association with the American Army's occupation
of Japan; Gordon was an agricultural specialist so, as jobs go, his assign-
ment was not politically sensitive. Nevertheless, during the cold war
witch-hunts, everyone was vulnerable, especially government employees.
In early 1950 he asked that his father stop sending him journals like the
Worker and the *National Guardian,* both of which had communist connections. Apparently Gordon was concerned that his mail was being
screened, for he insisted that his father remove identification from clip-

pings taken from radical journals.[21] In the spring of 1950 Gordon also asked to be deleted from the subscriber list of the MFSA's *Social Questions Bulletin* "because of the anti-communist hysteria and the wild charges that have been made against the MFSA."[22] Not long after that word came that Harry was to join the *Daily Worker*'s board of directors. Gordon's frustrations exploded in a letter to his brother and sister-in-law: "As I wrote to Dad yesterday, I can see only ill effects and harm to us all without any offsetting benefits to anyone if Dad were to have anything to do with the DW. . . . I can see no gain for Dad fronting for the commies on the board of directors and everything to lose. Serving on the board of directors would be taken as positive proof of his being a communist."[23]

Harry Ward recognized that he and like-minded folk were under surveillance:

> ▉▉▉▉▉▉▉ *advised that Rev. Harry F. Ward, in speaking at the Community Church, Boston, Mass., on 12/17/50, urged the use of underground hand presses to print real news that regular newspapers would not print. He also urged small meetings in each others homes, because "the FBI can't attend all these meetings yet."*[24]

In Ward's judgment, these were dangerous times. In an article titled "Back to Barbarism?" he worried aloud about the technological devastation in the hands of the "scientific savage."[25] As the horrors of Nazi Germany's genocidal juggernaut became public knowledge, Ward lamented "the increase of anti-Semitic, anti-Negro, and anti-democratic, fascist, tendencies in a 'class-riven society,'" and he blamed these tendencies primarily on the capitalist system. "The capitalist economy operates on the basis of functional inequality. That is the way it gets its leadership. It raises the strong to power. It keeps the Jew, the Negro, woman, most of the children of the low income group in a subordinate position."[26]

During this period Ward worked with the Civil Rights Congress, a leftist civil rights organization, and in 1950 he was named its national honorary co-chair, along with Benjamin Mays, president of Morehouse College. When the Department of Justice sought to prosecute W. E. B. DuBois—at eighty-three a respected scholar, the cofounder of the NAACP, and the patriarch of many black American freedom efforts, including the Civil Rights Congress—under the McCarran Act for his leadership in the Peace Information Center, Ward was not afraid to point an accusing finger. "To the officers, the prosecutor and the court, this was just routine. To an astonished world it was a revelation of the barbarism of United States justice." Because of the parallels to Nazi tactics and the obvious racism of the case, Ward issued a call to arms: "This prosecution is warning all unpopular minorities that the day has come when they have to stand up and live together or crawl on their knees and die together in concentration camps."[27]

Over the subsequent months Gordon Ward pointed out in correspondence to his father the specific excesses of North Korea and the Soviet Union. Harry did not acknowledge these to his eldest child, but to Lynd he lamented Moscow's blunders and its "desire for monolithic organization which means concentration of power of course and the [word indecipherable] party democracy corrective isn't working."[28] Would that Harry Ward had made such statements in the public realm so as to provide some credible evidence of the soundness of his critical faculties. He refused, for as he reminded his MFSA successor Jack McMichael: "The demand for an anti-communist statement is both a snare and an unethical position. What followers of Jesus have to do is to find out what common ground there is on which we can live in the same world with communism[,] not how to damn it. That only helps the enemies of all that Jesus stood for."[29] If one holds a dualistic worldview, one must stand by allies, no matter what their transgressions. Tragically, in many eyes this was the undoing of Ward's credibility.

Though Harry enjoyed a good fight and though he had persevered through some controversial times over the decades, the hysteria of the McCarthy era stunned even him: "This nation is literally going crazy, with a fear mania induced by propaganda. Last night a 350 million defense program announced for New York City—mostly underground shelters. More jobs for the boys and more gravy for the right contractors. Making even first grade kids lie down and crawl, and teaching them all to obey commands and be little yes men and women."[30]

More grief came when Ward heard from California that his longtime best friend, George Coe, had died on 9 November 1951 at the age of eighty-nine. Ward had many fond memories of this friend of half a century, but perhaps most vivid in his mind were those summers in camp, when around the campfire or in a boat on the lake their moral passions flamed brightly in conversation with one another: "It was one of the delights of our years together, around the campfire or in front of the blazing hearth, to hear the pungent words with which he would strip the cloak of hypocrisy from the Pharisees of our day. The smear tactics of our red baiters and witch hunters, the threats of our fascist fanatics, never drove him to cover."[31]

Harry remembered George Coe as not only a worthy colleague, fellow camper, and stimulating conversationalist, but more importantly as "a never failing friend."[32] In 1915 Coe had written an article, "On Having Friends: A Study in Social Values," for the *Journal of Philosophy, Psychology and Scientific Methods*. Though scholarly and thought provoking, the article is also illuminating in its expression of the richness of the Ward-Coe friendship, even in its early days. (By 1915 they had known each other about twenty years.) The article distinguishes carefully between the concept of "friendship" and the concrete experience of "having a friend." Coe found that the difference could be best explained with an illustration obviously taken from Canadian summers at Lonely Lake: "My friend and I, chatting by an open fire, now and then fall into the silence, well recognized in the literature of affection, in which each friend 'has' the other in an intimacy closer than conversation."[33]

In the last years of his life Coe continued to discuss Marxist philosophy with Ward in their correspondence. Though they did not see eye to eye on everything, Ward felt confirmed in his own commitment by Coe's observation that "what is splitting the world is the ethical core of Marxism, not the political system that has developed in Russia. . . . Marx raised the fundamental ethical questions whether it is humane or just that a man's sustenance should depend upon his contributing by his labor to the private profit of another."[34] Such defense of Marxism and the Soviet Union was a moral cause for which Harry was fighting, and in Coe he found a like-minded general who "never counselled retreat."[35] And yet there continued to be casualties, even close to home.

In December of 1951 Gordon wrote to his brother and sister-in-law that he could not be employed by the U.S. government or even, perhaps, by the U.N. because of "my connections with Dad and with six organi-

George Albert Coe and Daisy Ward on one of the benches surrounding the Coe campfire pit where Lonely Lake families gathered on Sunday evenings. Coe, Ward's "never failing friend," and Daisy, Harry's life partner, were Harry's closest confidants. (Courtesy of Nanda Ward and Robin Ward Savage)

zations later included in the Attorney General's list of Communist organizations."[36] It was time to confront his father, and so he wrote to him. Muriel watched as her father opened Gordon's letter, started reading it, and then became obviously agitated, telling Daisy and Muriel that the letter was too long to read out loud. "You can read it to yourselves later!"[37] Harry read to himself his eldest's impassioned words.

I feel impelled to remind you that one factor in the Army['s] consideration of my loyalty was my guilt by association with you on account of your activities with communist organizations. I realize that the damage was done on the basis of the past and part of it years ago when we had no inkling of what was in store for us. But any continuation of associations with Communists and communist organizations by you is going to work further damage to my professional career. So I ask your consideration when you get further requests for speaking and writing from the Communists and their organizations and fronts.[38]

Gordon also tried to point out the benefits of this approach for his father's goals. "Only those who are above suspicion can attract any following for the vital campaign to put men of broad vision and character into power in Washington."[39] Harry was not persuaded, and after reading the letter, he growled to Daisy and Muriel, "It's all about how I can get the Communist taint off of me and how I can get a united front started without the Communists."[40]

In his next letter to Gordon, Harry did not even allude to the effects of his activities on his son's career. Gordon was stunned and mentioned this to his brother Lynd.[41] Though Lynd talked with his father about the matter, and though Harry assured Gordon that he would not accept speaking engagements or become involved in activities that might "endanger" Gordon's situation, the old warrior's behavior belied these assurances; he continued to speak on behalf of radical causes. Gordon was exasperated and wrote Lynd: "I have no desire to cause tension in the family and am not going to keep harping on the matter. I have simply used the recent action against me to try to impress on Dad that he endangers all his children's livelihood when he associates with communists and fellow travelers in organizations."[42] In a letter written the same day to his sister Muriel, Gordon lamented that "Dad has never acknowledged to me any recognition that his activities are part of my problem."[43] Muriel assured her brother that their father was "deeply concerned"; she probably recognized how difficult it was for this Victorian Englishman to express his feelings even to family members. Gordon admitted how difficult it would be for Harry to withdraw from his cherished causes: "I know he feels lost when he is not active."[44]

That spring Gordon described to his parents how he had missed out on a U.S. Department of Agriculture job in Lebanon. "The doors of possible government employment are shut tight." He wondered if he would need to go into farming "if this loyalty business keeps spreading like a strangling insidious vapor."[45] Meanwhile Harry continued to be involved in controversial activities—e.g., addressing a November meeting of the (Ethel and Julius) Rosenberg Committee for Clemency. In letters to his parents well into 1953, Gordon continued to discuss his career problems and comment sharply about communist abuses in North Korea, China, and the Soviet Union. Still, a Father's Day letter that year was full of recollections of father-son canoe trips in the Canadian wilds as well as admiration for Harry's work on civil liberties and his "application of the teachings of Jesus to socio-economic activities, especially in leadership of the MFSA."[46] No records survive of Harry's responses, but someone was privy to these family exchanges:

> *Newark Confidential Informant T-27 advised that subject had denied to his son, GORDON HUGH WARD, that he was a member of the CP. The subject had also told his son that he had never been a member of the CP, according to the informant.*[47]

Trouble was brewing, and the Ward family correspondence quickly became dominated by the House Un-American Activities Committee (HUAC) instead of Gordon's problems. Witnesses testifying before HUAC named Harry Ward as a key player in the communist conspiracy to overthrow America. One witness described him as "the Red dean of the Communist party in the religious field. . . . [T]he chief architect for Communist infiltration and subversion in the religious field."[48] Jack McMichael, Harry's MFSA successor, became a target of HUAC hearings in July of 1953. That same month a HUAC witness fingered Harry Ward as a member of the Communist Party. The HUAC report on Ward spans almost nine pages of single-space type and lists various events, organizations, sponsorships, petitions, articles, and books that might be construed as connecting him to communists or communist "fronts."

Harry told his family that he intended to demand a hearing before HUAC, but Lynd advised against such exposure. On 11 September 1935, Ward released a statement to the press asserting that he was not a member of the Communist Party as charged by HUAC: "My judgment and actions concerning political and economic issues are derived from the basic ethical principles of the religion of Jesus, of which I am minister and teacher. At the beginning of my ministry I made the decision that it required complete independence of all political parties, and I have never deviated from this position."[49] The following day he sent the press release and a letter to his accusers in Congress, with a forceful accusation of his own: "By attempting to spread into the churches fear, prejudice and hate, you are weakening the power of Protestant conscience and intimidating the voice of its pulpit." This not only violated the Constitution, Ward argued, it also stifled all voices of religious dissent—Jews and Catholics as well as Protestants.[50]

Concurrently, Ward and his MFSA allies were getting less and less support from the Methodist Church; this is not surprising in light of the anticommunist hysteria and the perception that Ward's successor, Jack McMichael, was too high-handed. There was an abundance of negative publicity. Widely read articles in Scripps-Howard newspapers and *Readers Digest* accused the MFSA of communist infiltration. Most of the influential Methodist leadership had exited the organization in the late 1940s and early 1950s, and in 1952 the Methodist General Conference formally dissociated itself from the MFSA and set up its own Board of Social and Economic Relations. The General Conference asked the MFSA to drop "Methodist" from its name and altered the "Social Creed" by removing the line, "subordination of the profit motive to the creative and cooperative spirit."[51] In 1953 the Committee for Preservation of Methodism, Houston, Texas, published a booklet titled "Is There a Pink Fringe in the Methodist Church?" In this booklet Ward was identified as a member of over fifty communist front groups.

But perhaps most unpleasant of all that year was the release of Ralph Roy's *Apostles of Discord*, which described Harry Ward and his MFSA successor Jack McMichael in HUAC-like terms: "While they are both intelligent and sincere, they follow faithfully the ideological routes charted by the Kremlin, blind alleys and all. . . . Ward and McMichael sought to steer the Methodist Federation straight along the narrow Communist Party line . . . [lest] they should permit [the *Social Questions Bulletin*] to deviate from the Moscow version of 'truth.'"[52] Harry Ward was infuriated not only by specific statements but by the very focus of the book. Roy seemed to portray right-wing and left-wing forces in the contemporary church as equally harmful.

Since Roy was a Union Theological Seminary graduate, Ward protested to Union colleagues John Bennett and Reinhold Niebuhr. Their responses must have tasted bitter in Harry's mouth. Bennett, Ward's successor and Roy's dissertation supervisor, was not sympathetic to Ward's protests; indeed, he expressed confidence in Roy's "competence and his fairness." He insisted that Roy had not labeled Ward a Communist Party member but rather had demonstrated the "remarkable consistency" of Ward's support of the communist line and Ward's failure to balance this commitment "with discriminating criticisms concerning Communism in Russia or elsewhere." The final paragraph of Bennett's response is forthright:

> It is very distasteful to me to write in this way and to reflect upon the extent to which you and I have had to take different paths in recent years. I still honor the things which you represented and which you did in an earlier period and am puzzled about what seems to me to be your lack of critical attitude toward policies and behavior of Communist governments and parties. I personally accept your own statement that you were never a member of the Communist Party, but membership in the party seems to be far less important that what one does about particular decisions which involve aid to, or discouragement of the Communist movement.[53]

Niebuhr's response was more indirect. He granted that the book was unfair in its coupling of groups of the right and left, though he insisted that Roy "specifically refuted that the left-wing groups were on a par with the hate groups of the right." Yet Niebuhr insisted that he agreed with Roy "that many of the groups on the left . . . were so committed to a political cause that they judged all things from the standpoint of that cause rather than from the standpoint of their Christian faith." He concluded with a personal note of sympathy for his former colleague: "I am sorry to hear that you must again appear before the House Un-American Activities Committee. I wish you could have been spared this ordeal."[54]

Ward was spared the ordeal, but he was still boiling about the Roy book. Communication with Bennett continued on the matter, with Bennett trying to smooth the ruffled feathers and assure Ward that the young scholar was fair-minded.[55] The old warrior was hardly pacified, and he continued to try to set the record straight. He wrote a response to Roy's book, though there is no record that it was ever published. It is clear that Ward was most offended by the accusation that he was somehow beholden to a party line, communist or whatever.

[T]he only line that I have followed is one that I discovered for myself in my student days before there was a communist party in the U.S. or Russia. That is the line that Jesus took up from the social sections of the Hebrew law. . . . If this line touches the communist line at any points it is not because either the followers of Marx or those of Jesus have so willed but by the operation of the same historic force. What those who cry fellow traveller and party line at the religious left need to do is to show, if they can, where the interpretation and attempted development of the religion of Jesus is incorrect.[56]

In an October 1955 letter Ward accused Roy of more than careless errors: "It was a vicious and intentional lie."[57] Six months later Harry was writing to Methodist officials about Roy's ministerial status, questioning his advancement in light of the injury he had done to fellow ministers.[58] The incident remained a bitterly painful one for Harry, for he now felt betrayed by the seminary. From then on he would have little to do with Union Theological Seminary.

Ward's reaction to attacks against himself and other left-leaning clergy during the McCarthy years were expressed in more than letters and manuscripts. For example, he served as an active consultant to the Religious Freedom Committee, an organization particularly devoted to defending ministers who were being attacked in the communist witch-hunt.

Though Harry did not have to testify before HUAC in 1953, Jack McMichael did. This was a difficult experience, for Ward as well as for McMichael, especially because it followed the HUAC appearance of G. Bromley Oxnam, the former Boston University student and baby-sitter for Harry's children. Oxnam was now a prominent Methodist bishop and had been counted among Ward's allies. Though Oxnam did not cave in to HUAC—in fact, he stood up to them with articulate force and courage—he specifically distanced himself from Ward and his ilk.[59] This was not easy for Harry to bear.

The year brought further disappointment as another publisher rejected Ward's thoroughly revised "Jesus and Marx" manuscript. The long manuscript had become Ward's comprehensive apologia for Marxism in at least four ways. In it he: (1) attempts to clear up common misunderstandings of Marxist logic (e.g., by explicating what is meant by "materialism"); (2) introduces the reader to a wide range of Marxist writings; (3) demonstrates Marxism's promise as realized in the Soviet Union, China, and the "New Democracies" of Eastern Europe; and (4) sets forth the complementary natures of Marxism and the religion of Jesus.

Though Ward was repeating here themes that recur throughout his writings over the last two decades, he had never drawn together in a single book his years of reading in Marxist texts. Through the use of numerous lengthy quotations of primary sources, he sought to introduce his readers to Marxist philosophy and practice. The reader encounters not only the published works of Marx and Engels—including the *Economic and Philosophical Manuscripts* of the young Marx as well as "The Communist Manifesto" and *Capital*—but also their correspondence, the works of Lenin, speeches and essays by other communist leaders, and the writings of numerous other Marxist authors and interpreters.

Despite the fact that the revised manuscript dates from the early 1950s, Ward includes—apparently without flinching—more than a few sources by and about Stalin. Perhaps here we see best the sort of uncritical doublespeak to which Ward allowed himself to give blessing. One example of this is a clever rationalization by Stalin on repression in the name of democracy: "Under the dictatorship of the working class, democracy is *workers'* democracy, the democracy of the exploited majority, based upon the restriction of the rights of the exploiting minority and directed against this minority" (87).[60] Moreover, Ward could argue that "The compulsion to develop the force and violence of state power against outside threats keeps its repressive functions alive beyond their due time. The ups and downs of civil liberties in the Soviet Union coincide with peaceful or warlike relations abroad" (91). The blame always seemed to lie elsewhere.

Revelations about Stalin's murderous rampages against "counterrevolutionaries" apparently did have some impact on Ward. In the final version of the "Jesus and Marx" manuscript, certain passages from later drafts have disappeared—e.g., "Stalin, next to Lenin the most influential disciple of Marx."[61] Still, there is precious little evidence that Ward was carefully scrutinizing the unsettling turn of events in the Soviet Union. When these matters arise he quickly reverts to the theoretical. Soft questions are pondered; no difficult conclusions are entertained. For example, in the midst of a section in which he heavily quotes Stalin on how dictatorship necessarily restricts the freedoms of some persons in order to realize the well-being of the many, Ward rather lamely suggests: "For those who believe that the principles of Jesus require the democratic way of life[,] the moral question is whether restrictions and repressions go beyond what is necessary to protect the new order from violent overthrow and its economic development from sabotage."[62]

From Ward's background notes for this manuscript, it is clear that friendly critics had encouraged him to focus primarily on the writings of Marx and Engels, but he concluded that a theoretical approach was inadequate—that the experiences of socialist countries must be part of the argument. The problem, of course, was that his "facts," as he relentlessly labeled them through the decades, were based on extrapolations of his 1931–32 experiences, reports from folk with similar pro-Soviet sympathies, and official documents promulgated by Soviet and Eastern European leaders. Coupled with these "facts" was his persistent refusal to concede the mountain of damning evidence that had accumulated against the Soviet system. Whatever his private feelings, he would not betray an ally in public. In his dualistic worldview, the historical examples of the trajectory toward hope—socialism—must be publicly supported without reserve. Never give aid and comfort to the enemy. "[T]here is only one highway into the more abundant life for all peoples" (281).

The manuscript also represents Harry Ward's grandiose effort to argue the *moral case* for Marxists and followers of the religion of Jesus to join forces to achieve their commonly desired goal: a just democratic order, with a planned economy in the hands of the people. As he often insisted, Marxism and the religion of Jesus represent the best of science and idealism, respectively. Their convergence means that "[t]echnical necessity and moral judgement unite, economic and spiritual need join, in proclaiming that the end of an era has come, the transition to another stage of human living has begun" (167).

What sets the "Jesus and Marx" manuscript apart from Ward's other writings (in addition to its lengthy engagement with Marxist primary texts) is its meticulous comparison of Jesus of Nazareth and Karl Marx as historic figures and as representatives of significant historical movements. Among the *many* similarities Ward uncovers between these two men is a "moral indignation" consonant with their Jewish heritage. As true prophets, both men identified with the oppressed. Both knew poverty firsthand, and their ideas were grounded in the situation of the workers. Both were dangerous to the status quo of their times. Both called for revolutionary changes in human life and pronounced judgment on those who would not follow the new courses for humanity they advocated. They sought the same end for humanity, argues Ward, whether it is described as a classless society or the brotherhood of humanity. They firmly believed in the possibilities of humankind and thus tenaciously held on to their conviction that their causes were invincible. Because neither viewed humans in the abstract, they linked personal ethics with social morality. The vision that they shared "makes Marx a fellow traveler with Jesus" (206).

While the similarities between the two great men are many, there are some important differences as well, Ward notes, especially with respect to the issue of the existence of God. Marx was an ethical humanist, and Jesus advocated an ethical religion with an ethical God, yet Ward does not believe this difference will keep their adherents from joining forces; it is a legitimate issue that followers of Jesus and followers of Marx can pursue in dialogue. One of the obvious goals of the manuscript is to demonstrate the common ground that can enable this dialogue to yield common action.

On the question of God, Ward follows a theological line he pursued most of his adult life: God is neither a transcendent, autocratic being nor a mental concept. Rather, the God of the Judeo-Christian heritage is "a personalized spiritual force requiring a certain way of living"; God is an ethical God (212). The deity whose worship is an opiate of the people is not the God of the religion of Jesus; the religion of Jesus does not believe in a God of the status quo. Ward points out certain parallel ideas on the Marxist side: "From the same source, regardless of whether they call it

God, or laws of motion in history, nature and the mind, there emerge the same categorical moral imperatives for all life" (214). Living under the ominous cloud of nuclear weapons, such possibilities for common ground cannot be ignored, argues Ward. Furthermore, he asserts that it is foolhardy for Marxists to oppose belief in an ethical God if that belief encourages people to pursue the course proposed by Marxism. This ethical God is not the imperialist God promulgated by the state churches of Europe, although, Ward insists, this concept of God is the backdrop against which one should evaluate the traditional Marxist rejection of religion.

While it is clear that Ward rejects the church's exaltation of the man from Nazareth to divine being, he does think that Christians and Marxists ought to give Jesus a closer look. Marxists need to see the significant role of Jesus in the evolving history of human morality: "Jesus was something more than a teacher of ethics. He was the voice of ethical religion," which promoted ideals central to the Marxist vision (209). Addressing Christians, Ward claims that Jesus had more in common with Marx than with Plato or Aristotle—the two men whose philosophical frameworks were appropriated by Christian theologians. What Marx offers to Christians (and liberal Protestants are obviously Ward's primary audience for this manuscript) is an invaluable economic analysis to complement the moral values of the religion of Jesus. Not only are Jesus and Marx compatible, they represent fundamental components of humanity's future.

At points such as these Ward typically turns poetic, which provides quite a contrast to the pages and pages of his detailed discussion of Marxist terminology and citations of Marxist sources. The book's conclusion reads like the end of one of Ward's stirring speeches: "[Behind science and religion's] joint actions to bring the life more abundant to mankind is belief in the possibilities of human living that is justified by the long course of human history and supported by the moral law of the universe" (291–92).

The problem was that Harry Ward was allowing himself to be used by persons who were not sympathetic to his eloquently expressed aspirations. Reinhold Niebuhr diagnosed the issue astutely: "The realities of Communist politics are in such vivid contrast to the moral motives for original allegiance that those converts who have not broken with Communism have become more and more pathetic in seeking to cover their mistaken loyalty with ever more implausible interpretations of present realities."[63] No doubt Niebuhr had persons like his former colleague specifically in mind when he wrote this, for clearly Harry was driven by moral motives. Ward was no armchair Stalinist who simply found the Soviet system logically or fashionably promising. As he would later say, "No 'thorough-going Marxist' [as he had been labeled] would be trying to reconcile the truth in the Bible with anything; neither would he be combining idealism with anything; and certainly he would not be looking upon events in the Soviet Union as an experiment in Christianity."[64] Yet Niebuhr was right: the public utterances of this grand old warrior for workers' well-being and for civil liberties, this eighty-year-old man who could still bring audiences to their feet with his powerful rhetoric and brilliant mind, had taken on a "pathetic" quality when he spoke about the Soviet system.

Josef Stalin died on 5 March 1953, and by mid-September Nikita Khrushchev was named first secretary of the Soviet Communist Party's Central Committee. Later that year Ward finally acknowledged some of the abominations of those Stalinist years and pointed the way toward a more accurate evaluation of that period:

> [T]he unreal picture of the USSR as portrayed by cold war propaganda, and the equally unreal opposite cherished by some of its friends has to be replaced by a truthful portrait. . . . Some of them [the Soviet leaders] have surrendered and others will surrender to the evil tendencies to which all flesh is heir. What nation or system has no evil men in its records? Recent Soviet admissions reveal the inadequacy of the friendship which blindly assumes that the socialist system and its leaders can do no wrong. They admit serious mistakes and, because they are human, others will be made. The socialist state shares enough of the nature of all states to make it fall under the judgment that there is none that is altogether righteous, no not one.[65]

Despite Harry Ward's concession, his reputation continued to be a significant issue in his elder son's life. Gordon Ward was still struggling with the Army Loyalty Board, trying to get clearance for a government job in agriculture. A certain resignation had come over him about his job prospects and his father's behavior: "I guess there is no stopping Dad when he has his mind set on doing certain things."[66] "I know that he is quite set in his thinking on certain subjects and that I have to recognize he will not change."[67] Yet somehow or other, in May of 1955 the Army finally gave Gordon clearance.[68]

That same year also saw the formation of the Warsaw Pact as the cold war bred political posturing and military buildup. Once again the world was becoming a dangerous place. Then in late February of 1956 Khrushchev uttered his first strong public denunciation of Stalin. Harry seized upon this event, insisting that this new openness was evidence that repressive excesses had ended in the Soviet Union. He acknowledged that Stalinist "terror went far beyond the need for national survival," though he also insisted that the "gains reached where the repression did not."[69] Within a year Ward conceded the existence of a serious flaw in the previous Soviet regime: "no matter how high the humanitarian objectives, a nation that cannot train leaders dominated by the spirit of service will fall back into the ways of imperialist powers."[70]

By the time this statement was published, the hopes attached to Khrushchev's announcement had been all but erased by a new crisis in Eastern Europe. On October 23 there was a Hungarian uprising against the Soviet policy, and Hungary left the Warsaw Pact. Within two weeks, Soviet tanks rolled into Hungary and crushed the rebellion. How could this be construed as evidence of democracy? A few days later Harry Ward addressed supporters of the National Council for American-Soviet Friendship at a meeting attended by at least one FBI informant.

████████████ *advised that [at] an annual rally for peace and friendship sponsored by the* NATIONAL COUNCIL OF AMERICAN-SOVIET FRIENDSHIP *. . . [Ward] pointed out that the socialists must not be separated from the Democratic process and that they [the audience] should not pass judgment on the Hungarian situation until all the facts are known. . . .* WARD *blamed the Hungarian situation on Stalinism. . . . He stated that Russia administratively made mistakes but that these mistakes can never be repeated because everything now has been brought out in the open. There is no longer any fear of public*

expression; nor is there any fear of the secret police. He stated that the
secret police has lost its power.[71]

Two years later Harry Ward suffered a grievous personal loss. In August of 1957, in the midst of the family's Canadian summer, Muriel became very ill. Lynd and May accompanied her on the train back to New Jersey, and within days she was dead: Daisy and Harry's brilliant, hardworking, insecure but successful daughter dead at fifty. Daisy was particularly devastated, and she was never the same. The suddenness of her daughter's death seemed to exacerbate the effects of her already evident mental deterioration (probably related to Alzheimer's disease), and she became difficult to control. Harry, Daisy, and Muriel had shared the New Jersey home for years, but suddenly Harry's daughter was dead and his wife often mentally deranged. More than ever Harry found retreat and consolation in his flower gardens:

▇▇▇▇▇▇▇▇ *stated that Ward Nursery School, which the subject's*
daughter operated at 1116 Arcadian Way prior to her death, continues
to function on week day mornings having an enrollment of approxi-
mately forty children. [T]he subject spends a great deal of his time
working in the gardens around his home.[72]

Daisy became more than Harry could handle, and the family placed her in a nursing home. He wrote his son Gordon about the transition: "the house seems empty despite the fact that a good deal of her vivid personality left us over two years ago."[73] Lynd and May hired a woman appropriately named Grace to help Harry manage the house. Grace, an African American, enjoyed listening to baseball games with Harry, especially the achievements of the Brooklyn Dodgers' Jackie Robinson. Harry was pleased that some positive social change was taking place, but the pace was too slow to satisfy him, and it certainly did not represent the transformation of the social order he had worked so hard to bring about.

Changes were also taking place elsewhere in the world. In 1958 Khrushchev consolidated his power by becoming premier of the Soviet Union in addition to head of the Soviet Communist Party, and in 1959 he visited the United States. Harry's pamphlet, *The Story of American Soviet Relations, 1917–1959,* published in November 1959 by the National Council of American-Soviet Friendship, sought to persuade readers that peaceful coexistence between the Soviet Union and the United States was not only practical for peace but valuable for the development of democracy. Much of Ward's energy is devoted to correcting historic American distortions of the U.S.S.R. He repeats his familiar defenses of the Soviet Union's early withdrawal from World War I (the Soviets lacked resources, and they were taking the lead in a negotiated peace), the Nazi-Soviet Nonaggression Pact (the Allies sold out at Munich, so the Soviets had no other options), the Soviet invasion of Finland (a defensive maneuver by the Soviets because they needed Finland as a base for fighting the Nazis), and Soviet dominance in Eastern Europe (the Soviets needed a defensible border). Ward portrays the United States as the primary instigator of the cold war and the Soviet Union as a consistent advocate for peace. His reference to Stalinist internal violence is illuminating: "the *sudden* revelation of the shocking violations of the Soviet *constitution* in the *last years* of Stalin."[74] The highlighted words expose Ward's beliefs: that this was new evidence (though, of course, it was the first time that Stalin's brutality was officially verified by the Soviet Union); the word choice that emphasizes violation of the constitution, not of persons; and the occurrence of those violations only at the *end* of Stalin's regime. Ward reminds his readers of the good relationships between Americans and Soviets during their common war against Hitler's Germany, and he warns that the cold war would deter disarmament efforts. He concludes with a flourish: "The truth is mighty and will prevail—when the minority who know it are able to convince a sufficient majority to see it and put it into effect."[75]

In November 1959 Daisy's mind was released from torment. At the family memorial service, Harry recalled her sacrifices and persistence throughout their years together: "From the time Mother left her comfortable suburban home in Kansas City to come into one of Chicago's tough districts. . . . I took her into a good deal of discomfort and sometimes, in distant lands, into what to many people would have been real hardships. Not once did she complain and always she did more than her part in making the situation bearable."[76]

The family funeral rituals that began with Muriel's death continued as Lynd and Harry scattered Daisy's ashes on Lonely Lake. Sometime after Muriel's death Harry had started sleeping in the room over his garage, the room used by Muriel's preschool. With Daisy's departure he returned to the couple's old bedroom again. He was sad, but the old warrior, now in his late eighties, fiercely maintained his independence. In Canada he not only continued to work his large garden, he insisted on staying in the cabin by himself.

Even at ninety, Harry was attentive to world events and setting forth solutions to problems. The title of his Carnegie Hall speech on the occasion of his ninetieth birthday—"What Needs Now to Be Done?"—reflects his activist mentality. He encouraged his audience not only to apply political pressure with regard to matters such as banning nuclear tests, but also to engage their neighbors in conversations that just might change minds and generate action. Harry railed against the U.S. cold war strategy supporting totalitarian regimes, including "the participation of our government in, and its responsibility for—I choose my words carefully—the murder of innocent men, women and children in Viet Nam."[77]

It is revealing that Ward expressed gratitude to Union Theological Seminary at the beginning of this speech, for he was alienated from that community. However, in the final years of his life, the seminary made overtures, and Harry responded politely. Roger Shinn recalled an afternoon when Ward, Niebuhr, President Bennett, and others shared tea together in Bennett's apartment. "That day Dr. Ward was an old man among friends from his past years, genial, humorous, reminiscent—yet occasionally uttering strong opinions as if to remind us that, in the midst of such cordiality, he was still a radical."[78] Ward had deservedly gained a reputation among his students that he was not about to abandon even in the twilight of his life. As Stephen Fritchman put it, "There are hundreds of men in pulpits today who studied under him, and live with troubled consciences ever since, for he [Ward] is a gadfly extraordinary."[79] Under the tutelage of Harry Ward, Reinhold Niebuhr, and others Union had produced its fair share of ministers with troubled consciences, men and women who really made a difference in communities and the nation. John Bennett wrote Harry a note after the visit, for he had been touched by the old ethics profs once again engaged in serious conversation.[80] Meanwhile, the FBI kept up its surveillance.

Observations were conducted in the neighborhood of the subject's residence on 7/2/62, 7/3/62 and 7/10/62, but no pertinent information was developed concerning subject.[81]

*In September, 1962, subject described as a subscriber to "The Worker."
In March, 1963, subject listed as a sponsor of a reception for ELIZABETH
GURLEY FLYNN, National Chairman, CP, USA.*[82]

*Observations were conducted in the neighborhood of the subject's resi-
dence on May 20, 21, 28, 1963, June 4, 1963, but no pertinent information was developed concerning the subject.*[83]

For all his misguided assumptions about the Soviet Union, Ward was
right on target about a number of domestic issues, including the abuse of
power by Hoover's FBI and the increasing threats to free speech and
open public debate. The only known surviving recording of Ward's
speeches comes from late in his life, probably the mid-1950s, and allows
one to hear the person Benjamin Mays described as "the little man with
a big voice."[84] Despite his advanced years, Ward's voice here is passionate and confidently measured. His analysis is razor-sharp as he identifies "four cornerstones" already in place for making America a police
state: the FBI lists, HUAC's inquisition, the U.S. attorney general's list
of subversive organizations as a test of employee loyalty, and paid in-
formers. Harry's speech is a call to defend the Bill of Rights with perseverance and discernment. He is wary that well-intentioned folk do
not understand what is at stake: "We've been fighting a series of battles,
and we haven't realized that Reaction is fighting a war, a carefully
planned war and a longtime war; and that you can't win wars by simply
fighting a series of battles. You have to have a strategy that goes as wide
and as deep as that of the people who are your opponents. Otherwise,
they win and you lose." But the old warrior was not discouraged, and he
concluded with a rallying cry: "It's the old, old story, you know. United
we stand and united we win!"[85] As it deactivated its file on Harry Ward,
the FBI composed a terse account of his life.

*Subject's file has been reviewed at the Bureau. He is a white male, 90
years of age, who is a retired minister. He studied in Russia between
1924 and 1932 and was reportedly a Communist Party member between 1943 and 1945. Since 1945 he has supported various Communist party front organization. Subject's name is being deleted from the
Security Index at the Bureau. You should make appropriate disposition
of his Security Index cards in your field division.*[86]

Harry F. Ward backstage at Carnegie Hall. According to the *Social Questions Bulletin* (December 1966), one thousand people were present to celebrate Harry F. Ward's ninetieth birthday. (Photo by Nanda Ward, Courtesy of Nanda Ward and Robin Ward Savage)

Like most of his life, Harry Ward's death in December of 1966 was a struggle. His last two years were lived in excruciating agony due to repeated spinal fractures. His spirit was anything but broken, however, for he insisted on knowing the doctors' prognosis: "If something is going to kill me, I want to know what it is."[87] The family itself did not know about all of Harry Ward's final wishes, which, unknown to them, he had put into writing.

Cremation desired. Everything as simple and inexpensive as possible.

No flowers except one or two red roses on coffin.

No "viewing of remains."

No lying eulogy—especially to the Lord in an all worship Memorial Service at Union.

As to the ashes I've always wanted what Coe did and got: except that I've long had a fancy to let the northwest wind take them where it will from on top of the bluff between our camp and Lynd's, maybe where I finished writing *Our Economic Morality*. If the wind were strong enough they might get out to the lake. But in this matter, as in the others except the first, I think the living should do what will give them the most pleasure, I mean satisfaction.
Dad[88]

His body was cremated, the arrangements were simple and inexpensive, and it seems that the memorial service on 4 January 1967 at Union Seminary was not a "lying eulogy." Among those leading the service were recent allies, including the MFSA's Lee Ball and Richard Morford, director of the National Council of American-Soviet Friendship. Like Harry, Ball and Morford were ordained ministers laboring on the fringes of liberal-radical politics. Lynd chose two hymns by long-deceased Social Gospelers—Frank Mason North and Washington Gladden—to frame the service. Bishop Herbert Welch, now 104 years old and one of the five founders of the Methodist Federation along with Harry Ward, had been scheduled to participate, but fragile health would not allow it. Roger Shinn, a former student of Ward's and subsequently an ethics professor at Union, evoked several vivid pictures of Ward in action at the seminary, at home, and in the public square. Shinn expressed well the valuable tension that Ward contributed to the seminary community and beyond:

Harry Ward was a man of controversy. I have rejoiced as his tongue lashed at the evil forces we both opposed. I have squirmed as he attacked positions closer to my own. Yet I remember with special gratitude that he never showed me more respect than on one occasion when our convictions clashed. Men of controversy are often a trial to institutions. And Harry Ward served Union Seminary, perhaps not always as it wished to be served, but as he profoundly believed it should be served.[89]

Harry Ward was a scholar who thrust his faith into the center of life, a fearless warrior, a man who identified himself with the oppressed of the world.[90]

The family did distribute Harry's ashes at Lonely Lake, though not from the top of the bluff that he associated with his finest manuscript, his 1929 *Our Economic Morality and the Religion of Jesus.* It is instructive that Ward would focus on the writing of *Our Economic Morality*, for that book represents the period of his greatest prestige and influence. Recent decades had not been so kind.

As they cleaned out the home overlooking the Hudson River, the family discovered, in an obscure area of the attic, a hand-tooled leather photo album that none of Harry's now aged children could ever remember seeing. It was a gift from his London congregation, just before he embarked for America as a teenager in 1891. The names of the people shown in the photos are all preceded by the title "Brother" or "Sister," for this represented that intimate, countercultural Methodist chapel community where formal titles were meaningless, and all persons, regardless of social rank or age, were simply known as Christian "brothers" or "sisters." A newspaper clipping, dated 19 May 1891, was tucked into the album; it not only recounts the occasion for giving Harry the photo album but also the religious subculture that defined his growing-up years.

The Wesleyan Methodists had a field day at Acton Green on Bank Holiday, commencing at 10 o'clock in the morning by a prayer meeting led by Mr. Thornton. At 11 o'clock a consecration service was held conducted by Rev. G. H. Barker who founded his address upon John xvii.19. "And for their sakes I sanctify myself that they also might be sanctified through the truth." At two o'clock in the afternoon the mission band marched through the streets of the neighborhood, returning at 3 P.M for a praise meeting which was conducted by Mr. H. Ward, and taken part in by the members of the various mission bands represented. At 4:30 P.M a public tea was held, to which about 100 sat down. While tea was in progress a very interesting ceremony took place in the form of the presentation of a large album containing photographs of many of those connected with the work of the chapel, [to] Mr. H. Ward, jun[ior]. Mr. Ward has for some little time been a local preacher in the Wesleyan connexion and has assisted the work of the mission at Acton Green, as Sunday-school teacher, worker in the mission band, and deputy class leader. The presentation was made by Mr. George Thomas, and Mr. Ward suitably responded.[91]

How foreign this world was to the one in which Harry spent most of his adult life! No wonder this album was hidden in the attic, for Harry Ward had long separated himself from such an expression of religious belief and from folk like this. Still, the mind-set formed in those years had shaped his life. Despite his desire to be accepted in the mainstream, Ward's convictions and habits of thought pushed him into another sectarian subculture. And he remained until the end a crusading dualist, resisting the encroachments of the dominant culture, especially capitalism. He relished and lived the simple life and wanted to engage ordinary working folk, not the academic elites. Nearly a half century earlier he had written, "I have found that the best safeguard against the limitations of professionalism is to take some part, outside one's vocation, in the fight against injustice and tyranny."[92]

Harry Frederick Ward
Security Matter-C

"The Record" page A-6, Hackensack, New Jersey, daily newspaper, on December 10, 1966, in its Weekend edition carried the following article:

"Fort Lee—Dr. Harry F. Ward a retired professor at Union Theological Seminary, New York City, died yesterday at his home at 1116 Arcadian Way. He was 93.

"Born in London, Dr. Ward came to this country 76 years ago. He lived 40 years in the Palisade section of Fort Lee.

"He was predeceased by his wife, Daisy. Surviving are two sons, Dr. Gordon Ward of Beirut, Lebanon, and Lynd Ward of Cresskill, two grandchildren, and two great-grandchildren.

"There will be private funeral services Monday at the McCorry Brothers Funeral Home, 780 Anderson Avenue, Cliffside Park, at the convenience of the family. Cremation will follow at the Garden State Crematory, North Bergen."

This document contains neither recommendations nor conclusions of the FBI. It is the property of the FBI and is loaned to your agency; it and its contents are not to be distributed outside your agency.[93]

Epilogue

The Legacy of Harry F. Ward

The more necessary it is for us to think and act together, the more imperative it is that we should be able and willing to go it alone when others are not ready. If we have hit the right trail, they will come after.
—Harry F. Ward, "Why I Have Found Life Worth Living"

The work of applying the principles of Jesus to the social order requires those engaged in it to be continuously in the minority.
—Harry F. Ward, *Social Service Bulletin*, 15 June 1924 (cited by Milton John Huber, "A History of the Methodist Federation for Social Action")

HARRY F. WARD lived too long. More accurately, he lived too long for his place in history to remain secure. Had his frail body given out as everyone (including Harry!) expected, his decades of unapologetic pro-Sovietism would not have so greatly damaged his reputation as a radical Social Gospel prophet and defender of civil liberties.[1] To be sure, Harry Ward remains for history what he was in life—controversial. But except for the controversies that swirled around him he might not have vanished so easily from the institutional memories of American Protestantism, Union Theological Seminary, and the American Civil Liberties Union. Of course, good history is not defined by "what if?" inquiries. Assessments of Harry Ward and his place in history must take seriously all of his life.

Yet the question lingers: What clouded Ward's keen critical capacities with respect to some things even as he discerned so clearly other matters? Many folk make errors in judgment, but Ward's persistent refusal to acknowledge Soviet oppression violated some of his most cherished values. This is not to suggest that Ward was alone in his denial; cold warriors on both sides were just as myopic. Nor does this criticism suggest that Ward was a dupe. There were carefully considered reasons for his behavior, even if they led him to inconsistency and, more tragically, caused the demise of his reputation and influence as a warrior fighting for a just social order.

PERSONALITY TRAITS

It is a bit of common sense that with age our personal characteristics become "more so." As an adult Harry Ward was headstrong and stubborn. He was not likely to be persuaded by people who held different points of view; he believed that he had the right answers and the right strategies for virtually everything. He seems to have had difficulty admitting to mistakes. And it is likely that his carefully concealed sense of inferiority contributed to his unbending certainty. With the passing years, he became "more so." Harry's character traits seem to have been exacerbated by external factors. When he felt backed into a corner, he came out swinging. From at least the third decade of his life onward, he was condemned with a variety of negative labels—"troublemaker," "radical," "heretic," "communist." These accusations seem to have been made him more and more unyielding in his opinions. In the end his obduracy helped push Harry Ward from a position of integrity—a man known for standing by his convictions—into uncritical ideological rigidity. His best friend George Coe tried to warn him of this during the thirties, but to no avail.

DISPOSITIONAL OUTSIDER

Harry Ward inherited some habits of mind and heart from his family's sectarian religious heritage. Followers of the sectarian emphases of Christian tradition were predisposed to be suspicious of the larger culture—what they labeled "the world." Though they did not disengage from the larger culture, they never capitulated to its dominant values, for to do so would be "worldly." To be a faithful Christian meant to be forever an outsider of sorts; in the language of the New Testament one must be in the world but not of it. Though Ward abandoned the theology and practices of most of this religious heritage, he never abandoned its outsider mind-set. Sharing the perspective of the prophetic minority— whether it be the anti-liturgical and anti-public house mentality of his family's sectarian Methodism in Victorian England or the anticapitalist, antimaterialist mentality of Harry Ward's radical Social Gospel— remained an essential habit throughout his life. To be faithful to that habit necessarily entailed a certain disposition, one that demonstrates little interest in compromise. It is a mind-set unencumbered by personal concerns about being in the mainstream. From this perspective, the label of outsider is a badge of honor, and Harry wore this badge proudly throughout his life.

An outsider's disposition does not inevitably foster poor judgment, but outsider status does incline one toward a siege mentality that easily gives rise to a dualistic perspective, which, when coupled with a certain zeal, can in turn lead to a holy war mentality.

INSTRUMENTAL VIEW OF RELIGION

The evangelistic Methodism to which Harry's family of origin conformed regarded religion as primarily an instrument for "saving souls" and helping believers grow in holiness. It is not that religious practice or doctrine was unimportant to his family; they mattered a great deal. However, converting sinners and aiding believers to grow in holiness were of far greater significance. Thus his father's objection to read prayers, scripted sermons, and ornate chapels was not so much a matter of taste or theological debate as a concern for evangelistic effectiveness. Harry

Ward senior cared deeply about the religiously disenfranchised who were repulsed by things liturgical. The mission band went to those people where they were and used all manner of appeals to draw them in to hear the gospel.

Though Harry's system of religious belief and practice changed dramatically in America, this basic, instrumental orientation remained unaltered, especially when the church's beliefs and practice seemed utterly vacuous to him—beginning when he lived in Chicago and increasingly so by the mid-1920s. By then the religious telos had been reduced in Harry's perspective to the humane and just society: only as religion *works* to realize that end is it a viable human endeavor.

By the same token, civil liberties became valuable only as instruments for achieving the telos of a democratized economy, planned and guided by the people. Obtaining that end, especially in the Soviet Union, justified the suspension of civil liberties so as to protect what *had* been accomplished and what might yet *be* accomplished from the depredations of "counterrevolutionaries." Of course, the problem was that the "temporary" dictatorship in the name of economic democracy was neither temporary nor ultimately inclined toward anything remotely democratic. Absolute power did indeed corrupt absolutely, so there was no credible democratic firebreak against the abuses that ensued from this instrumental view of civil liberties. Only a democratic rhetoric survived, and this was to be manipulated as the dictators' propaganda machine saw fit. While Harry Ward clearly perceived the corrupting effects of J. Edgar Hoover's unchecked power on American democracy, he seemed unable to concede the fundamental flaws of Stalinism even to himself, blinded as he was by his zeal for economic democracy.

Experiences and Circumstances

It is important to recognize the lifelong impact of Ward's experiences in Chicago's back-of-the-yards, where Harry was confronted by the cruel effects of the reactionary agenda of capitalism's vested interests. The memories of brutal oppression against laborers, radicals, and the poor burned themselves into Harry's sensitive soul. He would never let them go. The cumulative effect of his unrelenting vilification at the hands of reactionary forces only reinforced his perceptions of the capitalist world's corrupt power arrangements.

These factors dovetailed and encouraged Harry Ward to maintain a dualistic outlook on life. Ideologically and existentially Harry Ward saw the world divided into two camps: right and wrong, good and evil. He inhabited a universe of either-or's, of life-and-death struggles. No wonder his favorite casual reading and movies came to be the "penny dreadfuls," especially the westerns, where good and evil characters are easily distinguishable by their white and black hats. More importantly, his dualism was not a matter of theory; right was worth fighting for. Thus Harry Ward came to embody the *unyielding dualism of a holy warrior,* and it is this mind-set and lifestyle that in the end led to his undoing, for the unyielding dualism of a holy warrior inevitably involves uncritical, partisan allegiance.

To some degree Ward's perspective on Marxism might have been vindicated at least in part by the late twentieth-century Christian movement known as "liberation theology." This movement took seriously Marxist insights on economic oppression and married them to the strong biblical and theological traditions of social justice and solidarity with the oppressed. However, Ward's limitations are evident even in this hypothetical case. Instead of being a promising precursor of liberation theology, his "Jesus and Marx" manuscript is corrupted by lengthy citations from Soviet leaders, including Stalin. The hard questions about economic power are all there, but they are colored by his loyalties that hardened during the cold war. It might be reasonable to assume that Ward would have rejoiced in developments in the late 1960s: the promise of a "Prague Spring"; an Eastern European Marxist writing a book titled *A Marxist Looks at Jesus;*[2] a conference on the Marxist-Christian dialogue at Union Theological Seminary; and surely Union Theological Seminary's hiring of persons like Beverly Wildung Harrison, a feminist-Marxist ethicist, and James Cone, an African-American liberation theologian. However, one has to wonder how Ward would have ultimately responded to all these events, given his relentless public support of the Soviet Union over Hungary in 1956. Would he have truly welcomed a "Prague Spring"? In the present climate of scholarship, with some liberation theologies under a cloud and Marxist-inspired efforts out of favor, most bets seem to be off on the promise of collaboration between Marxists and Christians.

Of course, Harry Ward did not start the culture wars nor the cold war in which he became embroiled. Given those conflicts, however, his holy warrior's unyielding dualism required that his alliance with the Soviet experiment be unwavering; a holy warrior does not break faith with the righteous cause, at least not publicly, and thereby give aid and comfort to the enemy. Ward was not the only one who fell into this trap, for holy warriors on both sides of the culture wars blindly adhered to party lines. For example, Reinhold Niebuhr, too, became a cold warrior, at least for a time, though he was outraged by the guilt-by-association tactics of Hooverism-McCarthyism. While Niebuhr retained some appreciation for Marxist analysis, it became for him an ideology forever tainted by utopianism and, worse yet, Stalinism. More importantly, his penetrating questions about economic structures and economic power became subservient to political issues, or they became all but irrelevant in his broad-brushed pronouncements about competing mythologies.

It was not just that Niebuhr had negotiated a peace settlement between Protestant ethics and the structures of capitalism. More significantly, his wariness of all things Marxist led him to dim the searchlights that had revealed the web of tangled political and economic arrangements in the West, both at home and abroad. Despite the remarkable insights and assets of Niebuhr's Christian realism, under its hegemony mainline Protestant ethics became a capitalistic framework for most economic issues. Moreover, Christian realism fostered the subservience of questions about economic power to questions about political power. It also led to the loss of careful structural analysis of the relationship between economic power and democratic institutions, an emphasis on foreign policy issues almost exclusively within an American-European framework, and the preservation of liberalism as the dominant mainline Protestant paradigm—albeit a chastened liberalism. As Beverly Wildung Harrison puts it, "An obvious limitation of political realism as a social theory is its total inability to focus [on] the role of economic activity in society, however one conceives that activity. Its imaging of human social relations simply leaves economic life out of [its] account. Ironically, much of Niebuhr's early prestige derived from his awareness that economic power was an irrevocable dimension of social power."[3]

Ward's approach fared no better, given his unrelenting holy war dualism. Thus the thirties culture wars and their successor, the cold war, severely damaged the critical apparatus of mainline Protestant ethics' approaches to economic justice.

What is remarkable about Ward is that he did not simply become a secular communist. He continued to try to do what virtually no one in his time believed was either helpful or interesting—uncover the common ground between Marxism and what Ward called "the religion of Jesus." In that respect this holy warrior was clearly no pro-Soviet clone. Harry's independence of thought and deeply held convictions would never allow that. If he had been able to let go of his holy war dualism, he might have remained a valuable contributor to the conversation, even if from the fringe—where, frankly, this dispositional outsider felt most comfortable anyway.

Many years after the American Social Gospel had become passé, Harry Ward would still refer to the "retreat from Rauschenbusch." He recognized that this patriarch of the Social Gospel had developed and promulgated a true understanding of reality. In some ways Ward himself had retreated from Rauschenbusch, though not in the same way as those Ward chastised. Rauschenbusch's Social Gospel was grounded in a rich spirituality that remained the anchor of his commitment and, perhaps more importantly, his discernment. In Rauschenbusch's *Prayers of the Social Awakening,* for example, one can recognize that his passion went beyond social concern and sympathy for the downtrodden. Rauschenbusch's almost mystical experience of the transcendent continued to generate fervor on behalf of the oppressed. The student of Harry Ward senses that such an experience of the transcendent evaporated from his life, or at least it seems to have become focused on the natural world rather than the human one.

Responding to critics who believed that he would be straightened out if he would just spend more time on his knees (in prayer), Ward chuckled as he described the time he did spend (literally) on his knees working in his garden. This was more than a clever pun, for it seems that Ward did believe and perhaps experience the transcendent in nature. However, the human side of religion, what he persistently labeled "the religion of Jesus," focused almost exclusively on societal improvement; it seemed to have nothing to do with the depths of reality that human

Harry F. Ward in his garden at Lonely Lake. (Courtesy of Nanda Ward and Robin Ward Savage)

beings have associated with the transcendent, even God. One has to wonder if Ward's critical apparatus might not have been more balanced if he had maintained some perspective on social realities grounded in more than an instrumental understanding of the religion of Jesus. Perhaps if Harry Ward's spirituality had retained that connection between a cosmic presence and the cherished value of individual human creatures, he might not have been able to slough off Julius Hecker's "disappearance" during the Stalinist purges. Ward's Social Gospel hero, Rauschenbusch, describes this sort of spirituality in his poem "The Little Gate to God," written late in his life when he, too, was harshly attacked by reactionary critics.

> When I am in the consciousness of God,
> My fellowmen are not far-off and forgotten,
> But close and strangely dear.
> Those whom I love
> Have a mystic value.
> They shine, as if a light were glowing within them.[4]

Still, as Third Reich Christian martyr Dietrich Bonhoeffer noted about his collaborative efforts with "good people" who had no interest in or appreciation for traditional religious claims, the work of justice, whether it is given religious warrant or not, is willy-nilly the work of a righteous God.[5]

On the positive side of the ledger was Ward's clear vision of what the cold war had done to American democracy. Only as the inside stories about the civil rights movement of the fifties and sixties become public through the release of FBI files under the Freedom of Information Act do many Americans finally grasp what Harry Ward and too few others saw quite clearly and warned about early in this century. Ward understood well how anticommunist hysteria gnawed away at the soul of American democracy.

No wonder that a whole range of persons, including folk singer Pete Seeger, would recall being radicalized by Harry Ward's speeches.[6] It was not just what Harry Ward said, it was also the place from which he spoke: outside the mainstream even as he sought to alter the mainstream. By disposition and by conviction, he recognized that outsider status—what he usually labeled the "minority" or "prophetic" stance—enabled one to maintain perspective. He understood quite well that any ethic of resistance is usually situated in the outsider's vantage point. Even the most sincere folk will probably be co-opted by the dominant cultural values, for it is hard to discern the limitations of the capitalist-anticommunist system if one is exposed to no other system.

Perhaps one day many folk, including this biographer, will move beyond personal struggles with consumerism and materialism and fully confront the corrupting effects of the capitalist ethos. Most of us who care about economic justice too easily paraphrase the prayer of the young St. Augustine: Lord, make me just, but not yet.[7] Ward's socialist solution to the corruption may not be the cure, but his diagnosis of the *systemic* illness deserves more careful attention. The words he penned in his lean-to overlooking Lonely Lake that summer of 1929 remain compelling.

Insistence upon the impracticality of the morality of Jesus is in effect the assertion of the supremacy of the economic appetites over the rest of life. It is after all but a refined form of the old cry

"Eat, drink and be merry for tomorrow we die." It tells us that the chief end of man is to make and enjoy goods, to manufacture and use conveniences and comforts—that is when it does not tell us that the chief end of man is to make money and thereby have power over others. But this is to assert the dictatorship of one part of life over the rest. . . . To accept this dictation means to give up the chance of living life whole. We are promised in return the comfortable life; but when was that ever the good life? Mechanical conveniences we have in abundance, but other values must go or stay in mutilated form. We can neither fulfill the struggle of the past for freedom and justice nor can we realize the possibilities of the future. . . . The social structure that proceeds from such a view of life is as jerry-built as the houses it provides for most of its population, and those who are content to dwell in it will of necessity leave little behind them but ruins.[8]

Harry Ward recognized that no person connected to the Christian tradition—whether he or she be orthodox, liberal, conservative, or seeker—who takes seriously Jesus' teaching, "You cannot serve God and Mammon," can ever be completely at home with capitalism. Surely Harry would have us add those religious humanists who take Jesus' teachings seriously as well as religious folk who are compelled by very different but compatible traditions, e.g., the warnings of the Bhagavad Gita and the Buddha about things that keep us attached to the superficial and materialistic. For all such persons there is value in never making peace with capitalism—or at the least in listening attentively to anticapitalist outsiders like Harry F. Ward.

One will have to separate the wheat from the chaff in Ward's life and thought. But like the homemade bread he loved to make and share with his family, students, and friends, Harry Ward's grain and leaven just may provide some of the nutrition for a healthier, more just social order. On the dedicatory page of his 1917 book, *A Social Theory of Education*, George Coe aptly described Harry Ward's legacy: "To Harry F. Ward, who sees and makes others see."[9]

ABBREVIATIONS

ACLU	American Civil Liberties Union
AFL	American Federation of Labor
ALPD	American League for Peace and Democracy
DK	Daisy Kendall
DKW	Daisy Kendall Ward
FOR	Fellowship of Reconciliation
FSC	Fellowship of Socialist Christians
GAC	George A. Coe
GPA	General Public Administration
HFW	Harry F. Ward
HUAC	House Special Committee to Investigate Un-American Activities
IWW	Industrial Workers of the World
MFSA Papers	Methodist Federation for Social Action Archives
MFSS	Methodist Federation for Social Service
NPC	National Policy Council of New America
NUH	*Northwestern University: A History, 1855–1905*
NYT	*New York Times*
RN	Reinhold Niebuhr
SHSW	State Historical Society of Wisconsin
UCCD	United Christian Council for Democracy
UKC	Ursula Keppel-Compton
UN	Ursula Niebuhr
UTS	Union Theological Seminary

NOTES

CHAPTER 1

1. *The Victoria History of the County of Middlesex,* 2, ed. William Page (London: Constable, 1911), 114.

2. C. J. Hamilton, "Chiswick, Past and Present," *English Illustrated Magazine* (1891):874.

3. Birth certificate for Harry Frederick Ward, Ward Papers, Burke Library, Union Theological Seminary, New York, New York (hereafter UTS).

4. Harry F. Ward (hereafter HFW) to Emily B. Kendall, 8 December 1895, Ward Papers, UTS.

5. According to the 1881 Chiswick census.

6. Headstone in Ealing cemetery, London, examined by the author.

7. Letter to Harry F. Ward, Salt Lake City, from his father, 29 December 1891, Ward Papers, UTS.

8. HFW to Daisy Kendall Ward (hereafter DKW), 20 April 1909, Ward Papers, UTS.

9. HFW to Emily B. Kendall, 8 December 1895, Ward Papers, UTS.

10. Gordon H. Ward, letter to author, February 1983.

11. As a young adult remembering those New Forest experiences, Ward would speak of it as a place where nature offers "a home," where "every tree carries human associations in its heart, the spirit of the hearthstone and the roof-tree is in the branches, and generations of forebears who have lived and died in these glades" (HFW, "The New Forest," typewritten MS, Ward Papers, UTS).

12. John R. Wise, *The New Forest: Its History and Scenery,* 3rd ed. (London: Henry Sotheran, 1880), 170.

13. HFW, "New Forest," 8.

14. Recollections by Lynd Ward transcribed in a letter from Gordon H. Ward to the author, 17 March 1983.

15. As recounted by Lynd Ward to Nanda Ward and included in a letter from Gordon Ward to the author, 17 March 1983. The rough character of many New Forest inhabitants is verified by a report of one Methodist preacher, who in 1790 proposed to do some open-air preaching near Cadnam, the home of

Harry's grandfather. According to the account, a number of local folk "sent a threatening letter declaring that they would . . . murder the individual" if he chose to pursue his preaching in their homeland. No wonder this area was part of what was called the "Methodist Wilderness." Like many of those rough folk, the Ward ancestor's life was dramatically changed by his conversion. He gave up rum-running and poaching and settled down to farm in the New Forest area.

16. Donald Read, *England, 1868–1914: The Age of Urban Democracy* (London: Longman, 1979), 73.

17. 1879 minutes of the Second London District, John Rylands Library of Manchester.

18. See, for example, "A Cold Church and the Liturgy," *Methodist Times*, 7, 29 January 1891, 112; "Liturgical Services," *Local Preacher's Magazine* (1889):373.

19. "The Local Preacher," *Local Preacher's Magazine and Christian Family Record*, 36 (1886):181.

20. Ealing and Acton Circuit Plan for Ealing and Acton Chapels, 26 April–25 July 1891, Ward Papers, UTS.

21. Information from an advertisement in the *Methodist Times*, 6, 3 April 1890, 333, and a report of the meetings in the following week's issue, "The London Mission Bands on Bank Holiday," 10 April 1890, 351.

22. Ibid.

23. Cited in Maldwyn Lloyd Edwards, *Methodism and England: A Study of Methodism in Its Social and Political Aspects during the Period 1850–1932* (London: Epworth Press, 1943), 220.

24. Read, *England 1868–1914*, 267–68.

25. HFW to Daisy Kendall (hereafter DK), 28 February 1898, Ward Papers, UTS.

26. Cited in William H. Scheuerle, "Amusements and Recreation: Middle Class," *Victorian Britain, an Encyclopedia*, ed. Sally Mitchell (New York: Garland, 1988), 17.

27. Cited from the *Methodist New Connexion Magazine* (April 1886):234, by Robert Currie, *Methodism Divided* (London: Faber, 1968), 133.

28. Peter Bailey uses the effective term "counter-attractions" to describe these various attempts at rational recreation. Cf. his *Leisure and Class in Victorian England: Rational Recreation and the Contest for Control, 1830–1855* (London: Routledge and Kegan Paul, 1978), 170. He states that lawn tennis was created in the mid-1870s as a sport for suburbia (75).

29. See, for example, *Methodist Times*, 6, 20 March 1890, 273; 17 April 1890, 367.

30. John Wesley, *A Collection of Hymns for the Use of the People Called Meth-*

odists with a New Supplement (London: Wesleyan-Methodist Book Room, 1888), no. 858, 256.

31. HFW, "Jesus and Marx," unpublished manuscript, loaned to the author by Robin Ward Savage.

32. Gail L. Savage, "Gentleman," in *Victorian Britain*, 326.

33. One hears the virtues of self-reliance, endurance, and hard work ringing through this text as well. "But always there is the issue of health, to make bright or gloomy the day, easy or hard, and sometimes good or bad, the work. The curse of poor health is that it turns too much of your attention in upon yourself. Also it asks for too much sympathy or gets too much consideration. The only remedy is work. . . . We can refuse to let pain disable us altogether. And as for courage, what is it but doing what has to be done whether you are fit or not, even though the rest quit?" (HFW, "Why I Have Found Life Worth Living," *Christian Century*, 1 March 1928, 281).

34. The certificate reads "Cambridge Local Examination, December 1887, Ealing Centre, presented to H. F. Ward as prize for Third Class Honours given by The Ealing Centre and awarded by the Syndicate" (Ward Papers, UTS). Fourteen was a typical age for working-class children to finish their education. After that, they usually learned a trade. Since Harry's schooling ended at age fourteen it is clear that his family intended for him to pursue the life of "small tradesmen, shopmen, clerks, upper artisans," with what was regarded as a "third grade" education. A "first grade" education, usually requiring the young person to pursue public school through age eighteen or nineteen, could lead to university admission. Cf. T. W. Bamford, *Rise of the Public Schools: A Study of Boys' Public Boarding Schools in England and Wales from 1837 to the Present Day* (London: Thomas Nelson, 1967), 172.

35. See, for example, Art Shields, "One Man's Quest," *Worker*, 14 January 1945, 1–5. Shields also mistakenly dates Ward's social concern to the London dock strike of 1889.

36. K. S. Inglis, *Churches and the Working Classes in Victorian England* (London: Routledge and Kegan Paul, 1963), 255.

37. *West London Observer*, 8 March 1890, 3.

38. *West London Observer*, 5 July 1890, 7.

39. Broadsheet in the Ward Papers, UTS, n.d.

40. Donna Price Paul, "Shopworkers," in *Victorian Britain*, 722.

CHAPTER 2

1. May McNeer Ward, conversation with author, 23 August 1992.

2. Listed as such on the quarterly circuit plan of the Ealing and Acton Circuit, 1891, Ward Papers, UTS.

3. One tradition states that he was twelve. Since the mission band associated with the Chiswick Methodist Church did not originate until 1889, it is more likely that this took place when he was sixteen or seventeen. More telling is the letter Daisy Kendall writes to her parents, 25 November 1895. She reports that Harry had been preaching since seventeen.

4. "25 Years of Social Gospel: Prof. Ward of Union Retires," *Newsweek*, 30 June 1941, 46.

5. Carl E. Hester III, "The Thought and Career of Harry F. Ward," student paper for Church History 446, Union Theological Seminary, 27 March 1961, 11. This paper was based in part on interviews with a very elderly Harry Ward.

6. H. Ward (father) to Harry F. Ward (son), Salt Lake City, 29 December 1891, Ward Papers, UTS.

7. HFW to Mrs. Kendall, 8 December 1895. Daisy Kendall writes to her parents in a letter of 25 November 1895: "He grieves his mother deeply and has been so lonely since her death about four years ago." Both letters are in the Ward Papers, UTS.

8. HFW to Mrs. Kendall, 8 December 1895, Ward Papers, UTS.

9. Harry Ward's son Gordon believed that Harry had more empathy with his mother than with his father. Gordon H. Ward, letter to author, 5 May 1983.

10. George Coe remembered USC in that period as "mostly raw edges and the financial management was wretched." Cf. Charles S. Braden, "In Evanston," *Religious Education* 47(2) (March–April 1952): 91.

11. James Dombrowski, *The Early Days of Christian Socialism in America* (New York: Columbia University Press, 1936), 50. Dombrowski is not guessing about Ward's experience, for Ward was his teacher and friend at Union Theological Seminary. Richard T. Ely, *Social Aspects of Christianity and Other Essays* (New York: Thomas Y. Crowell, 1889).

12. HFW to Mrs. (Emily) Kendall, 8 December 1895, Ward Papers, UTS.

13. HFW to Daisy Kendall, 28 February 1898, Ward Papers, UTS.

14. Apparently a statement made by Ward to Carl Hester in a 1961 interview.

15. HFW, "We Were Friends," *Religious Education*, 47 (March–April 1952): 88–89; Braden, "In Evanston," 92. Interestingly enough, the conversaziones seem to have developed among Victorian Methodists as an alternative form of recreation for their young people. No doubt American Methodists agreed with English Methodists that these alternatives were necessarily part of helping young people develop wholesome habits and relationships.

16. Braden, "In Evanston," 92.

17. George Hatheway Parkinson, "Intercollegiate Debates," *Northwestern University: A History, 1855–1905* (hereafter *NUH*), ed. Arthur Herbert Wilde (New York: University Publishing, 1905), 2:148.

18. Ibid., 148–49.

19. Ibid., 149; George Thomas Palmer, "History of Oratorical Contests of Northwestern University," *NUH,* 2:163–65.

20. Estelle Frances Ward, *The Story of Northwestern University* (New York: Dodd, Mead, 1924), 206–7.

21. George A. Coe (hereafter GAC), "The Religious Problem in Colleges," *Northwestern,* 19, 13 April 1899, 2.

22. "Our College Men's Meeting," *Northwestern,* 19, 13 April 1899, 4.

23. *NUH,* 3:160.

24. GAC, "Religious Problem in Colleges," 4.

25. HFW, "We Were Friends," 88.

26. GAC, "My Search for What Is Most Worthwhile," *Religious Education* (March–April 1957): 73.

27. GAC, "Religious Experience and the Scientific Movement," in *The Church and Christian Experience* (Western Methodist Book Concern, 1898), booklet in the Coe Papers, Yale Divinity School.

28. Cf. GAC, "Theory of Knowledge and Theism," *Methodist Review,* 80 (January 1898): 71.

29. GAC, *The Religion of a Mature Mind* (Chicago: Fleming H. Revell, 1902), 49.

30. Ibid., 172.

31. Ibid., 183, 186.

32. Ibid., 166.

33. Ibid., 168, 170.

34. Ibid., 288.

35. Historian Henry May observed, for example, that the Progressive program of President Woodrow Wilson "assimilated easily enough" Ely's "mildly reformist economics" (Henry F. May, *The End of American Innocence, A Study of the First Years of Our Own Time, 1912–1917* [New York: Knopf, 1959]), 113.

36. GAC to J. H. Wigmore, Secretary, Harvard Club, Ward Papers, UTS.

37. John Gray to the Committee on Scholarship of the Harvard Club of Chicago, Ward Papers, UTS.

38. HFW, "We Were Friends," 89.

39. HFW, "Why I Have Found Life Worth Living," 282.

40. Hester, "Thought and Career of Harry F. Ward," 25–26.

41. DK to her parents, 25 November 1895, Ward Papers, UTS.

42. HFW to DK, 10 July 1895, Ward Papers, UTS.

43. Letter to the Harvard Club in support of Harry's scholarship, Ward Papers, UTS.

44. "Kicks from the Kicker," *Northwestern,* 20 February 1897, Ward Papers, UTS. Though no author is identified for this column, it appears in a scrapbook recording all published references about or by him at Northwestern.

45. Ibid.

46. "Kicks from the Kicker," 27 February 1897.

47. W—— B—— (indecipherable) to HFW, 26 May 1897, Ward Papers, UTS. Eugene Link's book on Ward incorrectly associates this letter with Ward's termination at the Northwestern Settlement three years letter. However, the date of this letter is clear.

48. HFW to Mr. and Mrs. Kendall, 23 February 1899, Ward Papers, UTS.

49. HFW to DK, 25 October 1897, Ward Papers, UTS.

50. GAC, *Religion of a Mature Mind*, 429.

51. Ibid., 4, 418.

52. One who lives in this way—according to the moral content discernible in the life and teachings of Jesus—"somehow finds the facts of existence falling into order, is comforted and feels . . . not alone" (ibid., 130–31).

53. HFW to DK, 15 October 1897, Ward Papers, UTS.

54. Quoted by Ralph Barton Perry, *The Thought and Character of William James* (Boston: Little, Brown, 1935), 1:586.

55. HFW to DK, 15 October (1897), Ward Papers, UTS.

56. Perry, *Thought and Character of William James*, 1:586.

57. HFW to DK, 28 February 1898, Ward Papers, UTS.

58. Notes from James's lectures, in Perry, *Thought and Character of William James*, 2:331.

59. Ibid.

60. Ibid., 2:275.

61. Ibid.

62. HFW, "The Religion of Kipling," *Methodist Review* (March–April 1900): 262–69.

63. HFW to DK, 25 October 1897, Ward Papers, UTS.

64. Hester, "Thought and Career of Harry F. Ward," 22.

65. Dombrowski, *Early Days of Christian Socialism*, 70.

66. HFW to DK, 25 October 1897, Ward Papers, UTS.

67. Ibid.

68. HFW, "The Awkward Squad," *Evanston Press*, 7 May 1898, n.p., clipping in Ward Papers, UTS.

69. Ibid.

CHAPTER 3

1. "What Is the Settlement?" *Neighbor*, 15 November 1899, Ward Papers, UTS.

2. Jane Addams, *Twenty Years at Hull House* (New York: Signet, 1910), 126.

3. HFW, "Why I Have Found Life Worth Living," 282.

4. Upton Sinclair, *The Jungle* (New York: New American Library, 1905), 30. Since Sinclair researched this muckraking novel on the Chicago meatpacking industry during the same time as Ward's sojourn there, it is appropriate to incorporate some of Sinclair's observations into the Ward narrative.

5. HFW, "The Dreamers," typewritten sermon, 25 February 1900, Ward Papers, UTS.

6. Sinclair, *Jungle*, 34.

7. "Death Is the Reason," *Neighbor* (June 1900), Ward Papers, UTS.

8. "Summer Outings," *Neighbor* (May 1900), Ward Papers, UTS.

9. Addams, *Twenty Years at Hull House*, 346.

10. Sinclair, *Jungle*, 101.

11. Addams, *Twenty Years at Hull House*, 99.

12. "The Labor Situation," *Neighbor* (April 1900), Ward Papers, UTS. Jane Addams recognized that whether settlements liked it or not, they were linked to union activities in the public mind due to settlements' clear solidarity with the lives of working folk (Addams, *Twenty Years at Hull House*, 228).

13. "A Personal Appeal," Northwestern scrapbook, Ward Papers, UTS.

14. Ibid.

15. HFW, "Statement Presented to a Special Meeting of the Council of Northwestern University Settlement Association," 29 May 1900, Ward Papers, UTS.

16. HFW, "The Christian in Politics," typewritten sermon, 24 June 1900, Ward Papers, UTS.

17. More than a decade later he described this revelatory moment he could never forget in *The Gospel for a Working World* (New York: Missionary Education Movement of the United States and Canada, 1918). Encounters like this eventually radicalized his thinking and strategy for the rest of his long life, and therefore his own account of that night is worth careful examination. Ward writes about a preacher in the third person, though the account is transparently autobiographical.

18. HFW, *Gospel for a Working World*, xiii–xv.

19. HFW, "To the Ministers Meetings of Chicago," Ward Papers, UTS.

20. Shields, "One Man's Quest," 1.

21. HFW, "Jesus and the Future," typewritten sermon, 25 May 1902, Ward Papers, UTS.

22. (HFW), notes on trip, Ward Papers, UTS.

23. Ibid.

24. Two years earlier he had been ordained as a deacon.

25. HFW, "Two Aspects of Industrialism," Ward Papers, UTS.

26. HFW, "Revivals," sermon, 16 April 1905, 4, Ward Papers, UTS.

27. HFW, "Two Aspects of Industrialism."

28. HFW, "Christianity and the Anarchist Problem," sermon, 15 September 1901, 9, Ward Papers, UTS.

29. HFW, "Lincoln and the People," 14 February 1904, typewritten sermon, Ward Papers, UTS.

30. HFW, "The Spirit of Lincoln," 12 February 1905, typewritten sermon notes, Ward Papers, UTS.

31. Shields, "One Man's Quest," 3.

32. Cited by Robert T. Handy, *A History of Union Theological Seminary in New York* (New York: Columbia University Press, 1987), 148.

33. HFW, "Achieving the Impossible," typewritten sermon, 18 November 1906, Ward Papers, UTS.

34. "Union Ave. M. E. Conference," clipping, Ward Papers, UTS.

35. William McGuire King, "The Emergence of Social Gospel Radicalism in American Methodism" (Ph.D. diss., Harvard University, 1977), 190.

36. "Minutes of the Conference Called to meet in the Ebbit House, Washington, D.C., Tuesday and Wednesday, December 3rd and 4th, 1907," Methodist Federation for Social Action Archives, Drew University, Madison, New Jersey (hereafter MFSA Papers, Drew University).

37. Quoted from the Methodist Federation for Social Service (hereafter MFSS) minutes by Richard Diener Tholin, "Prophetic Action and Denominational Unity: The Function of Unofficial Social Action Groups in the Methodist Church and the Protestant Episcopal Church" (Th.D. diss., Union Theological Seminary, 1967), 21.

38. The MFSS minutes note that "While the 'Social Creed of the Church' as it has been called is the work of the sub committee of the larger committee on the State of the Church, it was prepared in close co-operation with the Executive Committee of the Federation for Social Service, members of which prepared several sections of the Statement. Mr. Harry F. Ward of the Executive Committee gave particular attention to the matter, both in composition and through conferences with the leaders of the General Conference Committee."

39. William McGuire King has observed that another statement in the document, a declaration about organized labor just prior to the "Social Creed," would come to have critical importance within a few years when the Methodist Church fiercely debated its relationship to organized labor: "We cordially declare our fraternal interest in the aspirations of the laboring classes, and our desire to assist them in the righting of every wrong and the attainment of their highest well-being. We recognize that the fundamental purposes of the labor movement are essentially ethical, and therefore, should command the support of

Christian men. We recognize further that the organization of labor is not only the right of the laborers and conducive to their welfare, but is incidentally of great benefit to society at large." (From the *General Conference Journal* [1908]), 198–99; cited by King, "The Emergence of Social Gospel Radicalism."

40. HFW, "Christian Socialism," *Unity*, 8 August 1907, 363–66; "Christian Socialism," *Unity*, 15 August 1907, 378–82, copy in Ward Papers, UTS.

41. King rightly asserts that it is better to understand Ward as a Fabian Socialist.

42. HFW, "*The Church and the Social Problem* by Samuel Plantz," *Northwestern Christian Advocate*, 20 February 1907, 9.

43. HFW, "Christian Socialism," *Unity*, 8 August 1907, 363.

44. Ibid., 364.

45. HFW, "Christian Socialism," *Unity*, 15 August 1907, 379.

46. Ibid., 381–82.

47. Ibid., 379.

48. Ibid., 380.

49. HFW, "Where Is Thy Brother?" typewritten sermon, 19 January 1908, Ward Papers, UTS.

50. HFW to DKW, 1 December 1908, Ward Papers, UTS.

51. HFW to DKW, 5 December 1908, Ward Papers, UTS.

52. HFW to DKW, n.d. (probably early October 1908), Ward Papers, UTS.

53. HFW to DKW, October 1908, Ward Papers, UTS.

54. HFW, "The Call of Lonely Lake," unpublished poem, 1908, Ward-McNeer Papers, Georgetown University Library Special Collections Division. An expanded, printed version is in possession of Robin Ward Savage.

55. HFW to DKW, 11 October 1908, Ward Papers, UTS.

56. HFW to DKW, 21 November 1908, Ward Papers, UTS.

57. HFW to DKW, 15 November 1908, Ward Papers, UTS.

58. Ibid.

59. HFW to DKW, 02 November 1908, Ward Papers, UTS.

60. HFW to DKW, 24 November 1908, Ward Papers, UTS.

61. HFW to DKW, 25 February 1909, Ward Papers, UTS.

62. HFW to DKW, 1 November 1908, Ward Papers, UTS.

63. HFW to DKW, 21 January 1909, Ward Papers, UTS.

64. HFW to DKW, 1 November 1908, Ward Papers, UTS.

65. HFW to DKW, 24 November 1908, Ward Papers, UTS.

66. HFW to DKW, 5 November 1908, Ward Papers, UTS.

67. HFW to DKW, 13 April 1909, Ward Papers, UTS.

68. HFW to DKW, 20 April 1909, Ward Papers, UTS.

69. HFW to DKW, 17 February 1909, Ward Papers, UTS.

70. HFW, "The Call of the Wild," sermon, 27 October 1907, Ward Papers, UTS.

71. Quoted by King, "Emergence of Social Gospel Radicalism," 201, from HFW, "Industrial Relations," *Christian City* 22 (March 1910):71, and "Social Reconstruction," *Christian City* 22 (June 1910):163.

72. HFW, "Social Reconstruction," 103.

73. Quoted from the MFSS minutes, 111, by King, "Emergence of Social Gospel Radicalism," 203.

74. Milton John Huber, "A History of the Methodist Federation for Social Action" (Ph.D. diss., Boston University, 1949), 91–93.

CHAPTER 4

1. Quoted from *Discipline* (1912), 512–14, by Tholin, "Prophetic Action and Denominational Unity," 23.

2. Of course, Rauschenbusch reflects his own Baptist bias in pointing to the democratic (congregational) polity of his own tradition as best evidence of a Christianized church.

3. By recent standards Rauschenbusch's familial egalitarism seems naive and outmoded.

4. HFW to Walter Rauschenbusch, 29 December 1913, box 27, Walter Rauschenbusch Papers, American Baptist Historical Society Archives, American Baptist-Samuel Colgate Library, Rochester, New York. Courtesy of American Baptist Historical Society.

5. "Report of the Secretary for 1912–1913," MFSS minutes, 127, MSFA Papers, Drew University.

6. From a variety of newspaper clippings in the MFSA Papers, Drew University.

7. "Dr. Ward in This Northwest," 21 February 1913, unidentified newspaper clipping in MFSA Papers, Drew University.

8. "Social Service Evangelism," *Pittsburgh Christian Advocate,* 1 May 1913, 20.

9. "Relation of Labor and Christianity Is Touched by Ward," 17 March 1913, n.p., clipping in MFSA Papers, Drew University.

10. Frances Wayne, "Christianity Such as Christ Taught before Theologians Muddled, Need," *Denver Post,* 19 March 1913, n.p., clipping in MSFA Papers, Drew University.

11. "Open Meeting Success," *Labor World* (Spokane, Washington), 28 February 1913, n.p., clipping in MFSA Papers, Drew University.

12. A. W. Swenson, *Labor World,* 1 March 1913, n.p., clipping in MFSA Papers, Drew University.

13. "Social Service" (probably a Terre Haute newspaper), 29 January 1913, clipping in MFSA Papers, Drew University.

14. "High Learning Need of Labor" (unidentified Denver newspaper), 24 March 1913, n.p., clipping in MFSA Papers, Drew University.

15. "A Climactic Campaign at Denver" (unidentified newspaper), 1 May 1913, n.p., clipping in MFSA Papers, Drew University.

16. "Christianity Such as Christ Taught."

17. Daniel Bell, *Marxian Socialism in the United States* (Princeton: Princeton University Press, 1952), 71; Robert K. Murray, *Red Scare: A Study of National Hysteria, 1919–1920* (New York: McGraw-Hill, 1955), 19. No one could know that this would be the zenith of American socialism, for a world war, the fears associated with the Bolshevik Revolution, and intraparty fratricide would relegate socialist groups to the fringe of the American political and social scene.

18. Ward quoted in "Speaker Shows Ties between Socialism and Christianity" (unidentified San Francisco newspaper), 5 February 1913, n.p., clipping in MFSA Papers, Drew University.

19. "Many Things for Muncie Set Out" (unidentified Muncie, Indiana, newspaper), n.d., clipping from MFSA Papers, Drew University.

20. "Ameliorate Wrongs of Working Class" (unidentified newspaper), 1 December 1913, n.p., clipping in MFSA Papers, Drew University.

21. "Social Movement Bears out Word of God, He Says," *Indiana Daily Times,* 30 April 1915, n.p., clipping in MFSA Papers, Drew University.

22. HFW, "The Challenge of Socialism to Christianity," *Ford Hall Folks,* 22 March 1914, 1–4.

23. "Social Service Campaign in Troy Conference" (probably Methodism's *New York Christian Advocate*) 30 October 1913, n.p., clipping in MFSA Papers, Drew University.

24. Elmer E. Higley (a MFSS field representative), "Harry F. Ward, D. D." (probably a Methodist paper), n.d., clipping in MFSA Papers, Drew University. There is no evidence that Ward had any sort of earned or honorary doctorate as the article's title claims. Some newspaper accounts refer to him as "Dr. Ward," though he received only an honorary doctorate from the University of Wisconsin in 1931. His highest earned degree was the M.A. from Harvard. There is no evidence that the attributed doctorate was Ward's idea. Even at the time of his death in 1966 the business cards in his wallet listed him as "Mr. Harry Frederick Ward." The wallet is among the Ward Papers, UTS.

25. "Good Health Is up to the Church" (a Toledo newspaper), n.d., clipping in MFSA Papers, Drew University.

26. "Ameliorate Wrongs of Working Class" (unidentified newspaper), 1 December 1913, n.p., clipping in MFSA Papers, Drew University.

27. Newspaper clipping reporting on the labor parliament at First Baptist Church in an unidentified city, n.d., clipping in MFSA Papers, Drew University.

28. "'How Charitable Are You?' Asks Social Worker of Church Folks," *Toledo Blade*, 2 December 1913, n.p., clipping in MFSA Papers, Drew University.

29. "Social Revival at Rock River Conference" (unidentified Methodist paper), 8 May 1913, n.p., clipping in MFSA Papers, Drew University.

30. "'When They March the Ground Will Shake,'" *Epworth Herald*, 5 July 1913, n.p., clipping from MFSA Papers, Drew University.

31. HFW, "Report of the Secretary for 1912–1913," 5, MFSA Papers, Drew University.

32. HFW to E. R. Graham, 19 September 1913, MFSA Papers, Drew University.

33. The Methodist seminary at Boston University was particularly indebted to McConnell's spirited defense of two B.U.S.T. professors against heresy accusations at the 1908 Methodist General Conference.

34. "An Admirable Selection," *Christian Advocate*, 19 June 1913, n.p., clipping in MFSA Papers, Drew University.

35. Lynd Ward, *Storyteller without Words* (New York: Harry N. Abrams, 1974), 78.

36. "Report of the Secretary," *Social Service Bulletin* 4 (November 1914):1.

37. Coe moved from Northwestern University to Union Theological Seminary in 1909 to become Professor of Religious Education and Psychology of Religion.

38. Letter from George P. Mains, Agent in Charge, The Methodist Book Concern, to HFW, 23 January 1915, MFSA Papers, Drew University.

39. HFW, *The Labor Movement from the Standpoint of Religious Values* (New York: Sturgis and Walton, 1917), 139.

40. Ibid., 153.

41. HFW (not signed but from his Boston address) to D. D. Vaughn, 4 March 1915, MFSA Papers, Drew University.

42. Frank Duffy to HFW, 18 April 1916, MFSA Papers, Drew University.

43. Charles L. Hand to HFW, 11 May 1916, MFSA Papers, Drew University.

44. William Balch to HFW, 20 April 1916, MFSA Papers, Drew University.

45. Cited by King, "Emergence of Social Gospel Radicalism," 221, from the *General Conference Journal* (1916).

46. Quoted from the *Daily Christian Advocate* 18, 13 May 1916, 220, by King, "Emergence of Social Gospel Radicalism," 225.

47. Quoted from the *General Conference Journal* (1916), 803, by Tholin, "Prophetic Action and Denominational Unity," 307.

48. Ibid., 141–42, an allusion to Rauschenbusch.

49. HFW, "The Relation of the Church to Industrial and Financial Enterprises," *Biblical Review* (n.d, reprinted as a pamphlet, but identifies author as professor at Boston University, which dates it between 1913 and 1918), 375–94, Union Theological Seminary Library, New York.

50. George M. Ambrose to HFW, 22 May 1916, MFSA Papers, Drew University.

51. Charles Sumner to HFW, 29 May 1916, quoted by Ward in his "Report: On the Controversy between the Methodist Book Concern and the Allied Printing Trades Council" (1917), MFSA Papers, Drew University.

52. Charles Sumner to Dr. Race, 14 July 1916, quoted by Ward in ibid.

53. James W. Kline to HFW, 5 February 1917, MFSA Papers, Drew University.

54. HFW to James W. Kline, 9 February 1917, MFSA Papers, Drew University.

55. HFW to Charles Sumner, 7 December 1917, MFSA Papers, Drew University.

CHAPTER 5

1. HFW, "Not Peace, But a Sword," *Epworth Herald* 13 (November 1915): 1089.

2. L. J. Birney to HFW, 26 January 1917, Ward Papers, UTS.

3. L. J. Birney to HFW, 16 February 1917, Ward Papers, UTS.

4. Cited by King, "Emergence of Social Gospel Radicalism," 252, from the *Social Service Bulletin* 7 (May and July 1917):2 and 2–3, respectively.

5. Telegram from L. J. Birney to HFW, 4 June 1917, Ward Papers, UTS.

6. Telegram from HFW to L. J. Birney, 5 June 1917, Ward Papers, UTS.

7. HFW, *The Christian Demand for Social Reconstruction* (Philadelphia: Walter H. Jenkins, 1918), 50.

8. Letter from President of Boston University (name indecipherable), 10 April 1918, Ward Papers, UTS.

9. J. Covington Coleman in "Harry F. Ward 90th Birthday," Ward Papers, UTS.

10. Quoted from G. Bromley Oxnam's diary by King, "Emergence of Social Gospel Radicalism," 177.

11. Ward probably looked much better than the previous occupant of the chair in Christian ethics, Thomas C. Hall. Hall had angered many Americans, especially one of the seminary's trustees, when he defended Germany's action in sinking the *Lusitania* as a necessary part of military strategy. Hall's appeal for American neutrality had worn thin with this unpopular argument. Fortunately for Hall, he began a sabbatical and later was granted a leave of absence to work among prisoners of war. The seminary board sacked Hall a month after the United States entered the war.

12. Cf. King, "Emergence of Social Gospel Radicalism," 245–46.

13. Cf. letter of Norman Thomas to HFW, 5 June 1917, ACLU Papers, reel 3, vol. 18.

14. "Travel Book," entry dated 22 March 1918, Ward Papers, UTS.

15. HFW to Pauline Rauschenbusch, 1 August 1918, box 91, Walter Rauschenbusch Papers, American Baptist Historical Society Archives, American Baptist-Samuel Colgate Library, Rochester, New York. Courtesy of American Baptist Historical Society.

16. HFW, "The Present Task of Christian Ethics," *Union Theological Seminary Bulletin* 2 (November 1918): 21, 24.

17. Daniel Bell, *Marxian Socialism in the United States* (Princeton: Princeton University Press, 1952), 105–6.

18. C. J. Bushnell, *American Journal of Sociology* 25 (March 1920), 645, quoted in M. K. Reely and P. H. Rich, ed., *Book Review Digest*, 1920, 16, 547.

19. Murray, *Red Scare*, 163.

20. Ibid., 64–65.

21. E. I. Chamberlin to the Department of Evangelism of the Methodist Episcopal Church, Philadelphia, n.d., MFSA Papers, Drew University.

22. Quoted by Robert H. Craig, "An Introduction to the Life and Thought of Harry F. Ward," *Union Seminary Quarterly Review* 24 (Summer 1969): 340.

23. Quoted by Huber, "History of the Methodist Federation," 138.

24. According to an article, "Bolshevism and the Methodist Church," *Current Opinion* 66 (June 1919): 380.

25. Huber, "History of the Methodist Federation," 132–33. Huber cites an editorial by James R. Joy, "An Account of the Controversy Precipitated by Professor Ward," *New York Christian Advocate* (13 March 1919), n.p.

26. Minutes of the Meeting of the Eastern Section of the Executive Com-

mittee and Advisory Council of the Methodist Federation for Social Service, 24 March 1919, MSFA Papers, Drew University.

27. "A Statement by Professor Harry F. Ward," *Christian Advocate*, 3 April 1919, 434.

28. Ibid.

29. Ibid.

30. HFW to The Senate Committee Investigating German Propaganda, Washington, D.C., 28 January 1919, Ward Papers, UTS.

31. HFW, "Consolation," unpublished poem, dated "about January 27, 1919," Ward Papers, UTS.

32. Pauline Rauschenbusch to HFW, 3 April 1919, Ward Papers, UTS.

33. Eugene L. Fisk, M.D., Medical Director of the Life Extension Institute, Inc., New York City, to HFW, 4 April 1919, Ward Papers, UTS.

34. HFW to Dr. Olsen, 30 April 1919, MFSA Papers, Drew University.

35. Eli Pittman to HFW, 9 May 1919, MFSA Papers, Drew University.

36. HFW, "Why I Have Found Life Worth Living," 281.

37. Quoted in *Book Review Digest*, 1919, 15.

38. HFW to Ralph E. Davis, 24 February 1921, Ward Papers, UTS.

39. HFW, "The Rauschenbusch Memorial," *Religious Education* 24 (April 1919): 298.

40. Apparently the column ran for about a year, from 23 October 1920 until at least the following September.

41. HFW, "Some Studies in Christian Fellowship" *Churchman*, 3 September 1921, 12.

42. HFW, "Some Studies in Christian Fellowship: XXXV—Things That Unite—Love," *Churchman*, 27 August 1921, 9–10.

43. HFW, "Some Studies in Christian Fellowship: XXXVI—Things That Unite—The Church," *Churchman*, 3 September 1921, 12.

44. HFW, "The Function of the Church in Industry," *Annals* 103 (September 1922): 96.

CHAPTER 6

1. Norman Thomas to Roger Baldwin, 20 June 1917, ACLU Papers, vol. 18. This correspondence took place in conjunction with their work for the Civil Liberties Bureau of the American Union Against Militarism, a predecessor to the National Civil Liberties Bureau (beginning 1 October 1917), which in turn became the American Civil Liberties Union (beginning 19 January 1920).

2. Samuel Walker, *In Defense of American Liberties: A History of the ACLU* (New York: Oxford University Press, 1990), 51, 57.

3. Huber, "History of the Methodist Federation," 151.

4. "Report on Visit with Rev. H. F. Ward," 25 March 1920, three typewritten pages, MFSA Papers, Drew University.

5. "Mr. Jerome Davis," n.d., MFSA Papers, Drew University. It is not known how this report came to be in the possession of the MFSA.

6. HFW to the Honorable Calvin Coolidge, 15 June 1921, Ward Papers, UTS.

7. W. J. Burns, Director, to the Honorable Martin B. Madden, House of Representatives, 7 April 1922, in FBI files on Harry F. Ward.

8. Memorandum from J. Edgar Hoover to Mr. Burns, 3 January 1924, with attached clipping, FBI file on Harry F. Ward.

9. HFW, "Free Speech for the Army," New Republic, 13 July 1927, 196.

10. A doctor's report of 28 May 1928, the year she graduated from Oberlin College, states that Muriel's poor eyesight was probably due to encephalitis. Cf. report of John Phillips, M.D., to Mrs. Ward, Ward Papers, UTS. A newspaper article by a person who knew Daisy and Muriel called it "sleeping sickness." Cf. Nora Rodd, "Daisy Kendall Ward: Woman of Her Day" (obituary), newspaper clipping in possession of Robin Ward Savage.

11. HFW, "The Function of Faith in the Modern World," in What Religion Means to Me (Garden City: Doubleday, 1929), 44.

12. John Dos Passos, The Big Money (Boston: Houghton Mifflin, 1933), 87.

13. Walter Muelder, Methodism and Society in the Twentieth Century (New York: Abingdon, 1961), 94.

14. "Report of the Secretary, Methodist Federation for Social Service, October 1, 1919 to October 1, 1920," 1, MFSA Papers, Drew University.

15. Ibid., 3.

16. (HFW), "Suggested Statement for General Conference. In Outline," MSFA Papers, Drew University.

17. Sean Dennis Cashman, America in the Twenties and Thirties: The Olympian Age of Franklin Delano Roosevelt (New York: New York University Press, 1989), 42.

18. HFW, "We Were Friends," 90.

19. HFW, Ethical Aspects of Industrialism (Peking: Leader Press, 1925), 74, 75, 77.

20. The language of utopia had been part of the language of turn-of-the-century Progressivism with popular works like Edward Bellamy's Looking Backward, which illustrated the value of industrial efficiency. By contrast, William Morris's idealization of the age of handicraft in his dystopian novel, News from Nowhere, caught the attention of those who feared modern technology. Ward rejected this sort of antimodern, nostalgic yearning as a dream of

intellectuals, not of working persons who valued the contributions of the machine age (77).

21. HFW, "Some Studies in Christian Fellowship: II—Is a Class Divided Society Christian?" *Churchman*, 30 October 1920, 13.

22. HFW, *Ethical Aspects of Industrialism*, 72.

23. Ibid., 55, 58–59.

24. The findings were published as *Revolutionary Radicalism: Its History, Purpose and Tactics with an Exposition and Discussion of the Steps Being Taken and Required to Curb It*, part I, vol. 1 (Albany, New York: J. B. Lyon, 1920), 1115. The other such place was "St. Stephens College at Annandale, N.Y., where the president is the Rev. (Bernard) Iddings-Bell, and the professor of economics the Socialist, Dr. (Lyford P.) Edwards" (1115).

25. Ibid., 1116.

26. Ibid., 1084.

27. Ibid., eighth photostat page following 992.

28. "Minister Reply to D.A.R. Protest," *LeRoy Gazette-News* (New York), 4 April 1928, n.d., clipping in Ward Papers, UTS.

29. For example, in the "Minutes of the Meeting of the Eastern Section of the Executive Committee and Advisory Council of the Methodist Federation for Social Service," 24 March 1919, Tippy was the only recorded negative voice. Cf. MFSA Papers, Drew University.

30. Worth M. Tippy to S. Earl Taylor, 7 February 1920, MFSA Papers, Drew University.

31. Worth M. Tippy to Francis McConnell, 24 November 1920, MFSA Papers, Drew University.

32. Quoted in a memorandum by Ward, 28 November 1920, MFSA Papers, Drew University.

33. William McGuire King, "An Enthusiasm for Humanity: The Social Emphasis in Religion and Its Accommodation in Protestant Theology," in *Religion and Twentieth Century Intellectual Life*, ed. Michael J. Lacey (Cambridge: Cambridge University Press, 1989).

34. HFW, "Foreword," in *An American Pilgrimage: Portion of the Letters of Grace Scribner*, ed. Winifred L. Chappell (New York: Vanguard, 1927), ix.

35. HFW, "Remarks at Scribner's Memorial Service," MFSA Papers, Drew University.

36. Ibid. Before the decade was over, Harry would hold up Grace Scribner as a model for his own daughter (HFW to Muriel Ward, 1 November 1928, letter in possession of Nanda Ward).

37. Miriam Crist, "Winifred Chappell: 'Everybody on the Left Knew Her,'" *Radical Religion* 5(1) (1980):22.

38. HFW to Hugh Hartsthorne (citing a statement from Ward's letter to Coe), 9 January 1927, George Albert Coe Papers, Manuscript Group Number 36, Special Collections, Yale Divinity School Library. (Hereafter Coe Papers)

39. HFW to G. Bromley Oxnam, 5 April 1921, MFSA Papers, Drew University.

40. HFW, "Some Studies . . . XXXVIII," 12.

41. HFW, "Foreword," *An American Pilgrimage*, ix.

42. HFW, "Place of Religion in New Social Order," three pages of typed lecture notes for summer student conferences, 1921, 3, Ward Papers, UTS.

43. HFW, "The Challenge of the Social Crisis to Christianity," notes from a lecture at a summer student conference, 1921, Ward Papers, UTS.

44. HFW to Muriel Ward, 19 January 1925, letter in possession of Nanda Ward.

45. HFW to Kenyon L. Butterfield, 10 October 1922, Ward Papers, UTS.

46. Kenyon L. Butterfield to HFW, 29 November 1922, Ward Papers, UTS.

47. Gordon Ward to "Mother and Dad," n.d. (though it is datable, since the Wards' twenty-fifth wedding anniversary was in April 1924), letter in possession of Robin Ward Savage.

48. HFW, "How Can Civilization Be Saved," *Christian Century*, 11 September 1924.

49. DKW to Lynd Ward, n. d., Ward Papers, UTS.

50. A recollection from the 1924 trip cited in HFW, "The Lenin Spirit," based on notes from his speech and printed in *Daily Worker*, 4 February 1945, 5.

51. DKW to Lynd Ward, 1924, Ward Papers, UTS.

52. HFW, "Spirit of Lenin," 5.

53. HFW, "Will Religion Survive in Russia?" *Christian Century* 42, 12 February 1925, 215–218.

54. HFW, "Civil Liberties in Russia," *Nation* 120, 4 March 1925, 234–37.

55. HFW, "Why I Have Found Life Worth Living," 282.

56. HFW, "The Future of the Intellectual Class" (based on shorthand notes taken by Haridas Chatterjee), *Calcutta Review* 14 (February 1925):232, 238–39.

57. Ibid., 234.

58. FBI files on Harry F. Ward.

59. "Saklatvala Calls British Our Enemy," *New York Times* (hereafter *NYT*), 4 October 1925, p. 19, col. 1.

60. DKW to her children, 1925, Ward Papers, UTS.

61. HFW to his children, 5 May 1925, Ward Papers, UTS.

62. HFW to his children, 3 June 1925, Ward Papers, UTS.

63. HFW to his children, 8 June 1925, Ward Papers, UTS.

64. HFW, "The Shanghai Strike," 25 July 1925, an account forwarded by the ACLU to the Federated Press, Chicago, ACLU Papers.

65. HFW to his children, 2 April 1925, Ward Papers, UTS.

66. HFW to George Coe, 28 March 1925, Ward Papers, UTS.

67. DKW to her children, 4 April 1925, Ward Papers, UTS.

68. DKW to Lynd Ward, 1924 in Moscow, Ward Papers, UTS.

69. Gordon Ward, letter to author, 5 July 1983.

70. HFW, "China's Anti-Christian Movement," *Christian Century,* 15 April 1926, 475.

71. HFW, "China's Anti-Christian Temper," *Christian Century,* 13 May 1926, 613.

72. HFW to his children, 26 March 1925, Ward Papers, UTS.

73. HFW, *Ethical Aspects of Industrialism,* 73.

74. Ibid., 31.

75. HFW to M. K. Gandhi, 9 November 1925, Ward Papers, UTS. After a lengthy imprisonment and difficulties with his followers concerning non-cooperation as a means of social change, Gandhi removed himself from the political arena, asserting that India's goodness mattered more than any shortcut to independence.

76. HFW, "Gandhi and the Future of India," *Christian Century,* 4 June 1925, 727–29.

77. Ward was not unique in this fascination, for an entire issue of the Protestant pacifist journal, the *World Tomorrow,* was devoted to Gandhi (C. Chatfield, *For Peace and Justice: Pacifism in America, 1914–1941* [Knoxville: University of Tennessee Press, 1971], 203).

78. As reported by a newspaper article after Ward's return to the States. Cf. "Saklatvala Calls British Our Enemy."

79. HFW, "Creative Ideas in the Orient," *American Review,* 4 December 1926, 522.

80. Ibid., 520–21.

81. HFW to M. K. Gandhi, 9 November 1925, Ward Papers, UTS.

82. Eugene P. Link, *Labor-Religion Prophet: The Times and Life of Harry F. Ward* (Boulder, Colorado: Westview Press, 1984), 126.

83. HFW to President Calvin Coolidge, n.d. (in folder, "Correspondence Related to Chinese Situation, c. 1924–1928"), Ward Papers, UTS.

84. Link, *Labor-Religion Prophet,* 126.

85. HFW, "Anglo-American Relations in China," *Christian Century,* 1 September 1927, 1016–18.

86. HFW, "The Future of Religion," *World Tomorrow* 8 (December 1925): 372–74.

87. HFW, "Why I Have Found Life Worth Living."

88. Kirby Page, ed., *Recent Gains in American Civilization* (New York: Harcourt, Brace, 1928).

89. HFW, "Twenty Years of the Social Creed," *Christian Century*, 19 April 1928, 502. Jane Addams's reputation, too, hung under a dark cloud because of her antiwar efforts.

90. Ibid., 504.

91. Ibid., 503.

92. Ibid.

93. King ("Enthusiasm for Humanity") has argued that the dominant mythos of the radical Social Gospel was, in fact, the God of battles. Ward was no exception, but severe personal and public challenges of the 1920s altered the way Ward appropriated this mythos.

94. HFW to Muriel Ward, 20 November 1924, letter in possession of Nanda Ward.

95. HFW, "Function of Faith in Modern Life," 533.

96. HFW, "Function of Faith in the Modern World," 48.

97. HFW, "Why I Have Found Life Worth Living," 282–83.

CHAPTER 7

1. HFW, review of *Does Civilization Need Religion?* in *World Tomorrow*, January 1928, 38–39.

2. The preface states Ward's "particularly heavy obligation to my friend Professor John H. Gray . . . my first and . . . my continuous teacher in economics" (vii).

3. HFW, *Our Economic Morality*, 283, 312.

4. Reinhold Niebuhr (hereafter RN), "A Religion to Save the World," *New York Herald Tribune*, 17 March 1929, sec. 11, p. 25.

5. HFW to George Coe, n.d., Coe Papers, Yale Divinity School Library. Ward was particularly displeased with the other appointment—John Baillie in theology. Baille was regarded as a representative of Barthian Neo-Orthodoxy, which Ward viewed as yet another form of theological escapism. The letter expresses disgust with President Coffin's desire for "balance" on the faculty. The letter's phrasing makes it unclear whether this "balance" applies only to Baillie or if it also is relevant to Niebuhr's appointment. Given other evidence of Ward's regard for Niebuhr during this period, his frustration with Niebuhr's appointment seems to be only to the quick promotion to full professor and occupancy of an endowed chair—that is, there may be some evidence of professional jealousy by Ward here.

6. Niebuhr's frequent visits were remembered by Mae McNeer Ward, HFW's daughter-in-law, and recounted in interviews with the author.

7. Cf. Richard Wightman Fox, *Reinhold Niebuhr: A Biography* (San Francisco: Harper and Row, 1985), 28.

8. "Urge Friendliness in Soviet Protests," *NYT*, 7 March 1930, p. 6, col. 3.

9. Yale theologian H. Richard Niebuhr.

10. RN to James Dombrowski, 29 August 1930, Dombrowski Papers, the State Historical Society of Wisconsin, Madison, Wisconsin (hereafter SHSW).

11. Fox, *Reinhold Niebuhr*, 123–24.

12. Charles C. Brown, *Niebuhr and His Age* (Philadelphia: Trinity, 1992), 42–43.

13. Dietrich Bonhoeffer, *No Rusty Swords*, ed. and trans. Edwin H. Robertson (London: Collins, 1965), 89.

14. Dietrich Bonhoeffer, *Gesammelte Schriften* (Munich: Kaiser-Verlag, 1965–69), 3:191. Writer's translation.

15. Handy, *History of Union Theological Seminary*, 191.

16. HFW, "The Handwriting on the Wall," *Christian Century*, 4 March 1931, 306. Cf. also HFW, "The Challenge of Unemployment Relief," *Religious Education* 26 (March 1931):202.

17. HFW, "The Futility of the Modern Spirit," stenographer's notes of class lecture, 3, Ward Papers, UTS.

18. HFW, "The Inadequacy of Liberal Christianity," stenographer's notes of class lecture, 1–3, Ward Papers, UTS.

19. Principles of the Fellowship of Socialist Christians listed in a form letter to HFW, Ward Papers, UTS.

20. GAC to HFW, 10 February (1930), Coe Papers, Yale Divinity School Library.

21. HFW to RN, 13 January 1931, including manifesto "To the Middle Class" and report of the meeting, Niebuhr Papers, Library of Congress.

22. HFW, *Which Way Religion?* 221.

23. RN to Ursula Keppel-Compton (hereafter UKC), 18 June 1931, Niebuhr Papers, Library of Congress.

24. RN to UKC, 8 August 1931, Niebuhr Papers, Library of Congress.

25. Letters and telegrams from June 1929 in folder, "Case of James Dombrowski," Ward Papers, UTS.

26. James Dombrowski diary, 1929 (quoting from Ward's *The Opportunity for Religion in the Present World* [New York: Woman's World, 1919]), 29, Dombrowski Papers, SHSW.

27. This summary is based on letters from HFW and DKW to their children during this visit and HFW's subsequent book, *In Place of Profit: Social Incentives in the Soviet Union* (New York, Scribner's, 1933).

28. DKW to her children, 10 September 1931, Ward Papers, UTS.

29. DKW to her children, 19 September 1931, Ward Papers, UTS.

30. HFW, *In Place of Profit*, 75.

31. Ibid., 93.

32. RN to UKC, 6 October 1931, Niebuhr Papers, Library of Congress.

33. RN to UKC, 1 October 1931, Niebuhr Papers, Library of Congress.

34. RN to UKC, 4 October 1931, Niebuhr Papers, Library of Congress.

35. HFW to James Dombrowski, 4 October 1931, Dombrowski Papers, box 14, SHSW.

36. RN to UKC, 16 October 1931, Niebuhr Papers, Library of Congress.

37. RN to UKC, 18 October 1931, Niebuhr Papers, Library of Congress.

38. RN to UKC, 23 October 1931, Niebuhr Papers, Library of Congress. Here, "they" are the Scotts, and the other guests are the Burkitts. The full quote reads: "Had dinner last night at the Coffins with the Burkitts. . . . The Scotts had told the Burkitts that Coffin was altogether too sympathetic to radical opinion in the seminary so you may imagine what they told them about me."

39. H. S. Coffin to RN, 15 July 1933, Niebuhr Papers, Library of Congress.

40. RN to UKC, 3 November 1931, Niebuhr Papers, Library of Congress.

41. RN to UKC, 20 October 1931, Niebuhr Papers, Library of Congress.

42. RN to UKC, 24 November 1931, Niebuhr Papers, Library of Congress.

43. HFW, *In Place of Profit,* 382.

44. Ibid., 51.

45. Ibid., 107.

46. Ibid., 239.

47. Ibid.

48. RN, *Moral Man and Immoral Society* (New York: Scribner's, 1932), xxiii.

49. HFW to GAC, 19 February 1933, Coe Papers, Yale Divinity School Library.

50. HFW to GAC, 19 March 1933, Coe Papers, Yale Divinity School Library.

51. GAC, letter to the editor of *Christian Century,* 15 March 1933, 362–63.

52. Arthur W. Calhoun to RN, Niebuhr Papers, Library of Congress.

53. Cited by Fox, *Reinhold Niebuhr,* 136.

54. RN, "After Capitalism—What?" *World Tomorrow* 16 (March 1933):203.

55. RN, "Optimism and Utopianism," *World Tomorrow* 22 (February 1933):180.

56. HFW "A Statement of Our Position," *Social Questions Bulletin* 23 (November 1933):1–4.

57. HFW to GAC, Coe Papers, Yale Divinity School Library.

58. HFW to GAC, 19 February 1933, Coe Papers, Yale Divinity School Library.

59. Ibid.

60. GAC to HFW, 26 February 1933, Coe Papers, Yale Divinity School Library.

61. Ibid.

62. HFW to GAC, 5 May 1933, Coe Papers, Yale Divinity School Library.

63. Ibid.

64. GAC to HFW, 11 May 1933, Coe Papers, Yale Divinity School Library.

65. GAC to HFW, 11 May 1933, Coe Papers, Yale Divinity School Library.

66. HFW to GAC, 25 June 1933, Coe Papers, Yale Divinity School Library.

67. Minutes of the MFSS Executive Committee and General Council, 2 October 1933, MFSA Papers, Drew University.

68. "Statement of Our Position."

69. No doubt Ward's friendship with Coe, who taught at Columbia Teacher's College until 1927, provided opportunities to become associated with likeminded professors at Columbia such as George S. Counts, Goodwin Watson, and Walter Rauschenbusch.

70. HFW (proposal for New America), typewritten MS, 1933, Ward Papers, UTS.

71. Minutes of the MFSS Executive Committee and General Council, 27 October 1934, MFSA Papers, Drew University.

72. J. King Gordon (Union student in the 1930s), "Reinhold Niebuhr, Portrait of a Christian Realist," seventeen-page typewritten MS, Niebuhr Papers, Library of Congress.

73. Handy, *History of Union Theological Seminary*, 184–85.

74. Ibid., 187.

75. "Stalin Not Dictator, Prof. Ward Declares," *NYT,* 9 October 1934, p. 8, col. 5.

76. Reported in a letter from RN to Ursula Niebuhr (hereafter UN), 23 January 1935, Niebuhr Papers, Library of Congress.

77. See, for example, Donald Meyer's *The Protestant Search for Political Realism*, 2nd ed. (Middletown: Wesleyan University Press, 1988), which is in many ways a profound analysis of American Protestant political thought in the twenties and thirties. However, his description of Ward as an idealist without strategy does not match the facts, e.g., "Ward exhibited the extreme logic of opposing the sorry present with an ideal future; tactics were secondary" (188). Ward's tactics may have been wrong-headed or naive, but if anything, he was more concerned with tactics than Niebuhr at this stage of the 1930s. One problem with this otherwise brilliant book is that the author's analysis seems so thoroughly Niebuhrian (witness even the book's title) that other political options of the 1930s are read through Niebuhr's eyes. The issue here is not whether Niebuhr's own strategy was better but the tendency of historians persuaded by Niebuhrian categories to be seduced by his compelling rhetoric about radicals.

78. RN, *Reflections on the End of an Era* (New York: Scribner's, 1934), 23.

79. Ibid., 169.

80. J. King Gordon quoting a letter from Niebuhr in his typed manuscript of a review of Paul Merkley's *Reinhold Niebuhr: A Political Account,* Niebuhr Papers, Library of Congress.

81. GAC to Adelaide Case, 28 May 1934, Coe Papers, Yale Divinity School Library.

82. RN to James Dombrowski, 22 January 1934, Dombrowski Papers, box 22, SHSW.

83. HFW to Lynd Ward and May McNeer Ward, 5 June 1932, Ward Papers, UTS.

84. HFW, "Christians and Communists," *Christian Century,* 25 December 1935, 1652.

85. Ibid.

86. "News of New America" (mimeographed newsletter) (October 1935), Ward-McNeer Papers, Georgetown University Library Special Collections Division.

87. *National Newsletter—New America,* 1 December 1934, Ward-McNeer Papers, Georgetown University Library Special Collections Division.

88. "From the N.P.C.," *New American News* (August 1935):2, Ward-McNeer Papers, Georgetown University Library Special Collections Division.

89. "What Does the Election Mean?" *New American* (a monthly public newspaper) 1 (December 1936):4, Ward-McNeer Papers, Georgetown University Library Special Collections Division.

90. Typewritten outline titled "Prof. Ward, NA Training School, April 4, 1935, BASIC POINTS IN WINNING POWER," Ward Papers, UTS.

91. HFW to GAC, 3 June 1936, Coe Papers, Yale Divinity School Library.

92. RN to UN, 19 April (1936), Niebuhr Papers, Library of Congress.

93. RN to June Bingham, 14 January 1957, Niebuhr Papers, Library of Congress.

94. Cited in the Brown and Fox biographies of Niebuhr.

95. Roger Shinn, conversation with author, 21 September 1977.

96. Safford in HFW 90th Birthday program, Ward Papers, UTS. This recollection is verified by the writer's interview with Roger Shinn, a student beginning in 1938, later professor of ethics at UTS, and therefore a person keenly aware of the Union dynamics in those days.

97. RN to UN, 19 May (1936), Niebuhr Papers, Library of Congress.

98. HFW to GAC, 19 February 1933, Coe Papers, Yale Divinity School Library.

99. RN, *Reflections on the End of an Era,* ix.

100. Jack R. McMichael, letter to author, 19 July 1979. Another student recalls that "Ward, on his part, felt that Niebuhr had sold out and been taken in by that right-wing theologian Karl Barth." Cf. J. King Gordon, typewritten review of Paul Merkley's *Reinhold Niebuhr: A Political Account* in Niebuhr Papers, Library of Congress.

101. RN to UN, n.d., Niebuhr Papers, Library of Congress. Niebuhr's emphasis.

102. RN to UN, 13 October (1939), Niebuhr Papers, Library of Congress. Niebuhr appears to use the phrase "travelling with" in the sense of "associating with."

103. RN, "Ten Years That Shook My World," *Christian Century,* 26 April 1939, 543.

104. RN, "Ideology and Pretense," *Nation,* 9 December 1939, 645.

105. Ibid., 646.

106. RN to UN, 18 September 1939, Niebuhr Papers, Library of Congress.

107. RN to UN, 11 October 1939, Niebuhr Papers, Library of Congress.

108. John Bennett, letter to author, 25 June 1979.

109. HFW to Thomas Wright, 4 December 1938, Ward Papers, UTS.

110. There is considerable correspondence between Ward and other New America leaders over this matter, and a letter submitted as evidence during the 1939 Dies hearings indicates that Harry Ward left New America because of two "tendencies": anticommunism and over-intellectualism. Cf. letter from John C. Bobbitt to Thomas H. Wright in *Investigation of Un-American Propaganda Activities in the United States: Hearings before a Special Committee on Un-American Activities,* House of Representatives, Seventy-Sixth Congress (1939), vol 10., 16–21, 23–25, 28 (Washington D.C.: Government Printing Office, 1940), 6305–6.

111. Ward indicates (in a letter to Elizabeth L. Fackt, 27 September 1939, Ward Papers, UTS) that the ALPD was an issue in the break with New America.

112. HFW to Thomas Wright, 2 January 1938, Ward Papers, UTS.

CHAPTER 8

1. Formerly the American League Against War and Fascism. The name was changed in November 1937, contrary to some erroneous descriptions that link the name change to the time of the Nazi-Soviet pact (August 1939), an event to which the league responded ambivalently, which many understood as a pro-Soviet response.

2. Roger N. Baldwin to The National Committee, The American League for Peace and Democracy, 17 October 1939, Reinhold Niebuhr Papers, Library of Congress.

3. Statement quoted by Ward in his appearance before the House Committee on Un-American Activities in 1939 (undated transcript in Ward Papers, UTS).

4. Norman Thomas to HFW, 10 October 1939, Ward Papers, UTS.

5. *Investigation of Un-American Propaganda Activities in the United Sates, Hearings before a Special Committee on Un-American Activities, House of Representatives, Seventy-fifth Congress,* vol. 1 (Washington D.C.: United States Government Printing Office, 1938), 911.

6. For example, when quizzed by Matthews about certain controversial league statements, Ward retorted, "There were some expressions of that character in the program of the American League Against War and Fascism when I went in, and I was told that you put it there. We took it out as soon as we could" (*Investigation of Un-American Propaganda Activities in the United States,* 10:6224).

7. Ibid., 6262.

8. Ibid., 6289.

9. Ibid., 6264–65.

10. Ibid., 6265.

11. Ibid., 6315.

12. Ibid., 6318.

13. Two otherwise helpful historians of the ACLU have a different take on the events: They describe Dies as calling off the HUAC hearings on the ACLU and pronouncing the organization free from communist influence. They seem to imply that Ward was never allowed to give testimony. Cf. Walker, *In Defense of American Liberties,* 129; Jerold Simmons, "The American Civil Liberties Union and the Dies Committee, 1938–1940," *Harvard Civil Rights-Civil Liberties Law Review* 17 (1982):196–97. Still, the proceedings did seem to end abruptly, though given the committee's frustration with Ward's evasiveness and challenges to their assertions, it is a fair guess that they had had enough of him. Harry Ward had sufficiently damned himself in their eyes both before and after the proceedings to make their case.

14. *Investigation of Un-American Propaganda Activities in the United States,* 10:6303.

15. Ibid., 6309.

16. E.g., Robert H. Dolliver to HFW, 17 January 1941, Ward Papers, UTS.

17. Halford Luccock to HFW, 11 January 1941, Ward Papers, UTS.

18. Holmes to Roger Baldwin, 3 January 1940, cited by Simmons, "American Civil Liberties Union," 203–4.

19. Resolution cited by Corliss Lamont, ed., *The Trial of Elizabeth Gurley Flynn by the American Civil Liberties Union* (New York: Horizon Press, 1968),

42–43 (a book dedicated "to the memory of Dr. Harry F. Ward, Chairman, 1920–1940, Board of Directors of the American Civil Liberties Union").

20. Letter from HFW to Myles D. Blanchard, 1 October 1940, Ward Papers, UTS. The full text of Ward's resignation letter is included as an appendix in Lamont, *Trial of Elizabeth Gurley Flynn*, 209–11.

21. HFW to "the National Committee and the Board of Directors of the American Civil Liberties Union" (four-page mimeographed statement), 4 March 1940, copy in Alexander Meiklejohn Papers, box 30, SHSW.

22. Walker, *In Defense of American Liberties*, 131.

23. "Policy on Faculty is Given by Coffin," *NYT*, 22 May 1940, p. 24, col. 4.

24. HFW, "Impending Changes in the U.S.," lecture notes from Union Theological Seminary course, Christian Ethics 44, "Tactics of Social Change" (Spring 1941), Ward Papers, UTS.

25. According to Roger Shinn, then a UTS student, and Ward family members in interviews with this writer.

26. "Peace League Dies in Secret Session," *NYT*, 2 February 1940, 1.

27. HFW, *Democracy and Social Change* (New York: Modern Age, 1940).

28. Ward referred specifically to the United Christian Council for Democracy, a coalition of nine Protestant groups that had organized to undermine the profit system in order to develop an economic democracy.

29. According to an FBI check (26 July 1950, FBI files), Ward "registered to vote on November 5, 1940 and has voted since 1941, though he has never declared a preference for any political party."

30. Meyer, *Protestant Search for Political Realism*, 201.

31. Elliot Field to HFW, 25 March 1941, carbon copy in Niebuhr Papers, Library of Congress; Field's emphasis.

32. HFW, "Protestants and the Anti-Soviet Front," *Protestant* 4 (December 1941–January 1942):67.

33. I was first alerted to the fate of this student and friend of Harry Ward in a kind of throw-away comment by May McNeer Ward, Harry's daughter-in-law. She mentioned Hecker with a soft-spoken wistfulness, saying something like, "How could he [Harry Ward] forget him?" A 1997 Associated Press story briefly described the results of the one-hundred-page file on Hecker that had been recently released—"Soviet files indicate American leftists executed" (http://www.thonline.com/News/110997/National/national.htm).

34. RN, "Fellow Travelers," *Radical Religion*, 7, my emphasis. Niebuhr does not mention Ward by name, but certainly his former colleague was one such person as described here.

35. "Hisses and Cheers Evoked at Rally," *Baltimore Sun*, 24 May 1941, newspaper clipping in FBI files.

36. There is a reference to this letter of protest in the FBI file.

37. "Hisses and Cheers Evoked at Rally."

38. As with all informants listed in the file, this person's name is blacked out.

39. Unsigned internal memorandum, 24 May 1941, FBI files. Later references in the FBI files on Ward indicate that an active investigation of Ward began in 1941; cf. an 11 March 1955 internal memorandum. Black bars correspond to those used by censors before release of these documents under the Freedom of Information Act.

40. HFW, "Christianity, An Ethical Religion," *Union Review* 2 (May 1941):7.

41. Ibid., 8.

42. Ibid., 9.

43. Marx's statement is, "The philosophers have only *interpreted* the world in various ways; the point is, to *change* it" ("Theses on Feuerbach," in *Writings of the Young Marx on Philosophy and Society,* ed. Lloyd D. Easton and Kurt H. Guddat [New York: Anchor, 1967], 402).

44. HFW, "Christianity, An Ethical Religion," 9; my emphasis.

45. HFW, "Some Things I Have Learned While Teaching," *Alumni Bulletin of the Union Theological Seminary* 16 (June 1941):12.

46. Report, 10 July 1941, FBI files on HFW.

47. James Dombrowski to HFW, 6 May 1941, Ward Papers, UTS.

48. Sam H. Franklin to HFW, 3 May 1941, Ward Papers, UTS.

49. Frank W. Herriott to HFW, 7 May 1941, Ward Papers, UTS.

50. HFW, "Protestants and the Anti-Soviet Front"; my emphasis.

51. Report, 18 May 1943, FBI files.

52. Report, 9 May 1945, FBI files.

53. Memorandum, 18 May 1943, FBI files.

54. Card in HFW's wallet, dated 1 May 1943, Ward Papers, UTS. The card was still in his wallet at the time of his death in 1966.

55. FBI files.

56. Memorandum, 18 May 1944, FBI files.

57. Report, 19 June 1944, FBI files.

58. Memorandum, 16 October 1944, FBI files

59. Only identified as "during World War II," according to FBI report, 19 May 1955, FBI files.

60. Ibid.

61. HFW, "The Lenin Spirit," *Worker,* 4 February 1945, 5.

62. HFW, "Will America Change after the War?" *Reader's Scope* (September 1944):78.

63. HFW, "The Coming Struggle Within the Victorious Nations," Published article. No date or other publication information, but content indicates at least 1945. Copy in Ward Papers, UTS, 328–330.

64. See, for example, "Debs, Bourne, and Reed," *New Masses* 38, 4 March 1941, 13.

65. HFW, "The Task Before Us," *Social Questions Bulletin* (October 1944):3.

66. HFW, "The Future of the Profit Motive," *Christian Century*, 31 March 1943, 390.

67. HFW, "Judgment Day for Churches," *Christian Leader*, 7 April 1945, 151–52.

68. HFW, "Pulpits in War," 17.

69. HFW, "Fascist Trends in American Churches," *Christian Century*, 19 April 1944, 490–92.

70. For example, see his "Vatican Fascism," *Christian Century*, 12 June 1944; also his letter to GAC, 20 May 1943, Coe Papers, Yale Divinity School Library.

71. HFW, "Fascist Trends in American Churches," 492.

72. HFW to Jack McMichael, 29 May 1945, MFSA Papers, Drew University.

CHAPTER 9

1. Report, 11 June 1946, FBI files.

2. FBI files, 1946.

3. HFW to GAC, 6 January 1946, Coe Papers, Yale Divinity School Library.

4. Report, n.d., FBI files.

5. RN, "Our Relations to Russia," in *Toward a Better World*, ed. William Scarlet (Philadelphia: John Winston, 1946), 123–32.

6. HFW, "Our Relations to Russia," *Witness*, 27 February 1947, 9.

7. Ward is referring to language of the 1948 Amsterdam statement by the World Council of Churches. A newspaper clipping about the conference, emphasizing Niebuhr's use of this language, is included among Ward's manuscript preparation papers. The phrase seems to have been coined by William Temple, archbishop of Canterbury.

8. HFW, "Behind the Headlines: Our Policy Toward the Soviet Union," *Social Questions Bulletin* 37 (April 1947):55.

9. HFW, "Faith, Phrases, and Facts," *Zion's Herald*, 125, 17 December 1947, 1205, 1222–23.

10. HFW, "Behind the Headlines: Our Policy Toward the Soviet Union," 56.

11. HFW, "Behind the Headlines," *Social Questions Bulletin* 38 (April 1948):57.

12. HFW, "Behind the Headlines," *Social Questions Bulletin* 39 (January 1949):6–7.

13. HFW, "Behind the Headlines," *Social Questions Bulletin* 38 (November 1948):123. See similar statements in his other "Behind the Headlines" columns that year. Ward clearly recognized the shifting sands that accompanied the cold war.

14. HFW, "Socialist Democracy in the U.S.S.R.," *Protestant* (June–July, 1948), 18, 20.

15. Report, n.d., FBI files.

16. Gordon Ward to HFW, 25 July 1948, Ward-McNeer Papers, Georgetown University Library Special Collections Division.

17. Gordon Ward to Muriel Ward and Lynd Ward, 15 August 1948, Ward-McNeer Papers, Georgetown University Library Special Collections Division.

18. Statement by Louis F. Buedenz, 26 June 1950, FBI files.

19. The Ward Papers, UTS, contain at least three rejection letters: Harper and Brothers, 4 January 1950; Macmillan, 1953; Oxford University Press, 21 July 1955.

20. DKW to Raymond Robins, 21 March 1949, Raymond Robins Papers, State Historical Society of Wisconsin, Madison, Wisconsin.

21. Gordon Ward to HFW, 14 January and 1 February 1959, Ward-McNeer Papers, Georgetown University Library Special Collections Division.

22. Gordon Ward to his parents, 30 April 1950, Ward-McNeer Papers, Georgetown University Library Special Collections Division.

23. Gordon Ward to Lynd Ward and May McNeer Ward, 8 November 1950, Ward-McNeer Papers, Georgetown University Library Special Collections Division.

24. Report, n.d., FBI files.

25. HFW, "Back to Barbarism?" *Zion's Herald*, 18 January 1950, 51.

26. HFW, "Anti-Semitism and the Social Order," *Jewish Life* 2 (August 1948):13.

27. HFW, "The Case of Dr. DuBois," *Jewish Life* 5 (July 1951): 23–24.

28. HFW to Lynd Ward, n.d. (but context makes it clear that it is the early 1950s), Ward-McNeer Papers, Georgetown University Library Special Collections Division.

29. HFW to Jack McMichael, 20 June 1951, MFSA Papers, Georgetown University Library Special Collections Division.

30. HFW to Lynd Ward, 11 February 1951, Ward-McNeer Papers, George-town University Library Special Collections Division.

31. HFW, "We Were Friends," 89.

32. Ibid., 88.

33. GAC, "On Having Friends: A Study in Social Values," *Journal of Philosophy, Psychology and Scientific Methods* 12 (March 1915):156.

34. HFW, "We Were Friends," 90–91.

35. Ibid., 89.

36. Gordon Ward to Lynd Ward and May McNeer Ward, 2 November 1951, Ward-McNeer Papers, Georgetown University Library Special Collections Division. Indeed Harry Ward's FBI files refer to Army records, which mention HFW's participation in the Civil Rights Congress, the American League for Peace and Democracy/the American League Against War and Fascism, the Methodist Federation for Social Action, the ACLU, and the National Council of American-Soviet Friendship, plus the fact that he was "active in Front Organizations" and signed various petitions in behalf of Communist Party members.

37. Muriel Ward to Lynd and May Ward, n.d., Ward-McNeer Papers, Georgetown University Library Special Collections Division.

38. Gordon Ward to HFW, 16 January 1952, Ward-McNeer Papers, George-town University Library Special Collections Division.

39. Ibid.

40. As reported by Muriel. Cf. letter from Muriel Ward to Lynd and May Ward, n.d., Ward-McNeer Papers, Georgetown University Library Special Collections Division.

41. Gordon Ward to Lynd Ward, 17 January 1952, Ward-McNeer Papers, Georgetown University Library Special Collections Division.

42. Gordon Ward to Lynd Ward, 31 January 1952, Ward-McNeer Papers, Georgetown University Library Special Collections Division.

43. Gordon Ward to Muriel Ward, 31 January 1952, Ward-McNeer Papers, Georgetown University Library Special Collections Division.

44. Gordon Ward to Muriel Ward, 30 March 1952, Ward-McNeer Papers, Georgetown University Library Special Collections Division.

45. Gordon Ward to Harry and Daisy Ward, 25 March 1952, Ward-McNeer Papers, Georgetown University Library Special Collections Division.

46. Gordon Ward to HFW, n.d. (but the letter's internal evidence indicates 1953 Father's Day), Ward-McNeer Papers, Georgetown University Library Special Collections Division.

47. Report, n.d., FBI files.

48. "ExReds Tag Ward," newspaper clipping in Ward Papers, UTS.

49. HFW, statement to the press, 11 September 1953, MFSA Papers, Drew University. He also sent a copy to the *Christian Century*, probably the most frequently read weekly ecumenical journal among mainstream American Protestants.

50. HFW to Harold H. Velde, House of Representatives, 12 September 1953, MFSA Papers, Drew University.

51. King, "The Emergence of Social Gospel Radicalism," 2, 10–11; Tholin, "Prophetic Action and Denominational Unity," 442; Lonise L. Queen,, "Ward, Harry Frederick," in *The Encyclopedia of World Methodism*, 2 vols., ed. Nolan B. Harmon (Nashville: United Methodist Publishing House, 1974), 2:2450.

52. Ralph Roy, *Apostles of Discord: A Study of Organized Bigotry and Disruption on the Fringe of Protestantism* (Boston: Beacon, 1953), 317–19.

53. John C. Bennett to HFW, 9 October 1953, Ward Papers, UTS.

54. RN to HFW, 8 October 1953, Ward Papers, UTS.

55. John C. Bennett to HFW, 20 October 1953, Ward Papers, UTS.

56. HFW, an untitled, eleven-page typed manuscript, n.d., Ward Papers, UTS.

57. HFW to Ralph Roy, 18 October 1955, Ward Papers, UTS.

58. HFW to the Reverend Theodore R. Bundy, 10 March 1956, Ward Papers, UTS.

59. G. Bromley Oxnam's testimony before HUAC is quoted in his *I Protest* (New York: Harper and Brothers, 1954), 128–29.

60. Quoting Stalin's *Foundations of Leninism*, but, as is usually the case in the manuscript, Ward does not provide page numbers.

61. Box of notes and papers for preparation of "Jesus and Marx" manuscript, n.d., in possession of Robin Ward Savage.

62. HFW, "Jesus and Marx," 87.

63. RN, "Liberals and the Marxists Heresy," *Nation*, 21 October 1953, 14.

64. HFW to David P. McPhail, 14 April 1961, Ward Papers, UTS.

65. November 1953 statement by Ward, quoted by Jessica Smith, "Dr. Harry Ward at 90," *New World Review* 31 (October 1963):14.

66. Gordon Ward to Muriel Ward, 13 January 1954, Ward-McNeer Papers, Georgetown University Library Special Collections Division.

67. Gordon Ward to Lynd Ward, 3 September 1954, Ward-McNeer Papers, Georgetown University Library Special Collections Division.

68. Gordon Ward to Lynd Ward, 10 May 1955, Ward-McNeer Papers, Georgetown University Library Special Collections Division.

69. HFW, "The Basis of Socialist Democracy," *New World Review* 24 (November 1956): 25.

70. HFW, "Yesterday, Today, and Tomorrow," *Social Questions Bulletin* 47 (November 1957):29–30.

71. FBI report, 6 June 1957, FBI files.

72. Report, n.d., FBI files.

73. Quoting letter from HFW, Gordon Ward to May and Lynd Ward, 18 June 1960, Ward-McNeer Papers, Georgetown University Library Special Collections Division.

74. HFW, *The Story of American-Soviet Relations, 1917–1959* (New York: National Council of American-Soviet Relations, 1959), 58; my emphasis.

75. Ibid., 80.

76. From four typewritten pages recording remarks made by Lynd Ward and Harry Ward at her funeral, from Ward family archives maintained by Robin Ward Savage.

77. HFW, "What Needs Now to Be Done," *Social Questions Bulletin* 54 (March 1964):17–19.

78. Roger Shinn quoted in "Harry F. Ward—1873–1966," *Union Seminary Tower* (Winter 1967):1.

79. Stephen H. Frichman, "Remarks at the Harry F. Ward 90th Birthday Tribute," *Social Questions Bulletin* 54 (March 1964):21.

80. John Bennett to HFW, 9 February 1964, Ward Papers, UTS.

81. Report, 26 July 1962, FBI files.

82. Report, 15 August 1963, FBI files.

83. Ibid.

84. Benjamin Mays, in conversation with the author, 1978.

85. Transcribed by the author from "Does This Nation Want a Bill of Rights or a Police Nation?" sound recording (Americord, n.d. [during the Eisenhower administration]), kindly shared with the author by Nanda Ward.

86. Memorandum from the Director, FBI, 2 June 1964, FBI files.

87. May McNeer Ward, conversation with author, 1993.

88. "Instructions for Funeral in Case of Fatal Accident," n.d., Ward Papers, UTS.

89. Shinn's comments are included along with other excerpted eulogies from the memorial service in "A Prophet Was among Us," *Social Questions Bulletin* 57 (January 1967):3.

90. Shinn's remarks at the Ward memorial service as recorded in the Union alumni magazine. Cf. "Harry F. Ward—1873–1966," *Union Seminary Tower* (Winter 1967):1.

91. Newspaper clipping, "Wesleyan Convention," 18 May 1891 (no information on publication) in photo album of Ward family archives maintained by Robin Ward Savage.

92. HFW, "Why I Have Found Life Worth Living," 282.
93. Report, 5 January 1967, FBI files.

EPILOGUE

1. However, even Reinhold Niebuhr, who found Ward's Soviet sympathies "pathetic" and dangerous, could say about his former colleague in the end: "Dr. Ward . . . had the courage to challenge every form of social evil. . . . He became a historic figure in the encounter of the church with the social evils of modern industrialism. This generation owes him gratitude and respect." This message was sent by Niebuhr, who was in poor health, to the Ward memorial service. Cf. "Harry F. Ward—1873–1966," 1.

2. Milan Machovec, *A Marxist Looks at Jesus* (Philadelphia: Fortress, 1972).

3. Beverly Wildung Harrison, "The Role of Social Theory in Religious Social Ethics," in *Making the Connections: Essays in Feminist Social Ethics*, ed. Carol S. Robb (Boston: Beacon, 1985), 59. Christopher Lasch puts the matter this way: "The most instructive aspect of Niebuhr's career was the rapidity with which his realism degenerated, under the pressure of the cold war, into a bland and innocuous liberalism almost indistinguishable—for all its neo-orthodox overtones, and for all Niebuhr's unwillingness to apply the world 'liberal' to himself—from the liberalism against which he had initially rebelled.

"Like many others, Niebuhr decided, in the late forties, that Soviet totalitarianism was a greater menace than American capitalism; but the effect of defining the choice as a choice between rival systems was to blind him to the possibility that systems as such were neither moral nor immoral and that the choices confronting an American intellectual in the late forties were not questions of ultimate allegiance, not questions of allegiance at all, but questions of tactics and strategy. Niebuhr had all along shown a tendency to exalt political issues beyond their real importance even while attacking the 'utopians' for doing so . . . and in the latter part of his career this habit of rhetorical inflation got completely out of hand. As a result, rhetoric increasingly took the place of social analysis in Niebuhr's writings. [He misrepresented both the United States and U.S.S.R., for his] thought remained frozen in the polemical patterns of the late forties" (*The New Radicalism in America: The Intellectual as Social Type* [New York: Vintage, 1965], 300–301).

4. *Walter Rauschenbusch, Selected Writings*, ed. Winthrop S. Hudson (Mahwah, New Jersey: Paulist Press, 1984), 46–48. A fuller treatment of the connections between Rauschenbusch's spirituality and his social agenda can be found in my "Theology Converses with the Biographical Narrative of W. Rauschenbusch," *Perspectives in Religious Studies* 18 (Summer 1991):143–58.

5. Dietrich Bonhoeffer, "Christ and Good People," in *Ethics*, ed. Eberhard Bethge (New York: Macmillan, 1955), 60–63.

6. Robin Ward Savage recalled an experience at one of Seeger's concerts in the 1970s. She had sent a message to the performer, informing him that she was Harry Ward's granddaughter and wondering if he recalled the connection. (She remembered hearing Seeger sing in her grandparents' living room when she was a little girl.) Seeger invited her backstage enthusiastically, saying that he had been radicalized after hearing one of Harry Ward's speeches in Madison Square Garden.

7. Augustine's actual prayer had to do with another sort of unbridled desire: "Lord, make me chaste, but not yet."

8. HFW, *Our Economic Morality and the Ethic of Jesus*, 21–22.

9. GAC, *A Social Theory of Education* (New York: Scribner's, 1917).

REFERENCES

Addams, Jane. *Twenty Years at Hull House.* New York: Signet, 1910.

American Civil Liberties Union Papers. Seeley G. Mudd Manuscript Library, Princeton University Library, Princeton, New Jersey.

Bailey, Peter. *Leisure and Class in Victorian England: Rational Recreation and the Contest for Control, 1830–1855.* London: Routledge and Kegan Paul, 1978.

Bamford, T. W. *Rise of the Public Schools: A Study of Boys' Public Boarding Schools in England and Wales from 1837 to the Present Day.* London: Thomas Nelson, 1967.

Bell, Daniel. *Marxian Socialism in the United States.* Princeton: Princeton University Press, 1952.

Bellamy, Edward. *Looking Backward.* New York: New American Library, 1960.

Bennett, John. Letter to author. 25 June 1979.

"Bolshevism and the Methodist Church: An Account of the Controversy Precipitated by Professor Ward." *Current Opinion* 66 (June 1919): 380–81.

Bonhoeffer, Dietrich. "Christ and Good People." *Ethics.* Ed. Eberhard Bethge. New York: Macmillan, 1955.

———. *Gesammelte Schriften.* Munich: Kaiser-Verlag, 1965–1969.

———. *No Rusty Swords.* Ed. and trans. Edwin H. Robertson. London: Collins, 1996.

Book Review Digest. Ed. M. K. Reely and P. H. Rich. 1919.

Book Review Digest. Ed. M. K. Reely and P. H. Rich. 1920.

Braden, Charles. "In Evanston: [G. A. Coe at Northwestern University]." *Religious Education* 47(2) (March–April 1952): 91–94.

Brown, Charles C. *Niebuhr and His Age.* Philadelphia: Trinity, 1992.

Cashman, Sean Dennis. *America in the Twenties and Thirties: The Olympian Age of Franklin Delano Roosevelt.* New York: New York University Press, 1989.

Chatfield, Charles. *For Peace and Justice: Pacifism in America, 1914–1941.* Knoxville: University of Tennessee Press, 1971.

Chiswick Census, 1881.

Coe, George Albert. Letter to the editor. *Christian Century* (5 March 1933): 362–63.

————. "My Search for What Is Most Worthwhile." *Religious Education* 46(2) (March–April 1951): 67–73.

————. "On Having Friends: A Study in Social Values." *Journal of Philosophy, Psychology and Scientific Methods* 12 (18 March 1915): 155–61.

————. *The Religion of a Mature Mind.* Chicago: Fleming H. Revell, 1902.

————. "Religious Experience and the Scientific Movement." *The Church and Christian Experience.* Western Methodist Book Concern, 1898. Booklet.

————. "The Religious Problem in Colleges." *Northwestern* 19(23) (13 April 1899): 1–4.

————. *A Social Theory of Education.* New York: Scribner's, 1917.

————. "Theory of Knowledge and Theism." *Methodist Review* 80 (January 1898): 68–76.

Coe, George Albert. Papers. Record Group No. 36, Special Collections, Yale Divinity School Library, New Haven, Connecticut.

Craig, Robert H. "An Introduction to the Life and Thought of Harry F. Ward." *Union Seminary Quarterly Review* 24 (Summer 1969): 331–56.

Crist, Miriam. "Winifred Chappell: 'Everybody on the Left Knew Her.'" *Radical Religion* 5(1) (1980): 22–28.

Currie, Robert. *Methodism Divided.* London: Faber, 1968.

"Does This Nation Want a Bill of Rights or a Police Nation?" Sound recording. Americord. n.d.

Dombrowski, James. *The Early Days of Christian Socialism in America.* New York: Columbia University Press, 1936.

————. Papers. State Historical Society of Wisconsin, Madison.

Duke, David N. "Theology Converses with the Biographical Narrative of W. Rauschenbusch." *Perspectives in Religious Studies* 18 (Summer 1991): 143–51.

Easton, Lloyd D., and Kurt H. Guddat, eds. *Writings of the Young Marx on Philosophy and Society.* New York: Anchor, 1967.

Edwards, Maldwyn Lloyd. *Methodism and England: A Study of Methodism in Its Social and Political Aspects during the Period 1850–1932.* London: Epworth Press, 1943.

Ely, Richard T. *Social Aspects of Christianity and Other Essays.* New York: Thomas Y. Crowell, 1889.

FBI Files for Harry F. Ward. National Archives and Records Administration, Washington, D.C.

Fox, Richard Wightman. *Reinhold Niebuhr: A Biography.* San Francisco: Harper and Row, 1985.

Frichman, Stephen H. "Remarks at Harry F. Ward 90th Birthday Tribute." *Social Questions Bulletin* 54 (March 1964): 21–23.

Hamilton, C. J. "Chiswick, Past and Present." *English Illustrated Magazine* (1891): 874–85.

Handy, Robert T. *A History of Union Theological Seminary in New York.* New York: Columbia University Press, 1987.

Harrison, Beverly Wildung. "The Role of Social Theory in Religious Social Ethics." *Making the Connections: Essays in Feminist Social Ethics.* Ed. Carol S. Robb. Boston: Beacon, 1985.

"Harry F. Ward—1873–1966." *Union Seminary Tower* (Winter 1967): 1, 5.

Hester, Carl E., III. The Thought and Career of Harry F. Ward. Student paper for Church History 446, Union Theological Seminary. 27 March 1961.

Huber, Milton John. A History of the Methodist Federation for Social Action. Ph. D. diss., Boston University, 1949.

Hudson, Winthrop S., ed. *Walter Rauschenbusch, Selected Writings.* Mahwah, New Jersey: Paulist, 1984.

Hughes, Hugh Price. *Social Christianity: Sermons Delivered in St. James' Hall.* London: Hodder and Stoughton, 1889.

Inglis, K. S. *Churches and the Working Classes in Victorian England.* London: Routledge and Kegan Paul, 1963.

Investigation of Un-American Propaganda Activities in the United States: Hearings before a Special Committee on Un-American Activities. House of Representatives. 75th Congress. 1938. Washington, D.C.: Government Printing Office, 1938.

Investigation of Un-American Propaganda Activities in the United States: Hearings before a Special Committee on Un-American Activities. House of Representatives. 76th Congress. 1939. Washington, D.C.: Government Printing Office, 1939.

John Rylands University Library. Manchester, England.

King, William McGuire. The Emergence of Social Gospel Radicalism in American Methodism. Ph.D. diss., Harvard University, 1977.

———. "An Enthusiasm for Humanity: The Social Emphasis in Religion and Its Accommodation in Protestant Theology." In *Religion and Twentieth Century Intellectual Life.* Ed. Michael J. Lacey. Cambridge: Cambridge University Press, 1989.

Lamont, Corliss, ed. *The Trial of Helen Gurley Flynn by the American Civil Liberties Union.* New York: Horizon Press, 1968.

Lasch, Christopher. *The New Radicalism in America: The Intellectual as Social Type.* New York: Vintage, 1965.

Link, Eugene P. *Labor-Religion Prophet: The Times and Life of Harry F. Ward.* Boulder, Colorado: Westview Press, 1984.

"The Local Preacher." *The Local Preacher's Magazine and Christian Family Record* 36 (1886): 181.

Machovec, Milan. *A Marxist Looks at Jesus.* Philadelphia: Fortress, 1972.

May, Henry F. *The End of American Innocence: A Study of the First Years of Our Own Time, 1912–1917.* New York: Knopf, 1959.

Mays, Benjamin. Conversation with author. 1978.

McMichael, Jack R. Letter to author. 19 July 1979.

Methodist Federation for Social Action Archives. Methodist Archives and History Center, Drew University, Madison, New Jersey.

Methodist Times. London.

Meyer, Donald. *The Protestant Search for Political Realism.* 2nd ed. Middletown, Connecticut: Wesleyan University Press, 1988.

Morris, William. *News from Nowhere.* London: Routledge and Kegan Paul, 1890, 1970.

Muelder, Walter. *Methodism and Society in the Twentieth Century.* New York: Abingdon, 1961.

Murray, Robert K. *Red Scare: A Study of National Hysteria, 1919–1920.* New York: McGraw-Hill, 1955.

Newspaper clipping about 1948 Amsterdam conference by World Council of Churches. Among Ward's manuscript preparation papers.

Newsweek.

New York Times.

Niebuhr, Reinhold. "After Capitalism—What?" *World Tomorrow* 16 (1 March 1933): 203–5.

———. "Fellow Travelers." *Radical Religion* 5(1) (Winter 1940): 7–8.

———. "Ideology and Pretense." *Nation* (9 December 1939): 645–46.

———. "Liberals and the Marxists Heresy." *Nation* (21 October 1953): 13–15.

———. *Moral Man and Immoral Society.* New York: Scribner's, 1932.

———. *The Nature and Destiny of Man.* Vol. 1. New York: Charles Scribner's Sons, 1941.

———. *The Nature and Destiny of Man.* Vol. 2. New York: Charles Scribner's Sons, 1943.

———. "Optimism and Utopianism." *World Tomorrow* 16 (22 February 1933): 179–80.

———. "Our Relations to Russia." In *Toward a Better World.* Ed. William Scarlet. Philadelphia: John Winston, 1946: 123–32.

———. *Reflections on the End of an Era.* New York: Scribner's, 1934.

———. "A Religion to Save the World." *New York Herald Tribune* (17 March 1929). Sec. 11: 25.

——. "Ten Years That Shook My World." *Christian Century* (26 April 1939): 542–46.

Niebuhr, Reinhold. Papers. Library of Congress, Washington, D.C.

"Our College Men's Meeting." *Northwestern* 19(23) (13 April 1899): 4.

Oxnam, G. Bromley. *I Protest.* New York: Harper and Brothers, 1954.

Page, Kirby, ed. *Recent Gains in American Civilization.* New York: Harcourt, Brace, 1928.

Page, William. *The Victoria History of the County of Middlesex.* 2nd ed. London: Constable, 1911.

Palmer, George Thomas. "History of Oratorical Contests of Northwestern University." *Northwestern University: A History, 1855–1905.* Ed. Arthur Herbert Wilde. New York: University Publishing, 1905. 2:155–66.

Parkinson, George Hatheway. "Intercollegiate Debates." *Northwestern University: A History, 1855–1905.* Ed. Arthur Herbert Wilde. New York: University Publishing, 1905. 2:141–54.

Paul, Donna Price. "Shopworkers." *Victorian Britain, an Encyclopedia.* Ed. Sally Mitchell. New York: Garland, 1988, 721–22.

Passos, John Dos. *The Big Money.* Boston: Houghton Mifflin, 1933.

Peabody, Francis G. *Jesus Christ and the Social Question.* New York: Macmillan, 1900.

"Peace League Dies in Secret Session." *New York Times* (2 February 1940): 1, 8.

Perry, Ralph Baron. *The Thought and Character of William James.* Vols. 1–2. Boston: Little, Brown, 1935.

"A Prophet Was among Us." *Social Questions Bulletin* 57 (January 1967): 1–4.

Queen, Lonise L. "Ward, Harry F." *The Encyclopedia of World Methodism.* Vol. 2. Ed. Nolan B. Harmon. Nashville: United Methodist Publishing House, 1974.

Rauschenbusch, Walter. *Christianity and the Social Crisis.* New York: Macmillan, 1907.

——. *Christianizing the Social Order.* New York: Macmillan, 1912.

——. *Prayers of Social Awakening.* Boston: Pilgrim Press, 1910.

Rauschenbusch, Walter. Papers. American Baptist Historical Society Archives, Colgate Rochester Divinity School, Rochester, New York.

Read, Donald. *England, 1868–1914: The Age of Urban Democracy.* London: Longman, 1979.

Revolutionary Radicalism: Its History, Purpose and Tactics with an Exposition and Discussion of the Steps Being Taken and Required to Curb It. Part I, Vol. 1. Albany, New York: J. B. Lyon, 1920.

Robb, Carol S., ed. *Making Connections: Essays in Feminist Social Ethics.* Boston: Beacon, 1985.

Robins, Raymond, Papers. State Historical Society of Wisconsin, Madison.

Rodd, Nora. "Daisy Kendall Ward: Woman of Her Day." Obituary. Newspaper clipping in possession of Robin Ward Savage.

Roy, Ralph. *Apostles of Discord: A Study of Organized Bigotry and Disruption on the Fringe of Protestantism.* Boston: Beacon, 1953.

Savage, Gail L. "Gentleman." *Victorian Britain, an Encyclopedia.* Ed. Sally Mitchell. New York: Garland, 1988. 325–26.

Savage, Robin Ward. Recollections and boxes of notes and papers for preparation of Jesus and Marx manuscript. n.d.

Scheuerle, William H. "Amusements and Recreation: Middle Class." *Victorian Britain, an Encyclopedia.* Ed. Sally Mitchell. New York: Garland, 1988. 17–19.

Second London District Minutes. John Rylands University Library, Manchester, England. 1879.

Shields, Art. "One Man's Quest." *Worker* (14 January 1945): 1–5.

Shinn, Roger. Conversation with author. 21 September 1977.

Simmons, Jerold. "The American Civil Liberties Union and the Dies Committee, 1938–1940." *Harvard Civil Rights-Civil Liberties Law Review* 17 (1982): 183–207.

Sinclair, Upton. *The Jungle.* New York: New American Library, 1905.

Smith, Jessica. "Dr. Harry Ward at 90." *New World Review* (October 1963): 10–14.

"Social Service Evangelism." *Pittsburgh Christian Advocate* (1 May 1913): 20, 25.

Tholin, Richard Diener. Prophetic Action and Denominational Unity: The Function of Unofficial Social Action Groups in the Methodist Church and the Protestant Episcopal Church. Th. D. diss., Union Theological Seminary, New York, New York, 1967.

"25 Years of Social Gospel: Prof. Ward of Union Retires." *Newsweek* (30 June 1941): 46–48.

Walker, Samuel. *In Defense of American Liberties: A History of the ACLU.* New York: Oxford University Press, 1990.

Ward, Estelle Frances. *The Story of Northwestern University.* New York: Dodd, Mead, 1924.

Ward, Harry F. Papers. Burke Library, Union Theological Seminary, New York, New York.

Ward, Gordon H. Letter to author. February 1983.

———. Letter to author. 17 March 1983.

———. Letter to author. 5 May 1983.

———. Letter to author. 5 July 1983.

Ward, Harry F. "Anglo-American Relations in China." *Christian Century* (1 September 1927) : 1016–18.

———. "Anti-Semitism and the Social Order." *Jewish Life* 2 (August 1948): 10–14.

———. "Back to Barbarism?" *Zion's Herald* 128 (18 January 1950): 51–52.

———. "The Basis of Socialist Democracy." *New World Review* 24 (November 1956): 24–29.

———. "Behind the Headlines." *Social Questions Bulletin* 37 (April 1947): 54–56.

———. "Behind the Headlines." *Social Questions Bulletin* 38 (April 1948): 57.

———. "Behind the Headlines." *Social Questions Bulletin* 38 (November 1948): 122–23.

———. "Behind the Headlines." *Social Questions Bulletin* 39 (January 1949): 6–7.

———. "The Case of Dr. DuBois." *Jewish Life* 5 (July 1951): 23–24.

———. "The Challenge of Socialism to Christianity." *Ford Hall Folks* (22 March 1914): 1–4.

———. "The Challenge of Unemployment Relief." *Religious Education* 26 (March 1931): 200–205.

———. "China's Anti-Christian Movement." *Christian Century* (15 April 1926): 474–76.

———. "China's Anti-Christian Temper." *Christian Century* (13 May 1926): 611–16.

———. *The Christian Demand for Social Reconstruction.* Philadelphia: Walter H. Jenkins, 1918.

———. "Christianity, An Ethical Religion." *Union Review* 2 (May 1941): 7–9.

———. "Christians and Communists." *Christian Century* (25 December 1935): 1651–53.

———. "Christian Socialism." *Unity* (8 August 1907): 363–66.

———. "Christian Socialism." *Unity* (15 August 1907): 378–82.

———. "*The Church and the Social Problem* by Samuel Plantz." *Northwestern Christian Advocate* (20 February 1907): 8–9.

———. "Civil Liberties in Russia." *Nation* 120 (4 March 1925): 234–37.

———. "The Coming Struggle within the Victorious Nations." 328–30. Published article in Ward Papers, Burke Library, Union Theological Seminary, New York, New York. No publication information.

———. "Creative Ideas in the Orient." *American Review* 4 (December 1926): 520–22.

———. "Debs, Bourne, and Reed." *New Masses* 38 (4 March 1941): 13.

———. *Democracy and Social Change.* New York: Modern Age, 1940.

——. *Ethical Aspects of Industrialism.* Peking: Leader Press, 1925.

——. "Faith, Phrases, and Facts." *Zion's Herald* 125 (17 December 1947): 1203–5, 1222–23.

——. "Fascist Trends in American Churches." *Christian Century* (19 April 1944): 490–92.

——. Foreword. *An American Pilgrimage: Portion of the Letters of Grace Scribner.* Ed. Winifred L. Chappell. New York: Vanguard, 1927.

——. "Free Speech for the Army." *New Republic* (13 July 1927): 194–96.

——. "The Function of Faith in Modern Life." *Christian* 4 (12 July 1928): 532–33.

——. "The Function of Faith in the Modern World." *What Religion Means to Me.* Garden City: Doubleday, Doran, 1929.

——. "The Function of the Church in Industry." *Annals* 103 (September 1922): 96–100.

——. "The Future of Religion." *World Tomorrow* 8 (December 1925): 372–74.

——. "The Future of the Intellectual Class." *Calcutta Review* 14 (February 1925): 227–43.

——. "The Future of the Profit Motive." *Christian Century* (31 March 1943): 389–90.

——. "Gandhi and the Future of India." *Christian Century* (4 June 1925): 727–29.

——. *The Gospel for a Working World.* New York: Missionary Education Movement of the United States and Canada, 1918.

——. "The Handwriting on the Wall." *Christian Century* (4 March 1931): 304–6.

——. "How Can Civilization Be Saved?" *Christian Century* (11 September 1924): 1176–78.

——. "Industrial Relations." *Christian City* 22 (March 1910): 71.

——. *In Place of Profit: Social Incentives in the Soviet Union.* New York: Scribner's, 1933.

——. Jesus and Marx. Unpublished manuscript loaned to author by Robin Ward Savage.

——. "Judgment Day for Churches." *Christian Leader* 7 (April 1945): 151–52.

——. *The Labor Movement from the Standpoint of Religious Values.* New York: Sturgis and Walton, 1917.

——. "Lenin and Gandhi." *World Tomorrow* 8 (April 1925): 111–12.

——. "The Lenin Spirit." *Daily Worker* (4 February 1945): 5.

——. *The New Social Order: Principles and Programs.* New York: Macmillan, 1919.

——. "Not Peace, But a Sword." *Epworth Herald* 13 (November 1915): 1089.

——. *The Opportunity for Religion in the Present World.* New York: Woman's Press, 1919.

——. *Our Economic Morality and the Ethic of Jesus.* New York: Macmillan, 1929.

——. "Our Relations to Russia." *Witness* (7 February 1947): 8–10.

——. "The Present Task of Christian Ethics." *Union Theological Seminary Bulletin* 2 (November 1918): 18–27.

——. "Progress or Decadence?" *Recent Gains in American Civilization.* Ed. Kirby Page. New York: Harcourt, Brace, 1928. 277–305.

——. "Protestants and the Anti-Soviet Front." *Protestant* 4 (December 1941–January 1942): 62–69.

——. "Pulpits in War." *New Masses* 47 (15 June 1943): 15–17.

——. "The Rauschenbusch Memorial." *Religious Education* 24 (April 1919): 297–98.

——. "The Relation of the Church to Industrial and Financial Enterprises." *Biblical Review.* N.d., Union Theological Seminary Library, New York, New York. 375–94.

——. "The Religion of Kipling." *Methodist Review* (March–April 1900): 262–69.

——. "Report of the Secretary." *Social Service Bulletin* 4 (November 1914): 1.

——. Review of *Does Civilization Need Religion? World Tomorrow* 11 (January 1928): 38–39.

——. *The Social Creed of the Churches.* New York: Abingdon Press, 1914.

——. *Social Evangelism.* New York: Missionary Education Movement of the United States and Canada, 1915.

——. "Socialist Democracy in the U.S.S.R." *Protestant* (June–July 1948): 17–22.

——. "Social Reconstruction." *Christian City* 22 (June 1910): 163.

——. "Some Studies in Christian Fellowship: II—Is a Class Divided Society Christian?" *Churchman* (30 October 1920): 13–14.

——. "Some Studies in Christian Fellowship: XXXV—Things That Unite—Love." *Churchman* (27 August 1921): 9–10.

——. "Some Studies in Christian Fellowship: XXXVI—Things That Unite—The Church." *Churchman* (3 September 1921): 11–12.

——. "Some Studies in Christian Fellowship: XXXVI—Things That Divide—The Wage System." *Churchman* (9 July 1921): 12.

——. "Some Things I Have Learned While Teaching." *Alumni Bulletin of the Union Theological Seminary* 16 (June 1941): 4–12.

——. *The Soviet Spirit.* New York: International Publishers, 1944.

———. "A Statement of Our Position." *Social Questions Bulletin* 23 (November 1933): 1–4.

———. "A Statement by Professor Harry F. Ward." *Christian Advocate* (3 April 1919): 434.

———. *The Story of American-Soviet Relations, 1917–1959.* New York: National Council of American-Soviet Relations, 1959.

———. "The Task before Us." *Social Questions Bulletin* (October 1944): 2–3.

———. "To the National Committee and the Board of Directors of the American Civil Liberties Union." 4 March 1940. Copy in Alexander Meiklejohn Papers, Box 30, State Historical Society of Wisconsin, Madison.

———. "Twenty Years of the Social Creed." *Christian Century* (19 April 1928): 502–4.

———. "Vatican Fascism." *Christian Century* (12 June 1944): 693–95.

———. "We Were Friends." *Religious Education* 47 (March–April 1952): 88–91.

———. "What Needs Now to Be Done." *Social Questions Bulletin* 54 (March 1964): 17–19.

———. *Which Way Religion?* New York: Macmillan, 1931.

———. "Why I Have Found Life Worth Living." *Christian Century* (1 March 1928): 281–83.

———. "Will America Change After the War?" *Reader's Scope* (September 1944): 77–80.

———. "Will Religion Survive in Russia?" *Christian Century* (12 February 1925): 215–18.

Ward, Lynd. *Storyteller without Words.* New York: Harry N. Abrams, 1974.

Ward, May McNeer. Conversation with author. 23 August 1992.

———. Conversation with author. 1993.

Ward-McNeer Papers, Georgetown University Library Special Collections Division. Washington, D.C.

Ward, Nanda. Conversations with author.

Ward Family Archives. Maintained by Robin Ward Savage.

Wesley, John. *A Collection of Hymns for the Use of the People Called Methodists with a New Supplement.* London: Wesleyan-Methodist Book Room, 1888.

West London Observer

Wise, John R. *The New Forest: Its History and Scenery.* 3rd ed. London: Henry Sotheran, 1880.

INDEX

ABOUT THE AUTHOR

DAVID NELSON DUKE was professor of religion at William Jewell College in Liberty, Missouri, from 1980 to 2000. He published widely in the areas of religious ethics, religion and culture, and the Holocaust.